ACTIVIST
NEW YORK
A History of People, Protest, and Politics

This volume is published as a companion to the exhibition *Activist New York* organized by and presented at the Museum of the City of New York in the Puffin Foundation Gallery beginning on May 3, 2012.

This book was made possible through the generous support of the Puffin Foundation

Additional educational resources and lesson plans are available online at http://www.mcny.org/exhibition/activist-new-york-online

Book Design and Typography:
Michael Gericke, Justine Braisted and Yeryung Ko, Pentagram

NEW YORK UNIVERSITY PRESS
New York
www.nyupress.org

Washington Mews Books is an imprint that celebrates everything New York City has to offer. An eclectic mix of history and culture, the imprint embraces the cosmopolitan nature of America's most vibrant city.

References to Internet websites (URLs) were accurate at the time of writing. Neither the author nor New York University Press is responsible for URLs that may have expired or changed since the manuscript was prepared.

Library of Congress Cataloging-in-Publication Data

Names: Jaffe, Steven H., author.
Title: Activist New York : a history of people, protest, and politics / written by Steven H. Jaffe ; foreword by Eric Foner.
Description: New York : NYU Press, 2018. | Includes bibliographical references and index.
Identifiers: LCCN 2017051539 | ISBN 9781479804603 (cloth : alk. paper)
Subjects: LCSH: New York (N.Y.)—Social conditions. | Social movements—New York (State)—New York.
Classification: LCC HN80.N49 J34 2018 | DDC 306.09747/1—dc23
LC record available at https://lccn.loc.gov/2017051539

New York University Press books are printed on acid-free paper, and their binding materials are chosen for strength and durability. We strive to use environmentally responsible suppliers and materials to the greatest extent possible in publishing our books.

Manufactured in Canada

ISBN 978-1-4798-0460-3

Also available as an ebook

Activist New York

A History of People, Protest, and Politics

Steven H. Jaffe
Foreword by Eric Foner

WASHINGTON MEWS BOOKS
An Imprint of
NEW YORK UNIVERSITY PRESS
New York

Ban-the-bomb group march outside the United Nations 1962

Dick DeMarsico,

Using the streets for protest: Brooklyn resident Mrs. Donald Davidson and her daughter Denise march against US resumption of atomic bomb tests during the Kennedy administration.

Director's Foreword

Whitney W. Donhauser
Ronay Menschel Director & President of the Museum of the City of New York

New York has never been known as a place where people keep their views to themselves. Not only do New Yorkers speak their minds, they also have a long history of mobilizing around issues they believe in. *Activist New York*, the companion volume to the exhibition of the same name at the Museum of the City of New York, tells this quintessential New York story through the lives of some of the countless people who fought to advance the wellbeing of the city, nation, and world as they understood it. They struggled for such causes as equal rights, economic justice, gender equality, religious freedom, world peace, and the health of the environment, and to protect aspects of their lives that they felt were under threat. And they disagreed with each other—as good New Yorkers will—over which tactics to use, what strategies would be most effective, and what causes were worth fighting for.

The exhibition on which this book is based is the first in the Museum's Puffin Foundation Gallery for Social Activism. Since it opened in 2012, *Activist New York* has been visited by hundreds of thousands of people, including some tens of thousands of teachers and students who come for the programs offered by the wonderful staff of the Frederick A. O. Schwarz Education Center. Its companion website (www.mcny.org/exhibition/activist-new-york-online) has resources for teachers and learners of all ages. The stories in the *Activist New York* gallery change over time, enabling us to include a revolving selection of the many activist movements that have shaped this city and often the nation and the world.

Our huge gratitude goes to the Puffin Foundation Ltd., whose generous support makes all of this possible. Perry, Gladys, and Neal Rosenstein's commitment to preserving the legacy of generations of activists has enabled us to reach countless people with stories that might otherwise have been forgotten. They have not only supported the exhibition, website, and now the companion book, but they enable the ongoing work of its curator, Dr. Sarah Seidman, a rich array of public programs, and an innovative annual conference on teaching social activism in which educators can exchange ideas and experiences. Their vision and dedication is inspiring and deeply appreciated.

The book that you hold in your hands is the product of years of effort by Dr. Steven H. Jaffe, the curator of the inaugural version of *Activist New York*, working closely with the Museum's own Deputy Director and Chief Curator, Dr. Sarah M. Henry, and our indefatigable Director of Publications, Susan Gail Johnson. Steve vividly brings the stories of New York's activists to life in the pages that follow, interweaving in-depth looks at selected movements and leaders with the larger history of activism in our city, all energized by extraordinary images from our own collection and beyond, and engagingly designed by Michael Gericke, Justine Braisted, and Yeryung Ko, with the support of Amanda Kesner Walter, at Pentagram. At the Museum, Asher Kolman and Lauren Rosati provided vital editorial assistance. And we have Eric Zinner and his team at NYU Press to thank for their collaboration in making this book a reality.

Finally, we are deeply grateful to the scholars and public intellectuals who have served on the advisory committee for *Activist New York*, led by Peter Carroll, and to the many activists, photographers, collectors, curators, and archivists who graciously allowed us to exhibit their materials in the gallery and in this volume. Together they have helped us to tell the complex, important, and often challenging stories of activism in New York.

Malcolm X speaking at an outdoor rally in Harlem 1963
Unknown photographer

Issues of racial justice and activism have been intertwined over the centuries in New York. Harlem resident Malcolm X mobilized African Americans locally and nationally during the mid-20th century.

Foreword

Eric Foner

Activist New York offers vivid, eloquent evidence of the persistence and significance of political and social radicalism in New York City from the earliest days of colonial settlement to the present. Inspired by a path-breaking exhibition at the Museum of the City of New York, it reminds us that the city has always been an epicenter for movements that seek to enhance freedom and equality, in numerous forms, for New York's diverse population, and that events in the city have reverberated throughout the country. As Steven H. Jaffe notes, New York has long been the nation's "capital city of social activism." His account also makes clear that many of the liberties we take for granted—freedom of speech and religion; equality before the law regardless of race, gender, or ethnicity; the right to self-determination in the most intimate areas of life—would not have been achieved without activists' efforts.

Throughout our history, radical movements have challenged Americans to live up to their professed ideals and have developed penetrating critiques of social and economic inequality. They have done so in pursuit of numerous goals and using a variety of tactics. Some radical movements accept the society's prevailing emphasis on the ideal of the free, unfettered individual and seek to eliminate obstacles to its fulfilment, or extend it to excluded groups. Others insist on the necessity of community regulation of individual action, especially of economic activity, to ensure basic economic security and opportunity for the less fortunate. Some movements take as their task uplifting the condition of a single group of Americans; others envision a sweeping transformation of the entire social order. Occasionally radicals have resorted to violence, but most radical movements have reflected the democratic ethos of American life—they have been open rather than secretive and have relied on education, example, or "moral suasion," rather than coercion, to achieve their goals.

As the chapters that follow reveal, while often castigated as foreign-inspired enemies of American institutions, radicals have always sprung from American culture and appealed to some of its deepest values—facts that help to explain radicalism's survival even in the face of tenacious opposition. From 19th-century radicals who insisted that the inalienable rights enshrined in the Declaration of Independence were being undermined by slavery, gender discrimination, or the industrial revolution, to 20th-century advocates for women's suffrage and the empowerment of the city's disadvantaged black and Latino populations, radicals have adapted the language of American society to their own ends. In so doing, they have not only extended the benefits of American liberty to previously excluded groups, but have given American values new meanings.

Indeed, as this book shows, many ideas assumed to be timeless features of American culture originated with radical movements. It took the efforts of minorities such as Quakers and Jews to establish a right to religious toleration in Dutch New Netherland. The idea of freedom as a universal entitlement arose not from the founding fathers, who spoke of inalienable rights but made their peace with slavery, but from abolitionists, black and white, who invented the idea of equal citizenship irrespective of race. Despite New York City's close economic connections with the slave South before the Civil War, the Committee of Vigilance, founded by David Ruggles, helped to protect the city's black population from an epidemic of kidnapping and in assisting fugitive slaves who came to the city established the framework for the underground railroad.

The modern idea of privacy—the extension of individual rights into the most intimate areas of personal life—arose from the efforts of feminists and gay activists to secure for all Americans control over their own persons. Our modern understanding of free expression stems not simply from the Bill of Rights, but from the struggles of the labor, birth control, and civil rights movements throughout the 20th century to overturn laws and governmental practices that restricted the dissemination of ideas deemed radical, obscene, or socially dangerous, and from those activists who courageously combated governmental thought control during the era of the Cold War and McCarthyism.

New York has also been home to a vibrant labor movement, including the artisans who played a vital part in the run-up to American independence, early trade union leaders in the 1830s, and the young Jewish and Italian female garment workers whose "uprising of the 20,000" early in the 20th century inspired pioneering legislation regulating conditions of labor in the city. Larger-than-life radical orators and organizers populate the book, including Emma Goldman, who addressed thousands of New Yorkers on issues ranging from anarchism to free love and the right to birth control, and Marcus Garvey, who built the largest black mass movement before the civil rights revolution. But real pride of place goes to the often anonymous radicals who pioneered social change, including most recently gay and lesbian activists of the 1960s and '70s, and the young people of Occupy Wall Street, who put the issue of economic equality squarely on the national agenda.

Every generation of New Yorkers has witnessed the emergence of some kind of collective popular activism. Their movements have helped to make New York, and America, a freer, more equal society. The history of activism in New York City reinforces the insight of the sociologist Max Weber about how social change takes place: "What is possible would never have been achieved if, in this world, people had not repeatedly reached for the impossible."

"The Sailors' Strike—Scene on Peck Slip Wharf, New York City" 1869
Unknown artist, wood engraving from *Frank Leslie's Illustrated Newspaper*

As seaport, commercial center, and industrial hub, New York sparked movements by working people. These men were among over 1,000 seamen who went on strike for higher pay in 1869.

Midcentury Metropolis:
1918–1960   154

Chapter Ten   159

"The New Negro": Activist Harlem
— *To Drink or Not to Drink:*
  Prohibition, Pro and Con
— *Defending Civil Liberties:*
  The ACLU

Chapter Eleven   177

"Art is a Weapon": Activist
Theater in the Great Depression
— *Confronting Fascism*

Chapter Twelve   191

A Cold War: Activism and Anti-
Communism in New York
— *Blacklisting the Weavers*
— *Refusing to Hide: Anti-Civil*
  Defense Protests

The Sixties in New York:
1960–1973   206

Chapter Thirteen   211

"Gay is Good": The Rise of Gay
Power
— *Resisting the Vietnam War*
— *Women's Liberation in New York*

Chapter Fourteen   231

"¡Basta Ya!": The Young Lords and
Puerto Rican Activism
— *From Civil Rights to Black Power*
— *Asian American Activism*

Urban Crisis and Revival:
1973–2011   246

Chapter Fifteen   251

"Don't Move! Improve!": The New
Housing Activists
— *"Silence = Death": AIDS Activism*

Chapter Sixteen   265

"We Are the 99 Percent!":
Occupying Wall Street
— *A New Era of Activism*

Introduct
A City of

What is activism? And why has New York City played such an important role in its history?

These two questions are the starting point for this book and for the Museum of the City of New York's exhibition *Activist New York* on which it is based. People have defined "activism"— a word first used in the early 20th century—in many ways. This book proposes a definition that offers a way of understanding social and political movements both past and present: Activism is what happens when ordinary people mobilize in hope of shaping their society's future through collective public action.

That sentence helps us to grasp what connects a wide range of apparently unrelated events, efforts, and achievements, including ones that happened long before the word "activism" ever existed. The signing of a petition urging rulers to allow religious dissenters to live in peace; secret networks to help fugitive slaves reach freedom; strikes by laborers to pressure employers to grant higher pay, shorter hours, and the right to organize; protests by African Americans, Puerto Ricans, and Asian Americans seeking access to economic opportunities, good health, and political power; the fight by women to obtain the vote and gain full social equality: these actions and many more count as activism, and the people who engaged in them, either briefly or over a lifetime, were and are activists.

New York City has been a special place in the history of activism, and its importance is the result of a distinctive and ever-changing mix of human factors. Those factors have included extremes of wealth and poverty as in few other places; the dynamic of diverse religious, ethnic, and racial groups competing for rights, resources, and power; and the continual mingling of newly arriving people and ideas in one of the world's most densely crowded environments. The folksinger-activist Pete Seeger explained New York's role as an incubator for

:ion:
Activists

innovation by pointing to the power of this diversity to encourage the exchange and creation of ideas: "The extraordinary thing that cities do... is to bring together people who would not otherwise have met each other."[1]

Also critical in explaining the city's activist history is the sheer size of New York's population as it became the nation's largest city (1810), the world's largest (1925), and remained one of the top ten even when Tokyo, Mexico City, São Paulo, and others surpassed it (1970s-90s). The rise of New York as the nation's center of media, communications, and art is another crucial factor, enabling New Yorkers to broadcast their expressions of protest and plans for the future far beyond the city's borders.

New York has played an especially important role in the history of leftist and liberal activism, a byproduct of its history as a site of labor conflict, a crossroads for imported and homegrown avant-garde ideas, a laboratory for experiments in using

government to tame social ills, and a battleground for the rights of women and minorities. But activists can also fight to prevent, or roll back, change instead of promoting it, and these men and women have also been part of New York's history. Whether organizing to "protect" Protestant society from Catholic immigrants before the Civil War, speaking and writing against the woman suffrage movement during the 1910s, or forming neighborhood groups to resist the forced integration of local schools in the 1960s, conservative New Yorkers have used many of the same strategies and tactics embraced by those they have opposed, though often with less visibility and public celebration. At the same time, New Yorkers on the political left and center have also sought to block or roll back changes they have viewed as negative (such as overdevelopment, gentrification, and pollution) through movements to preserve landmarks, affordable housing, and a healthy urban environment.

Marcher, Union Square March 25, 2011
Steven H. Jaffe, photograph

A long activist legacy: A marcher carries a placard during the centennial commemoration of the Triangle Factory Fire.

Settled by Europeans in 1624 to earn income for Dutch investors, the town on Manhattan Island was blessed by a great natural harbor, access to rich natural resources, and the energy and ambition of generations of eager merchants, artisans, and laborers. It evolved steadily into North America's "capital of capital," the city where the pursuit of profit seemed more all-consuming and unashamed than anywhere else. In the 19th and early 20th centuries New Yorkers used these advantages to make their city the largest, busiest, and richest metropolis in the Western Hemisphere and then the world. The mid-20th century saw New York attain a position as the dominant global city, then suffer a period of declining fortunes and diminished resources in the 1970s before bouncing back as an acknowledged world center of finance and innovation in the late 20th and early 21st centuries.

Over those centuries, as this book will show, the nature of activism changed dramatically. In colonial Dutch New Amsterdam, and then English New York, those who challenged the status quo did so by petitioning authorities for special favors, defending themselves in court, or protesting in the streets. The American Revolution, itself a long episode of radical activism, created a new language of "inalienable natural rights." (Although in New York, as elsewhere, propertied white males initially enjoyed the lion's share of those rights to the exclusion of women, slaves, free African Americans, and the poor.) Additional "revolutions" that were part of the city's booming 19th-century economic growth—an explosion of mass-produced books and newspapers pouring off printing presses, an expanding school system, a vigorous and competitive party politics, and a growing labor movement—excited other New Yorkers with the possibilities of claiming the rights inscribed in the Declaration of Independence as their own.

Many prosperous 19th-century merchants, financiers, professionals, and manufacturers funneled money into crusades to reform the city and the world. But the question of money—and who controlled it—also became a flashpoint for conflict as immigration, industrial work, and urban crowding generated a type of mass poverty never seen before in America. Tensions over divisions between wealthy, middle-class, and working-class people stimulated further efforts to reform the existing economic and political system. In the case of anarchist, socialist, and other left-wing activists, these tensions also inspired radical visions for overturning the system altogether and starting afresh, whether through peaceful or violent means.

In the 20th century the groundwork for activism shifted as some of the agendas of grassroots protesters—including demands for decent housing and protection of the safety, health, and bargaining rights of wage earners—became incorporated into the realities of the political system. In the first decades of the century Manhattan became home to the world's most powerful and centralized business corporations. Partly in reaction to the power of expanding industrial capitalism—and then to the Depression that devastated the economy during the 1930s—New York City and State pioneered an unprecedented role for government involvement in the everyday lives of working people. This new urban liberalism satisfied some activist demands. But it also raised new expectations for further economic and political transformation, expectations that were sometimes rewarded and sometimes frustrated. In response, activists seeking new rights, freedoms, or opportunities—as well as those resisting change—found themselves trying to persuade, pressure, or fight government officials as well as business leaders in the city that had become the unofficial capital of the American economy.

Marcher with the American Civil Liberties Union at the Gay Pride Parade in New York City
2010
Cal Vornberger, photograph

New York's dense variety of communities and organizations have fueled the city's activist movements. The American Civil Liberties Union (ACLU), for example, founded in 1920 to defend the First Amendment and other rights, went on to help gay New Yorkers fight for legal recognition and equality.

Throng of women charge on New York City Hall to demand bread 1917
Central News Photo Service, photograph

New York's diversity meant that religious, ethnic, economic, and gender activism could combine in distinctive forms. Immigrant Jewish women, for instance, demonstrated against the high price of kosher meats in 1902 and rising food prices in 1917.

Today, in a world where media and electronic communications have become far more decentralized, New York is able to retain its wide influence. It remains a place whose sophisticated, inventive, "edgy" activists still attract attention. As has been true for generations, the very geography of the city's public spaces—its wide and straight avenues, open parks, squares, and bridges, and symbols like the Statue of Liberty and Wall Street—provide dramatic backdrops for marches, performances, and rallies. Unlike some other major American cities, New York affords ample elbow room in public spaces for such mass displays of popular democracy and for crowds of writers, broadcasters, and photographers to spread activist messages around the world.

At the same time, the city's dense networks allow the hidden, daily work of activism to go forward. That work includes behind-the-scenes planning sessions, fundraising drives, door-to-door canvassing, mass mailings, meetings with officials, arguments with allies and rivals, hard compromises, and countless other tasks demanding energy, time, patience, dedication, and often courage. The pressures and opportunities influencing the lives of ordinary New Yorkers continue to propel them into activism to shape the future for themselves and others. In the words of Lower East Side writer-activist Richard Kostelanetz, "inhabiting a hothouse influences receptive people to be what they've not been before and would not otherwise be."[2]

All these patterns can be found at multiple moments in New York's activist past. But the specifics of that history are not interchangeable any more than the lives of New Yorkers can be reduced to a two-dimensional stereotype. The experiences, emotions, frustrations, and accomplishments of different activists were profoundly shaped by the time and place they lived in and by the issues that drove them to act. Those details and those realities are what make the history of New York activism a living thing, today and into the future.

Colonial
Revolutio
New Yor

When the explorer Henry Hudson
sailed into New York Bay in 1609,
he claimed the island the Lenape
people called "Mannahatta" for
the Dutch.

and
nary
1624-
1783

At the time nobody could have predicted how important the area would someday become. Nor could anyone have imagined that New York City would become one of history's most influential places for imagining a better world. The process by which New York became a generator of new ideas about social and political change—a center of activism, radical ideas, and political protest—was long, unpredictable, and challenging.

The seeds of this future identity were planted as early as 1624. In that year European immigrants (soon joined by enslaved Africans) arrived to start settling the colony the Dutch had named New Netherland. They built its capital and trading center,

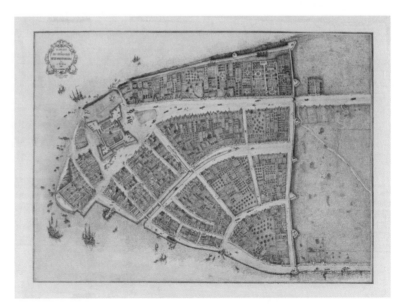

The Castello Plan. New Amsterdam in 1660
1916
John Wolcott Adams, drawing

The town of New Amsterdam, soon to become New York City, was built at the tip of Manhattan Island according to Dutch traditions of architecture, street and canal layout, and fortification.

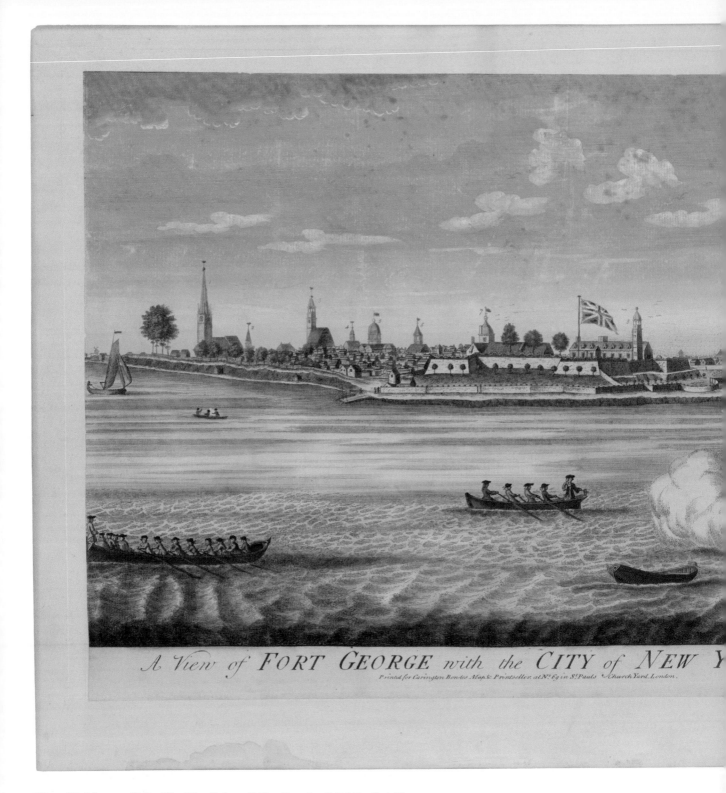

A View of FORT GEORGE with the CITY of NEW Y...

Printed for Carington Bowles Map & Printseller, at No. 69 in St Pauls Church Yard London.

A View of Fort George with the City of New York from the S.W. c. 1740

John Carwitham and Carington Bowles, color lithograph

Eighteenth-century British New York City was an ethnically diverse, politically turbulent colonial seaport.

?K from the S.W.

the town of New Amsterdam, at Manhattan's southern tip. During 40 years of Dutch rule, the social dynamics of the place helped set the stage for what would follow. New Amsterdam was a crossroads for starkly different national, racial, and religious groups: Dutch and Walloon Calvinists, German and Scandinavian Lutherans, Sephardic Jews, English Baptists and Quakers, Africans of many nationalities and religions, and others. This diversity sometimes created tensions, as the need to encourage settlers clashed with the authorities' desire for uniformity, and as conflicting Dutch traditions of toleration and religious orthodoxy brought people into collision. All of these factors helped to foster a distinctive culture, one in which the town's diverse residents proved themselves skilled at challenging each other, aggressively asserting what they believed, and questioning authority, whether it was political, religious, or economic.

After 1664, when an English fleet seized the colony from the Dutch and renamed it "New-York," the city's ethnic and religious mix grew even more complex. British New York City became one of the most diverse places in the world, filled with English, Scottish, Irish, French Huguenot, German, Jewish, and other newcomers, along with enslaved and free people from the Caribbean, West and Central Africa, and Madagascar. As the city mushroomed from 1,500 inhabitants in 1664 to some 10,000 by the 1730s, political and social conflicts spread. New Yorkers fought over questions of trade policy, civil and religious rights, freedom of the press, inequalities between rich and poor, ethnic resentments,

and access to power. The result was a city with competitive and contentious politics, home to rival political factions and parties earlier than most other places in North America.

Of course New York was not the only hotbed of debate in the British colonies. All of the larger towns, especially seaports, brought diverse people and ideas together, making them incubators of change as well. Nor was New York always more innovative or open than its sister cities. For example, while Quakers and Jews fought Dutch officials for the right to stay and worship in and around New Amsterdam in the 1650s, religious freedom was more attainable for Catholics in the Quaker city of Philadelphia: Priests were conducting public religious services there by 1707, 77 years before they won that right in New York. In the 1760s and 1770s, radicals protested Parliament's taxes in every American city from Savannah, Georgia to Portsmouth, New Hampshire, and Bostonians rather than New Yorkers often took the lead.

Yet New York's special character was already in play in the colonial era. In this city more than any other, friction, open rivalry, confrontation, and a wide variety of viewpoints became the lifeblood of public affairs. And after the Revolution—as Manhattan became the new nation's largest, busiest, and richest metropolis, a place whose ever-increasing number and diversity of immigrants dwarfed anything seen before—New York would come into its own as the activist city.

William Thorne senior

The marke of /W/ William Thorne Junior

Edward Tarte +   The marke of M[...]

John Stovor   The mark of P[...]

Nathaniel Hatfield   Philip[...]

Beniamin Hubbard

The marke X of William Pidgion

The marke D[...] of Edwere Alce[...]

Eliab Doughtie

Antonie Feild

Richard Horton

Edward Griffine

Nathaniell Tue

Robert Ffeild senior

~~Nicholas Parker~~

Robert feild Junior

Nicholas Parsall

Michaell Milner

~~Beniamin Hubbard~~

Henry Townsend

George wright

John . Soard

Henry Tarltee

Edward Heart

~~John maffine senior~~

[...] Townsend

[...]Harrington

CHAPTER ONE

Let Us Stay: The Struggle for Religious Freedom in Dutch New Netherland

Flushing Remonstrance 1657

The final page of the Flushing Remonstrance bears the signatures of 30 men who refused to turn away Quakers. The original document was partly burned in a fire that broke out at the New York State Library in Albany in 1911.

On December 27, 1657, 30 men living in the Dutch village of Flushing (in today's Queens) began a very public act of defiance.

The colony's governor, Petrus Stuyvesant, had barred all residents of New Netherland from opening their homes to Quakers, members of a religious group also known as the Society of Friends. The Flushing residents signed a petition to Stuyvesant, explaining that they could not obey his order: "If any of these said persons come in love unto us, we cannot in conscience lay violent hands upon them." Colonists had challenged Stuyvesant before, but rarely in so direct and confrontational a way. The petition, today known as the Flushing Remonstrance, shows how 17th-century New Yorkers disobeyed authority in order to stand up for what they believed to be right.[1]

Stuyvesant was infuriated by the petition, calling it "mutinous and detestable." He sent soldiers from New Amsterdam to arrest four officials of Flushing village—Tobias Feake, Edward Hart, William Noble, and Edward Farrington—and carry them off to jail in Manhattan. The governor believed that imprisoning these village leaders, all signers of the petition, would end the religious and political disorder. He soon learned that Quakers, and those defending them, were not so easily suppressed.[2]

The conflict over the Remonstrance was neither the first nor the last battle over religious toleration in New Netherland. Although they lost this first fight, Quakers and their sympathizers, along with other dissenters, stayed on. And they continued to make the colony the most religiously diverse place in 17th-century North America.

RELIGIOUS DIVERSITY

Just a few months earlier Flushing residents had first welcomed Quakers into their homes. This was a radical move because in the 17th century Quakers were considered very odd, even dangerous. The Society of Friends was a small Protestant sect founded in England in the 1640s, whose members interpreted Christianity in their own radical way. They were known as Quakers because of their practice of "quaking" in spiritual ecstasy when they preached or prayed in public, a behavior that was deeply disturbing to many mainstream Protestants. Their beliefs were disturbing as well: Quakers rejected all violence and war, refusing to perform military service. They also refused to remove their hats to acknowledge the authority of government officials and wealthy gentlemen, and they even permitted women to preach. Fleeing persecution in England, some Quakers crossed the Atlantic to North America in the 1650s.

They found an interested audience among some of the English Protestants who had settled in Dutch New Netherland. Seeking to expand the colony's population, Dutch officials had allowed English migrants to create new farming villages in western Long Island, in today's Brooklyn and Queens. Many

Petrus (Peter) Stuyvesant undated
Unknown artist, oil on wood panel

Religious dissenters faced a formidable adversary in New Netherland's governor, Petrus Stuyvesant, who ruled the colony from Fort Amsterdam at Manhattan's tip.

**Quaakers Vergade-
ring. Fronti Nulla
Fides. The Quakers
Meeting** undated
Unknown artist, engraving

Quakers shocked
17th-century officials
and others by
encouraging women
to preach, as shown
in this early view of a
Quaker religious meet-
ing in England.

of these English colonists had originally settled in
New England, but seeking to follow their own understanding of Christianity they had relocated to the
Dutch colony to escape the rigid religious control of
Puritan authorities in Massachusetts, Connecticut,
and the New Haven colony. In New Netherland some
followed "Independent" preachers who depart-
ed from the beliefs and practices of conventional
Puritanism. They had already created a precedent of
fringe religious communities in New Netherland by
the time the Quakers arrived.

In August 1657, 11 Quaker men and women from
England landed in the city and began preaching
loudly in the streets. Many inhabitants of New
Amsterdam, Stuyvesant included, were shocked.
According to the Dutch Reformed minister Johannes
Megapolensis two of the young women, Dorothy
Waugh and Mary Weatherhead, "began to quake...
preaching and calling out in the streets that the
last day was near." They "continued to cry out and
pray" even after being put in the city jail for disturbing the peace. To Governor Stuyvesant, this public
ranting—by women, no less—and the refusal of the

Quaker men to remove their hats before him were
acts of gross disobedience, warning signs that the
colony's political, social, and religious order was
under attack.[3]

Stuyvesant believed that the Quakers were
"heretics, deceivers, [and] seducers" who would lead
other colonists into error, sin, and disrespect for all
authority. He also believed that God would frown
on—and perhaps punish—the colony for tolerating
"heretics" within its boundaries. Stuyvesant was so
disturbed by the Quakers that in 1659 he ordered
a colony-wide day of prayer and fasting to seek
God's help in combating their "abominable Heresy."
Quaker beliefs, he concluded, were an infection
that had to be stopped from spreading throughout
the population.[4]

While some of the Quakers sailed off for
the English colony of Rhode Island, others left
Manhattan but remained in the area, preaching
to the English settlers on Long Island. Stuyvesant
soon had one of the preachers, Robert Hodgson,
arrested, brought to New Amsterdam, and flogged
for his refusal to perform forced labor while in jail.

A. Het Fort B. de Kerck C. de Wintmolen D. dese Vlagge wert op gehaelt als daer Schepen in de Haven k...

Nieuw Amsterdam op t Eylant Manhattans c. 1700
Unknown artist, colored engraving

New Amsterdam's Dutch Reformed Church (the large building at center left with a double-gabled blue roof) dominated the town's skyline as well as its official religious life.

The governor also reaffirmed an existing ban on all unauthorized religious gatherings, warning the colonists not to harbor any of the "erring spirits" (Quaker missionaries).[5]

"LIBERTY OF CONSCIENCE"

The challenge for Stuyvesant was how to enforce religious uniformity and at the same time encourage New Netherland's population growth, a balancing act that proved hard to maintain. The Dutch West India Company had learned as early as the 1620s that the way to grow the colony was to open New Netherland to an ethnically and religiously diverse array of settlers. Back at home, the Netherlands' own booming commercial economy was creating widespread employment and prosperity, and few Dutch men and women were willing to risk a 3,600-mile ocean voyage to a distant wilderness. In order to make their investment on the banks of the Hudson River profitable, company directors needed farmers, traders, artisans, soldiers, and taxpayers—regardless of their religious beliefs. This need for more settlers, along with his own personal religious convictions, had led Stuyvesant's predecessor, Governor Willem Kieft, to promise religious freedom to English newcomers during the 1640s. Even Stuyvesant, desperate for new settlers, asked the company directors to recruit "some homeless Polish, Lithuanian, Prussian... or Flemish farmers" for the colony in 1659. By then New Netherland's population embraced a variety of religious beliefs, and perhaps as many as half of the 10,000 colonists, including many of New Amsterdam's 1,500 inhabitants, were not Dutch.[6]

The Dutch people's own attitudes and religious situation grew increasingly complex on both sides of the Atlantic. The Dutch Reformed Church was the official "public" church, enjoying a privileged status and the support of government authorities. Dutch Reformed ministers held Sunday services and conducted baptisms, marriages, and funerals in their church, the only house of worship legally permitted in New Amsterdam. But at the same time, "liberty of conscience"—the idea that residents of Dutch territory should be permitted to follow their

TERDAM
hattans .

E . t'gevangen huys   F . de H. Generaels huys   G . t'Gerecht   H . de Kaeck   I . Compagnies Pachuys   K . Stadts Herberch

Iames Nailor Quaker fet 2 howers on the Pillory at Westminster whiped by the Hang
man to the old Exchainge London, Som dayes after, Stood too howers more on the Pillory
ur at the Exchainge, and there had his Tongue Bored throug with a hot Iron, &
Stigmatized in the Forehead with the Letter: B: Decemr 17 anno Domini 1656:

The Persecution of a Quaker in London
1656
Unknown artist, engraving

Early Quakers endured intolerance on both sides of the Atlantic. Petrus Stuyvesant had Robert Hodgson flogged, a punishment also inflicted on Friends in mid-17th-century England, as shown in this print.

Jews in a Synagogue
1648
Rembrandt van Rijn,
etching and drypoint

Although no surviving contemporary images portray New Amsterdam's first Jewish settlers, the Amsterdam artist Rembrandt engraved this view, which probably shows some of his own Jewish neighbors at around the time Recife refugees arrived in Manhattan. Like many other Amsterdam Protestants, Rembrandt accepted the Jewish presence in his home city.

own religious beliefs in private, without fear of persecution or expulsion—had also gained popularity. By the late 1650s the religious diversity of New Netherland resembled that of the Dutch seaport of Amsterdam, where Calvinist officials allowed Lutherans, Mennonites, Catholics, and Jews to live and hold religious services as long as they did so privately and inconspicuously. But Stuyvesant and those who thought like him felt that this was a dangerous policy; they believed that religious uniformity, not the more tolerant policy of cities like Amsterdam, was the key to ensuring a stable and strong community.

Religious hardliners and liberals battled over the same issue of toleration in Dutch colonies around the globe. Dutch outposts adopted a striking variety of policies, ranging from Batavia (today's Jakarta, Indonesia), where Dutch Reformed officials refused to tolerate any religious services—public or private—by Catholics or Muslims, to Recife in Brazil, where the Dutch allowed Catholic churches and the first synagogue in the Americas to open in the 1630s. Manhattan and its nearby village of Flushing became two of many far-flung settings for battles over Dutch religious policy.

In New Netherland dissenters of many religions drew courage from the situation in the colony and the emerging practice of toleration in the Dutch Republic, and they moved to undermine Stuyvesant's control. Sensing that they might appeal successfully for the right to remain

and practice their religion, Lutheran and Jewish settlers in New Amsterdam wrote their own petitions to Dutch West India Company officials in the Netherlands during the 1650s, before the arrival of the Quakers. The Lutherans failed in their effort to gain approval for a full-fledged public church, and the company backed Stuyvesant when he deported a Lutheran minister, Johannes Ernestus Gutwasser, in 1659. But officials in Amsterdam overruled Stuyvesant's attempt to discourage Jews from staying in New Amsterdam, and they instructed the governor to let them remain and worship in private.

Supporters of the Quakers followed suit. In December 1657 the Flushing villagers drafted and signed their petition, vowing to resist Stuyvesant's orders. Their document also spelled out their reasons: in welcoming Quakers into their midst, the petitioners noted that they were acting "according to the patent and charter of our Town." Indeed the charter issued by Governor Kieft to the original English settlers of Flushing in 1645 had promised them that they would "enjoy liberty of conscience, according to the custom and manner of Holland, without molestation or disturbance from any magistrates." Referring to the example set by Amsterdam, the Flushing petitioners reminded Stuyvesant that "the law of love, peace and liberty... extending to Jews, Turks, and Egyptians, as they are considered the sons of Adam... is the glory of the outward state of Holland." They insisted that they would welcome into their village any Christian, including

Petitioning for Freedom in New Amsterdam

In 1644 the governing Council of New Amsterdam received an unusual petition from 11 enslaved African men living on Manhattan Island. These men, including Anthony Portuguese, Simon Congo, and Paulo D'Angola, had spent at least 18 years as the human property of the Dutch West India Company. They had helped build Fort Amsterdam at the island's southern tip, farmed small plantations known as "boweries," served in the colony's military force, and performed other daily tasks for the company that controlled New Netherland. Now, they asked for their freedom.

The petitioners took advantage of the fact that slavery in New Amsterdam was not a rigid, carefully planned system. Instead, it had evolved gradually as a response to the colony's perpetual shortage of working people. With few Dutch families being willing to cross the Atlantic for an uncertain future in a remote colony, New Netherland's rulers resorted to buying or capturing Africans to help meet the labor shortage. But in 1643 several of these black men and women were granted their freedom. New Amsterdam's Africans and free Europeans also mingled in the town's Dutch Reformed Church, where many slaves were baptized and married as Christians. In 1650 that church would

Portrait of a young black woman with lacy head cap and matching collar 1645
Wenceslaus Hollar, etching

We have no authentic images of New Amsterdam's African inhabitants. But women such as Maria van Angola, wife of petitioner Anthony Portuguese, may have dressed like the woman portrayed in this 17th-century portrait engraved in Antwerp, Belgium.

bless the interracial marriage of German-born Harman Hanzen and
Angolan-born Maria Malaet.

Claiming that they had "long since been promised their Freedom,"
the 11 petitioners probably hoped that they would join six other
recently emancipated slaves—including two widows—whose outlying farms now served New Amsterdam as an informal buffer zone
against Lenape native attack. They got their wish, but liberation and
land grants came with conditions. Each man would have to make an
annual payment to the company, and his children would still serve
the company as slaves. In all, between 1643 and about 1662, 28 freed
African men and women would obtain Manhattan farmland totaling
at least 100 square city blocks today. Slavery remained a key institution; in 1664, about 300 of New Amsterdam's 1,500 people were slaves,
and only about 75 black inhabitants were free. But by advocating for
themselves, the petitioners of 1644 staked a claim to a life that offered
something more than chattel slavery: freedom for themselves and
their wives, and the ownership of land they could hand down to their
still-enslaved children. In a real sense, the long history of African-
American resistance to slavery in New York began with their petition.[7]

Map of the City of New York showing original high water line and the location of the different Farms and Estates 1852

D.T. Valentine and George Hayward, hand colored map

This map shows the location of farms (shaded in gray) granted to freed slaves between 1643 and 1662 in what are today Chinatown, the Lower East Side, SoHo, Greenwich Village, and Union Square.

Presbyterians, Baptists, and Quakers, and that they would "be glad to see anything of God in any of them, desiring to do unto all men as we desire all men should do unto us."[8]

But the Remonstrance failed to persuade Stuyvesant to change his views. Three of the arrested men—Flushing town clerk Edward Hart and magistrates William Noble and Edward Farrington—eventually backed down, apologizing to the governor and pledging to "offend no more." Stuyvesant released them from jail, although he suspended them from office, and kept the rule against Quakers. The Flushing Remonstrance itself was quickly forgotten, only to be rediscovered two centuries later by an American searching for Dutch colonial documents in Amsterdam archives. Since then it has been celebrated as one of the earliest American declarations of the principle of religious liberty and toleration.[9]

JOHN BOWNE TAKES ACTION

Although Stuyvesant's reaction temporarily put down the resistance of the Flushing villagers, it did not end the conflict over the Quaker presence. Five years later, in 1662, Stuyvesant ordered the arrest of John Bowne, an English-born Quaker, for holding illegal religious meetings in his farmhouse in Flushing. Bowne, officially banished from New Netherland, journeyed to Amsterdam, where he managed to convince the directors of the Dutch West India Company to hear his case. "We are known to be a peaceable people," he told them. Bowne asked the directors "to consider whether [Stuyvesant's] law… be according to justice and righteousness, or whether it be not quite contrary to it." He also reminded them that the 1645 charter of settlement guaranteed freedom of conscience to the residents of Flushing.[10]

HET WEST INDISCH HUYS.

The West India House in Amsterdam, constructed in 1642
1663
Unknown artist, engraving

Quaker John Bowne journeyed to the Dutch West India Company headquarters in Amsterdam, pictured here, to challenge Petrus Stuyvesant's religious intolerance.

**Bowne House,
c. 1850** c. 1955
Artvue Postcard Co.,
postcard

John Bowne's house,
built around 1661, long
remained a center of
religious and commu-
nity life for Flushing
Quakers. Today it still
stands as a museum,
a New York City land-
mark, and one of the
city's oldest surviving
buildings.

Bowne's argument persuaded the directors; they canceled his banishment and permitted him to return to New Netherland. They also drafted a set of explicit orders to Stuyvesant, instructing him to "allow every one to have his own belief, as long as he behaves quietly and legally, and gives no offence to his neighbors and does not oppose the government." In doing so, the directors forced Stuyvesant to bring New Netherland in line with Amsterdam's policy of toleration of private worship by dissenting groups.[11]

In the wake of John Bowne's visit in 1662, the company directors explained in a letter to Stuyvesant that they agreed with him in principle: they would prefer that Quakers "and other sectar- ians remained away from there." But in practical terms they could not "proceed against them rig- orously without diminishing the population and stopping immigration." The connection between the need to lure and keep newcomers, tolerating at least some of their religious practices, and enabling the colony to survive and prosper was too powerful an equation for Stuyvesant and other hardliners to overcome. Although Stuyvesant complied, he and his allies never truly accepted the "heretics and fanatics" whose presence they continued to view

as an insult to God and a trigger to social and spiritual chaos.[12]

The Dutch idea of freedom of conscience had played a role in creating a climate for toleration that persisted even after New Netherland became New York in 1664. The English conquerors brought their own religion with them, ultimately making the Church of England the colony's official church. They also outlawed Roman Catholic worship and priests from the colony after 1688, when the Dutch Protestant William of Orange became King of England by defeating the Catholic James II. But the English in New York continued to permit Jews and a wide array of Protestant sects, including Quakers and Lutherans, to stay. The diverse communities flourished, and by 1724, the churches and meeting houses of seven different Protestant confessions and a synagogue were open in British New York City. The Flushing petitioners, along with Jews and Lutherans, had helped to establish an enduring identity for New York City and its surroundings as a refuge for diverse believers, but also as a place where ideas of religious freedom would be repeated- ly fought over in centuries to come.

THE
New-York Weekly JOURNAL.

Containing the freſheſt Advices, Foreign, and Domeſtick.

MUNDAY February 18, 1733.

Mr. *Zenger*;

I beg you will give the following Sentiments of CATO, *a Place in your weekly Jourral, and you'll oblige one of your Subſcribers.*

Without Freedom of Thought, there can be no ſuch Thing as Wiſdom, and no ſuch Thing as public Liberty, without Freedom of Speech, which is the Right of every Man, as far as by it he does not hurt or controul the Right of another: And this is the only Check it ought to ſuffer, and the only Bounds it ought to know.

This ſacred Priviledge is ſo eſſential to free Governnments, that the Security of Property, and the Freedom of Speech always go together; and in thoſe wretched Countries where a Man cannot call his Tongue his own he can ſcarce call any Thing elſe his own. Whoever would overthrow the Liberty of a Nation muſt begin by ſubduing the Freeneſs of Speech; a Thing terrible to publick Traytors.

This ſecret was ſo well known, to the Court of King *Charles* the Firſt, that his wicked Miniſtry procured a Proclamation to forbid the People to talk of Parliaments, which thoſe Traytors had laid aſide.

To aſſert the undoubted Right of the Subjeƈt, and defend his Majeſty's legal Prerogative, was called Diſaffeƈtion, and puniſhed as Sedition.

That Men ought to ſpeak well of their Governours, is true, while their Governours deſerve to be well Spoken of, but to do publick Miſchief without Hearing of it is only the Prerogative and Felicity of Tyranny a free People will be ſhewing that they are ſo, by their Freedom of Speech.

The Adminiſtration of Government, is nothing elſe but the Attendance of the Truſtees of the People upon the Intereſt, and Affairs of the People. And it is the Part and Buſineſs of the People, for whoſe Sake alone all publick Matters are or ought to be tranſaƈted, to ſee whether they be well or ill tranſaƈted; ſo it is the Intereſt, and ought to be the Ambition of all honeſt Magiſtrates, to have their Deeds openly examined and publickly ſcanned.

Freedom of Speech is ever the Symptom as well as the Effeƈt of good Government. In old *Rome* all was left to the Judgment and Pleaſure of the People, who examined the public Proceedings with ſuch Diſcretion, and cenſured thoſe who adminiſtred them with ſuch Equity and Mildneſs, that in the Space of three Hundred Years, not five public Miniſters ſuffered unjuſtly. Indeed whenever the Commons proceeded to Violence, the great ones had been the Agreſſors.

Guilt only dreads Liberty of Speech, which drags it out of its Lurking Holes and expoſes its Deformity and horror to to Day light; the beſt Princes have ever incouraged and promoted freedom of Speech they know that upright Meaſures would defend themſelves and that all upright Men would defend them *Tacitus* ſpeaking of the Reign of good Princes ſays with extaſy; *A bleſſed Time, when you might think what you would, and Speak what you Thought.*

I doubt not but old *Spencer* and his Son who were the chief Miniſters and Betrayers of *Edward* the Second would have been glad to have ſtopt the Mouths of all the honeſt Men in *England*. They dreaded to be called Traytors becauſe they were Traytors. And I dare ſay Queen
Elizabeths

CHAPTER TWO

The Zenger Case: Fighting for Freedom of the Press

**New-York Weekly
Journal**
February 18, 1733

"Exhibit A" in the trial of John Peter Zenger: his
newspaper, the *New-York Weekly Journal*.

"How must a man speak or write, or what must he hear, read, or sing? Or when must he laugh, so as to be secure from being taken up as a libeler?"

Andrew Hamilton, an attorney, posed these questions in a crowded City Hall courtroom on August 4, 1735. On trial was a New York City printer, John Peter Zenger of the *New-York Weekly Journal*, who stood accused of publishing "many things tending to raise factions and tumults among the people of this Province, inflaming their minds with contempt of His Majesty's government, and greatly disturbing the peace thereof." Zenger's specific crime was publishing "seditious libels"—criticisms of the government—directed at the royal governor, William Cosby.[1]

Indeed the satirical attacks that Zenger had printed, most of them written anonymously by a New York lawyer named James Alexander, were designed specifically to anger Governor Cosby. "A governor [who] turns rogue, does a thousand things for which a small rogue would have deserved a halter [a hangman's noose]" was one *Weekly Journal* barb aimed at Cosby. Another suggested that Cosby was threatening New Yorkers with "SLAVERY," and implied that the governor might be "an overgrown criminal, or an impudent monster in iniquity." "Who is it then in [New York] that calls anything his own," the paper asked, "or enjoys any liberty longer than those in the administration will... let him do it?" Zenger's newspaper suggested that Cosby was an incompetent and corrupt tyrant who favored his inner circle while oppressing ordinary New Yorkers.[2]

The Zenger case would later come to involve high questions of popular rights, but at the beginning it was rooted in the kind of squabble over political power that New Yorkers had been having since the late 17th century. An alliance of wealthy merchants, lawyers, landlords, and land speculators had gathered under the leadership of a Bronx and Manhattan landowner named Lewis Morris. When

Governor Cosby arrived in New York in 1732, Morris and his friends quickly sided against him in a legal challenge to the new governor's salary. Cosby struck back by firing Morris from his position as chief justice of the New York Supreme Court. He also excluded Morris and his allies from the political jobs and other favors that the governor showered on his own supporters. Morris's followers were "a deluded and unreasonable mob," Cosby complained privately.[3]

As part of his effort to discredit Cosby and persuade London to recall him, in November 1733 Morris funded a new newspaper, the *Weekly Journal*, secretly edited by his ally James Alexander and published by John Peter Zenger, a German immigrant. Morris used the paper to help create something resembling what would today be called a political party. He appealed not only to his own crowd of wealthy anti-Cosby gentlemen but also to ordinary voters of artisan and "middling" status—as well as to Dutch New Yorkers who resented Cosby's treatment of Rip Van Dam, a prominent politician and merchant of Dutch descent. The *Weekly Journal* spoke directly to the "industrious poor," singling out wheelwrights, weavers, carters, furniture makers, builders, carpenters, and sailors to warn them that Cosby's "courtiers" looked down on them as "Dregs of the People." On the other side, as if to confirm the accusations that Cosby disdained common people, a pro-Cosby pamphleteer dismissed those New Yorkers being wooed by Morris as "unthinking" people "of no Credit or Reputation, rak'd out of Bawdy-Houses and Kennels."[4]

Newspaper journalism was less than a decade old in New York. Printer William Bradford had established his *New-York Gazette* in 1725, and by 1734 it was the official voice of the Cosby administration. While conflicts between rival newspapers

1 **_Portrait of General
   William Cosby_**
   undated
   Charles Jervas, oil on
   canvas

2 **_Governor Lewis
   Morris_** c. 1726
   John Watson, oil on linen

3 **_James Alexander_**
   c. 1750
   John Wollaston, oil on
   canvas

4 **Andrew Hamilton**
   undated
   Unknown artist

While no image of
John Peter Zenger
has survived, portraits of
the other central charac-
ters in his trial do exist.
The political feud between
Governor William Cosby
and Lewis Morris set the
Zenger case in motion.
James Alexander, writer in
Zenger's _Weekly Journal_ on
Morris's behalf, enlist-
ed Philadelphia lawyer
Andrew Hamilton to defend
Zenger.

The Art and Mystery of Printing Emblematically Displayed

Unknown artist, etching from *The Grub Street Journal*, October 26, 1732

Governor Cosby shared the low opinion of some Englishmen about the vulgarity and personal attacks of the "Grub Street" press. In this contemporary London cartoon criticizing the "excessive" freedom of the press, printers are caricatured as wild animals, devils, and a two-faced monster.

had already erupted elsewhere in the colonies, Zenger's *Weekly Journal* became the first deliberately planned opposition paper in North America. The paper helped to focus the efforts of Morris's supporters to elect opposition candidates to city and provincial legislatures.

"SECRET ARROWS THAT FLY IN THE DARK"

With its satirical assaults on Cosby's moral integrity, Alexander's slashing language echoed that of the press in London, where popular "Grub Street" publications, journalists, and pamphleteers freely insulted rival politicians as a way to score points with readers and voters. As Bradford's *Gazette* complained, the articles printed by Zenger were "secret arrows that fly in the dark, and wound the reputation of men much better than others." But Zenger's paper also raised larger issues, specifically about the right of political discussion. It reprinted several of "Cato's Letters," dramatic arguments for the freedom of expression written by two London political journalists. "Freedom of speech is the great bulwark of liberty," Alexander quoted Cato. "They prosper and die together, and it is the terror of traitors and oppressors and a barrier against them." The *Weekly Journal* also cited Cato's critique of self-interested officials who prosecuted opponents for libel: "the exposing... of public wickedness, as it is a duty which every man owes to truth and his country, can never be a libel in the nature of things."[5]

This defense of press freedom was actually in direct contradiction to British common law. In England any criticism of a public official in print was a crime because it could diminish popular respect for government and undermine "the king's peace." Under that theory, the truth or falsehood of the printed allegations was irrelevant; even accurate descriptions of corruption in high places could land writers or publishers in jail. Indeed some English jurists argued that critiques that were true were actually worse: "truth makes a libel the more provoking, and therefore the offense is the greater."[6]

But Zenger's fellow citizens in New York did not buy this argument: a grand jury refused to indict Zenger for seditious libel. A frustrated Cosby directed his attorney general, Richard Bradley, to indict the printer anyway. (They did not charge Alexander, fearing that they would not be able to prove the anonymous editor's complicity.) New York's sheriff arrested Zenger on November 17, 1734. Although Morris and Alexander could have bailed Zenger out, they left him in prison to draw publicity and to stir popular sympathy for the poor printer and his deprived family. He spent the next eight months in jail.

The jury's role in a libel trial was supposed to be simply to determine whether the defendant had actually published or written the printed matter in question; the judge got to decide whether the publication was, indeed, defamatory and whether the libeler would be fined, imprisoned, or both. This system stacked the deck against Zenger, since the trial judge in the case was an appointee and ally of the governor: Chief Justice James De Lancey. When Zenger's defense team, lawyers William Smith and James Alexander (himself the author of most of Zenger's inflammatory pieces), questioned De Lancey's ability to hear the case impartially, the judge disbarred them. The printer's conviction began to seem a foregone conclusion.

THE TRIAL OF JOHN PETER ZENGER

James Alexander turned to Philadelphia attorney Andrew Hamilton, who agreed to travel to New York and take the case without payment. On August 4, Hamilton rose in the courtroom to conduct Zenger's defense as the trial began. Over the next few hours Hamilton offered a novel and daring argument for the printer's acquittal. He freely admitted that Zenger had printed the articles in question. But, citing several British judges who dissented from legal tradition, Hamilton asserted that the truth of a printed allegation against an official should itself be a valid defense. Only allegations that were lies should be punished: "the words themselves must be libelous, that is, *false*, *scandalous*, and *seditious* or else we are not guilty." He further argued that "the just complaints of a number of men who suffer under a bad administration" should not be considered libel. Indeed, he claimed, the printer was performing a public service by exposing the dishonesty and incompetence of men holding power: the people needed "to be upon our guard against power wherever we apprehend that it may affect ourselves or our fellow subjects." Hamilton also maintained that colonial New Yorkers had a right to criticize their appointed governors. In London the right of the Court of King's Bench to punish detractors might be legitimate. But in New York, "a free people" and their elected assemblymen "were not obliged by any law to support a governor who goes about to destroy a province or colony… [which] he is bound to protect and encourage."[7]

Hamilton's provocative argument did not end there. He also maintained that the jury, rather than the judge, should have the right to acquit a defendant if his publication was truthful and intended for the public benefit. The precedent of "leaving it to the judgment of the Court *whether the words are libelous or not* in effect renders juries useless," he charged. Instead, "jurymen are to see with their own eyes, to hear with their own ears, and to make use of their own consciences and understandings in judging of the lives, liberties or estates of their fellow subjects."

Burning of Zenger's "Weekly Journal" in Wall Street, November 6, 1734
1908
Harry Fenn, half-tone photomechanical print from *Harper's Weekly*

In addition to arresting Zenger, Governor Cosby's officers symbolically burned his newspaper on Wall Street, near the pillory and stocks used for punishing wrongdoers.

John Peter Zenger Trial 19th century
Unknown artist, colored engraving

Andrew Hamilton (right) addresses the court in this 19th-century rendering of the Zenger trial.

Hamilton concluded with an emotional appeal to the 12 ordinary New York artisans and tradesmen sitting on the jury. "The question...is not of small or private concern," he contended:

> It is not the cause of a poor printer, nor of New York alone, which you are now trying: No! It may in its consequence affect every freeman that lives under a British government on the main of America....[N]ature and the laws of our country have given us a right—the liberty—both of exposing and opposing arbitrary power (in these parts of the world, at least) by speaking and writing truth.[8]

Within minutes of Hamilton's summation and the trial's conclusion, the jury, ignoring De Lancey's instruction that they merely determine whether Zenger had printed the articles, returned a verdict of not guilty. The courtroom, filled with anti-Cosby New Yorkers, resounded with three cheers of "Huzzah," and Zenger left jail the next day a free man.

THE ZENGER LEGACY

In the short term the Zenger verdict had virtually no impact in New York or anywhere else. Despite ongoing criticisms Cosby remained in office until his death in 1736. The Zenger arguments were invoked briefly in 1770, when the radical "Liberty Boy" Alexander McDougall was jailed after he criticized the Provincial Assembly for submitting to Parliament's demands that New York pay to house and supply British troops. But colonial courts continued to hold that even truthful publications could be punishable as libel and that judges, not juries, determined guilt or innocence. Even during the American Revolution, radical New Yorkers and others suppressed loyalist newspapers, rather than upholding the freedom of the press.

The "Zenger principles"—which held that truth was a defense against libel charges—were in fact largely ignored until 1798. In that year, ironically, they were incorporated into the federal Sedition Act, a law designed by congressmen in President

Educating the Enslaved in Colonial New York

In 1704, a French immigrant merchant named Elie Neau opened a ground-breaking and unsettling institution, "a Catechising School for the Slaves at New-York." It became the city's first school dedicated to educating people of color.[9]

Under English colonial rule, New York slavery had become harsher and more systematic than it had been under the Dutch, as local farmers, artisans, and traders came to rely more heavily on the unpaid labor of captive Africans. It also became harder for the city's black people to gain freedom or property, and strict laws increasingly regulated their daily lives. Even religion was withheld: many New York slaveholders resisted the idea of baptizing their slaves or teaching them to

Elias Neau *in the Dungeon, as described in Page 46.*

Elle Neau in the [Marseilles] Dungeon 1749
Unknown artist, from *A Short Account of the Life and Sufferings of Elias Neau*

Before teaching enslaved New Yorkers, Elie Neau was known on both sides of the Atlantic as a Protestant martyr. He was imprisoned by Catholic authorities in France for his religious views; after his release in 1698, he spent the rest of his life in New York.

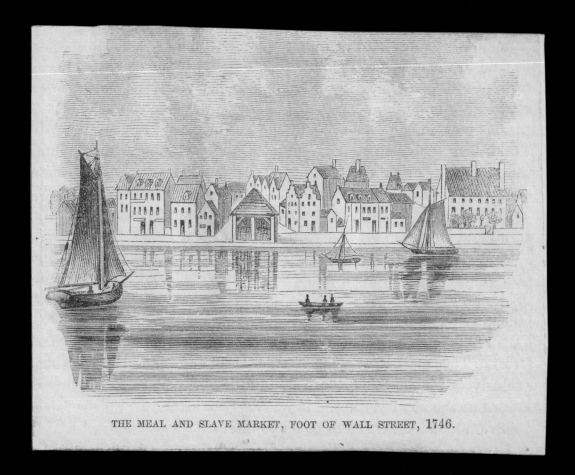

THE MEAL AND SLAVE MARKET, FOOT OF WALL STREET, 1746.

"The meal and slave market, foot of Wall Street, 1746"
1890–1934
Unknown artist, engraving

Slavery was everywhere in colonial English New York, with enslaved people making up about 20 percent of both Manhattan's and Brooklyn's populations by the time of Neau's death in 1722. In 1711 the city's meal market (center) on the East River shore became a venue for buying, selling, and renting human beings.

read the Bible, fearing that Christianity and literacy might embolden their human property to ask for freedom, or even try to seize it through violent rebellion.

Neau thought differently. A member of a French Protestant religious sect known as Huguenots, he espoused a fervent, evangelical form of Christianity, which taught that individuals could "be Born again by grace." In 1703, when the London-based Society for the Propagation of the Gospel in Foreign Parts offered to pay him a salary to educate slaves, Neau agreed, even though it meant leaving New York's French Church for Trinity Church, which was Anglican. Over the next 19 years he taught at least 122 men, 77 women, 12 boys, and 8 girls. Many, like Mingo, owned by merchant John Barberie, were enslaved, while some, such as Peter the Porter, were free. At least 85 of Neau's black students were baptized.[10]

Neau was not an abolitionist; in fact, he supported a colonial law that affirmed that baptism would not mean freedom. But at a time of great slaveholder hostility and in a rigid slave system, he insisted that enslaved men, women, and children were capable of being thinking, literate Christians, just as free white people were. Evangelical arguments against slavery itself would not be voiced openly until religious revivals in the mid-18th century. Yet Elie Neau's assertion of the spiritual equality of all believers, and their entitlement to literacy, would echo through the antislavery activism of later New Yorkers, both black and white.

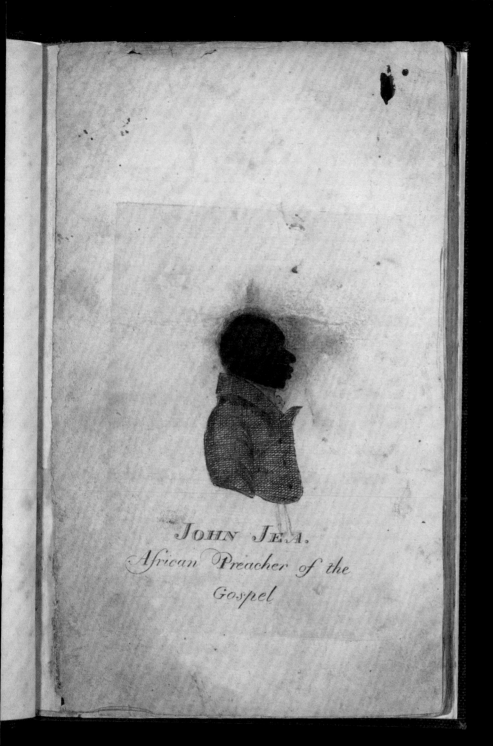

JOHN JEA.
*African Preacher of the
Gospel*

**John Jea. African
Preacher of the
Gospel** c. 1800
From *The life, history and
unparalleled sufferings
of John Jea, the African
preacher. Compiled and
written by himself.*

The kind of Protes-
tantism taught by
Elie Neau took root
among New York's
African Americans,
both enslaved and
free. John Jea, born
in what is now either
Nigeria or Cameroon
in 1773, was sold into
slavery in New York
City. Taught to read
the Bible, he gained
his freedom and
went on to become a
Protestant preacher,
author, and poet.

John Adams's Federalist Party specifically to suppress dissent printed by their opponents, the Jeffersonian Democrats. But the shortcomings of the new "truth defense" itself soon became apparent to journalistic foes of the president, since "truth" and "falsehood" themselves were subject to interpretation. Democratic writers found themselves facing Federalist juries and judges, who had a very different reading than they did on what counted as true.

By then the most radical advocates of a free press, like New York City's Democratic pamphleteers Tunis Wortman and John Thomson, were going beyond Andrew Hamilton to assert that all publications—true or false, fact or opinion, public-spirited or malicious—should be tolerated in order to allow for the freest possible questioning of authority and popular discussion of public issues. Wortman and Thomson, however, were ahead of their time, as Hamilton had been earlier. Even the idea that truthful publications should be protected, and the idea that a jury should decide all issues in a criminal prosecution for libel, only became the standard in American courtrooms through state libel laws (such as New York's of 1805), some seven decades or more after Hamilton had first asserted these criteria in Zenger's trial.

Beyond its specifics, the broader meaning of the Zenger trial was that it showed that New Yorkers were willing to challenge authority and discuss controversial topics even in the face of active governmental opposition. Indeed, even though the trial set no immediate legal precedents, New York's royal governors took notice and stopped trying to

Printing Office
c. 1800
Unknown artist, wood engraving

In the decades following Zenger's acquittal, New York City would become North America's leading city for publishing and communicating information, including controversial political and social ideas. This engraving shows an early 19th-century urban printing shop.

FLOAT — TRIAL OF JOHN PETER ZENGER

"Float—Trial of John Peter Zenger" 1909
Redfield Brothers, Inc., postcard

The Zenger acquittal later became part of New York folklore and a proud symbol of the city's role in extending American freedoms. This float appeared in a parade during a 1909 public celebration of the city's history.

prosecute other printers for seditious libel. After the Zenger trial, the spirit of contentiousness would never disappear from the city's public life, nor would the enthusiasm with which New Yorkers repeatedly turned to the printing press—and later to broadcasts and the internet as well—to debate issues and stir protest.

At moments when the right to free expression has been contested, the Zenger trial has resurfaced in public debate as an emblem of the rights of New Yorkers and other Americans on the political left, right, and center to scrutinize those in power and maintain open discussion. In 1947, during the Cold War, New York journalist William I. Nichols contrasted the American freedoms symbolized by Zenger with the one-party press of the Communist "Iron Curtain" nations. Critics of the anti-Communist campaign then spreading through American public life also cited Zenger. "Is there no modern [Andrew] Hamilton to defend freedom of speech now?" asked the liberal New York lawyer C.C. Burlingham in 1948,

protesting the Truman administration's denial of an entry visa to an English clergyman because of his alleged pro-Soviet views.[11]

The Zenger trial would go on to be invoked by the anti-Vietnam War activists known as the Catonsville Nine in 1968; by journalists defending *The New York Times*'s publication of the US government's top-secret Pentagon Papers in 1971; by a Brooklyn Supreme Court judge protecting the confidentiality of a *Daily News* reporter's informant in 1975; by the attorney William Kunstler in his defense of flag burners in 1990; and by the conservative online journalist Matt Drudge during the 1990s, to name only a few. The words spoken in a Manhattan courtroom in 1735 by Andrew Hamilton remained vivid and relevant to activists and their defenders: "All the high things that are said in favor of rulers... and upon the side of power, will not be able to stop people's mouths when they feel themselves oppressed, I mean in a free government."[12]

To

Mr. Evert Bancker
a Son of Liberty –
in New York
Pitt and Liberty and no Stampact

Leather Aprons & Silk Stockings: The Coming of the American Revolution in New York

Snuffbox c. 1765
Unknown maker, enamel
(fused coating)

The Sons of Liberty included merchants like Evert Bancker, who boycotted British imports, as well as ordinary artisans and laborers. Bancker's snuffbox is adorned with the phrase "Pitt and Liberty and no Stamp act," celebrating the English politician William Pitt's support for the colonists during the mid-1760s.

The tea tumbled into the harbor and floated alongside the hull of the ship *London.*

Above, on the ship's deck, the men who had broken open 18 chests and hurled the tea overboard acknowledged the cheers of the spectators on the adjoining wharf. It was the early evening of April 22, 1774, and New Yorkers had seized the opportunity to throw East India Company tea—hated symbol of parliamentary oppression—into the East River along the docks of lower Manhattan.

Several members of the New York Sons of Liberty, a semi-secret society of patriots, were dressed in Mohawk Indian garb, like their comrades in Boston four months earlier. They had planned to spill the tea in the dark of night. But the assembled throng was impatient to witness the historic act while there was still daylight, and they had sent men on board to find the chests below decks, haul them up, and throw their contents into the river. Members of the crowd then dragged the empty chests to a field north of the city where they burned them in the name of liberty and American rights.

The New York Tea Party symbolized many New Yorkers' active resistance to Parliament and, increasingly, to King George III. "You now hear the very lowest orders call him a knave or a fool," Manhattan lawyer William Smith Jr. wrote five months later. "The first act of indiscretion on the part of the army or the people... would light up a civil war." Within a year, colonists would in fact be in open rebellion against the British Empire.[1]

What was the source of the outrage and action? Patriots believed there was a growing English conspiracy to force Americans "to wear the yoke of slavery, and suffer it to be riveted about their necks," as printer John Holt's weekly *New-York Journal* put it in 1773. Over the course of the previous decade, a series of unprecedented regulations and taxes had burdened the budgets of working New Yorkers and reduced the profits of the seaport's merchants. The unrest began in 1764, when the Currency and Sugar Acts made money hard to borrow and required customs officers to suppress the port's lucrative trade in smuggled French Caribbean sugar. Both laws hurt New York's sailors and artisans as well as wealthy merchants. The Stamp Act (1765) and Townshend Duties (1767) imposed taxes that also hit the pockets of common tradesmen along with those of rich merchants and lawyers.[2]

These taxes also raised fears that the imperial government was denying colonists the most precious right of free-born Englishmen: the right to tax themselves through their own representative assemblies. The ongoing sequence of repressive British policies in the following years only seemed to add new pieces to an increasingly sinister and alarming puzzle. But also buried within the outrage was a feeling among some that all was not right at home—that inequality and privilege were corrupting New York society.

LEATHER APRONS

In the streets and on the wharves, workingmen and men of "middling" status accustomed to working with their hands—seamen, fishermen, carters, artisans with their journeymen and apprentices, small shopkeepers, laborers, servants—were the force that

Beaker 18th century
Hugues Lossieux and
Joseph Leddel, engraved
silver

This colonial silver beaker bears images of the Devil (seen here with a monster from hell) and the Pope, both of whom were mocked during New York's anti-Catholic Pope Day parades before the Revolution.

put muscle into demands for Parliament to recognize colonial rights. Artisan craftsmen in particular had become an important element in the city's economy and population. Such men—sometimes called "leather aprons"—had repeatedly taken to the streets to assert their rights. In 1764, in fact, a group of them had killed a British officer who was trying to round up civilians to force them into naval service, and workingmen rioted against a similar effort the following year.[3]

Although voting was reserved for white men who had paid a fee to qualify as "freemen," poor and middling New Yorkers together had long asserted their presence in the city's public life, often through rituals with long roots in English tradition. In the annual Pope Day parade on November 5, for example, workers commemorated the foiling of a Catholic plot to blow up the Houses of Parliament in London in 1605. Anti-Catholic paraders marched through the streets with effigies, including the Pope and the Devil, which they then burned in a public bonfire—much as they would symbolically burn the tea crates in 1774.

Mixing with these traditions were the new ideas of European Enlightenment philosophers, who were arguing that all men naturally shared the power to reason and had the right to life, liberty, and property, no matter what their social rank. These claims had radically democratic implications, and they circulated among New York's artisans and working people in conversations in workshops and taverns and through newspapers and pamphlets. Another influence was the "Great Awakening"—the waves of Protestant religious enthusiasm that swept through New York and other American towns between the 1730s and '50s. Encouraging white laborers, free blacks, and enslaved Africans to believe in the spiritual equality of all before God, the Great Awakening also spurred the "lowly" to question the existing religious, social, and political order.

Even New York women, barred from any formal role in the city's political and public life, were touched by the ideas of natural rights and American liberties. In 1774 a Manhattan teenager named Charity Clark, observing that "the Love of Liberty is cherished within this bosom," wrote to her cousin in England that she was part of "a fighting army" of women "armed with spinning wheels" who would free America from dependence on British imported textiles and parliamentary tyranny.[4]

Defense of the Liberty Pole in New York 1879
Felix Octavius Carr Darley and Albert Bobbett, wood engraving

This romanticized 19th-century view shows redcoats and "leather aprons" fighting over New York City's Liberty Pole before the American Revolution.

The Old Methodist Church 1768
Published by Richd. Butt, lithograph

During the mid-18th-century "Great Awakening," New York Methodists, shown here, and other evangelical Protestants sometimes challenged traditional religious and social authorities. The early Methodist church welcomed black as well as white believers.

NEW YORKERS TAKE TO THE STREETS

Where did loyal protest end and revolution begin? The line between parades in defense of British "liberty" and acts of outright rebellion proved thin. This became especially clear during the Stamp Act crisis, which brought working New Yorkers into the streets as never before. On November 1, 1765 about 2,000 seamen, artisans, women, and other New Yorkers amassed near lower Manhattan's southern tip, outraged at the new act, which placed a tax, in the form of a stamp, on every printed item in the colonies from playing cards to newspapers. They surrounded Fort George and confronted acting Governor Cadwallader Colden who had adamantly refused to hand over the hated stamps. One bystander watched as a sailor carried "an effigy of the governor made of paper," while others carried a companion figure of the Devil, as in the Pope Day processions.[5]

The crowd soon attacked the nearby home of a British army commander who had boasted that he would cram the stamps down New Yorkers' throats "with the end of my sword." According to an eyewitness, the crowd destroyed "windows and doors, the looking glasses, mahogany tables, silk curtains, a library of books, all the china and furniture… and at last burnt the whole," leveling the house in about

Quakers and Post-Revolutionary Reform

After the American Revolution, New York's Quakers—including descendants of religious dissenters who had once challenged Petrus Stuyvesant—devised an array of new institutions to address social ills and protect the city's most vulnerable populations. They were not alone in doing so: fellow Quakers and other Protestants across the United States collaborated with them in creating schools, asylums, and reform organizations. But the prosperity of the city's small Quaker community, and Manhattan's growing primacy as the nation's commercial and information center, made New York a hub of Quaker philanthropy and social innovation.

The core Quaker idea—that individuals should follow their God-given "inner light" to challenge injustice and remedy hurtful conditions—drove their efforts at urban reform. To improve the lives of poor children, Thomas Eddy helped found the Free School Society in 1805, the ancestor of the city's public school system, while Anna

A Quaker 1840–44
Nicolino Calyo, watercolor
on paper

A Quakeress
1840–44
Nicolino Calyo, watercolor
on paper

Unlike the street "ranters" of the 17th century, post-Revolutionary members of the Society of Friends (Quakers) were known for their quiet demeanor and distinctive, "modest" dress.

The Public School Society was dissolved in 1853, at which time George S Trimble had served as trustee 35 yrs. Wm H. Macy 16 and John J. Adams 14 yrs. New York, December 1870. For the Pupils of Public School No. 1

The Public School Society 1870
Unknown photographer

Quakers William H. Macy and George T. Trimble (probably the two men at left and center) helped manage the affairs of New York's Free School Society during the early 19th century.

Shotwell and May Murray established the Colored Orphan Asylum (1836) for African-American children in need. Believing that better prison conditions could reform convicted criminals, Eddy promoted and directed New York State's first penitentiary in Greenwich Village (1797). To encourage the city's poor to be thrifty, he also helped create the city's first Bank for Savings in 1819; by 1855 it had over $10 million in deposits, and the bank's loans had helped fund the building of the Erie Canal. Male Quaker merchants and doctors led many of these endeavors, but Quaker women—namely Shotwell, Murray, and Abigail Hopper Gibbons—also played key roles, foreshadowing the strong Quaker influence on the emerging women's rights movement in the 1840s and beyond.

Register of Manumissions of Slaves 1785–1809
Society for Promoting the Manumission of Slaves

This New York Manumission Society book records the freeing of local slaves. The society's founders included Quakers John Murray, William Shotwell, and Laurence Embree, as well as non-Quakers John Jay and Alexander Hamilton.

Ever since New Jersey Quaker John Woolman began speaking out against slavery during the 1750s, many (but not all) members of the Society of Friends embraced the causes of emancipation and racial equality. They were active in the New York Manumission Society, founded in 1785 to encourage masters to free their slaves. Quakers sometimes assumed attitudes of moral superiority and control when they "corrected" the behavior of those they wished to help. But their varied efforts helped set the stage for New York City's emergence as a nerve center of charitable reform in the years before the Civil War.

ten minutes. Within hours the shaken governor promised that he would back off from the tax, and as the witness put it, "the mob went home, every man to his home."[6]

Other episodes of popular resistance followed. In January 1770, in what is sometimes called the first battle of the Revolutionary War, British "redcoat" soldiers and New York laborers clashed on Golden Hill in lower Manhattan, a neighborhood of taverns and workshops. Soldiers swinging cutlasses and bayonets injured six civilians; one allegedly died of his wounds. The immediate trigger for the battle had been an attempt by redcoats to use gunpowder to blow up the "Liberty Pole," a lofty pine mast that New Yorkers had erected to celebrate Parliament's repeal of the Stamp Act four years earlier. Redcoats from Fort George had repeatedly torn it down only to have it put up again by sailors, artisans, and other "Liberty Boys."

News of events at Golden Hill traveled through the colonies. The reports further inflamed Boston's artisans and seamen in their own collision with redcoats, which culminated in the Boston Massacre a few weeks later. Four years later, in 1774, leather aprons would be among the "Mohawks" in New York's Tea Party, this time following Boston's lead.

SILK STOCKINGS

Seamen and artisans were not the only New Yorkers angered by parliamentary measures. Numerous gentlemen who wore silk stockings—patricians like the Bronx landowner Gouverneur Morris, the Westchester County landowner John Jay, and the Manhattan landowner John Morin Scott, all of them

lawyers—also objected to the taxes and regulations. These men and others fashioned their own tactics of opposition, tactics suited to the tastes and interests of "men of sense, coolness, and property," as one New Yorker put it in 1774.[7]

New York's moneyed and well-educated patriotic gentlemen voiced their grievances in newspapers, held public meetings in the city's taverns and coffeehouses to discuss strategy, and sent petitions across the ocean to ask Parliament to respect American rights. They also organized and hosted an important colonial meeting: the Stamp Act Congress in October 1765. Twenty-seven delegates from nine colonies attended the sessions in City Hall on Wall Street and formally rejected Parliament's right to impose the stamp tax. That same month, over 200 Manhattan merchants gathered at the City Arms tavern on Broadway to approve and sign a non-importation agreement, the first colonial boycott of British goods. Their goal was to force English exporters to pressure Parliament to repeal the Stamp Act.

Lawyers and merchants also relied heavily on their contacts in the Sons of Liberty to coordinate action with the city's "leather aprons." Artisan activists made sure that the petitions of protest circulated among common people (illiterate New Yorkers signed with an "X"). "Liberty Boys" also inspected the shops and homes of merchants to enforce the boycott, and on their own initiative in December 1765 created a Committee of Correspondence to coordinate action with like-minded patriots in the other colonies. Over the next decade, merchants, lawyers, artisans, and ship captains would work together (sometimes harmoniously, often not) on the Committee of 51, the Committee of 60,

the Committee of Inspection, the Committee of Observation, and other extra-legal bodies bent on resisting and overturning Parliament's policies.

But as agitation intensified, patrician New Yorkers often found themselves a step or two behind the crowds in the streets led by popular radicals like Alexander McDougall and John Lamb. Elite patriots scrambled to catch up, control, and channel the energies of the leather aprons. Many wealthy New Yorkers shared the patriotic outrage of "the Mob," but they also expected craftsmen, seamen, and laborers to know their place and not to question or challenge the existing social order. As John Jay saw it, "those who own the country ought to govern it." The problem for men like Jay was that popular anger at royal officials, tax collectors, and merchants trading with Britain could all too easily spill over into a more general disrespect toward all families of great property and position in New York, whatever their political views.[8]

For a generation, back to the era of the Zenger trial, competing factions of gentlemen running for office in New York had appealed to artisan voters by addressing them as the poor but virtuous and hard-working "bone and sinew" of the city and the province. Now, however, such rhetoric took on a new life in the hands of "Liberty Boys" themselves. Wealthy men probably squirmed uneasily when John Holt, the favored printer of the Sons of Liberty, used his *New-York Gazette* to assert in 1765 that "some individuals…can support the expense of good Houses, rich Furniture, and Luxurious Living. But is it equitable that 99, rather 999, should suffer for the Extravagance or Grandeur of one? Especially when it is considered that Men frequently owe their Wealth

to the impoverishment of their Neighbors?" In 1766 a group of working men shouting "Liberty, Liberty" chased an audience of well-to-do New Yorkers out of the Chapel Street Theater and tore it to the ground, justifying their action by declaring that playhouses catering to the rich were out of place at a time of patriotic self-denial and boycott, "when great numbers of poor people can scarce find subsistence."[9]

As the patriotic movement gathered momentum during the early 1770s, some New Yorkers—including about half of the city's merchants—pulled back

1 **Alexander McDougall** 1786
John Ramage, miniature, water-color on ivory

2 **John Lamb** 1777-1890
Joseph Napoleon Gimbrede, engraving from *The pictorial-field book of the Revolution*

3 **Marinus Willett** 1840–80
John Rogers, engraving

4 **Gouverneur Morris** 1783
Pierre Eugène Du Simitière, engraving

5 **John Jay** c. 1840–85
Unknown artist, engraving

6 **Alexander Hamilton** 1799–1808
John Trumbull, oil on canvas

A sometimes uneasy coalition of "low-born" men and established gentlemen organized New York City's revolutionary movement. Alexander McDougall, a Scottish immigrant and son of a milkman, was a ship captain and trader. John Lamb, son of a convicted burglar, became an optician and a wine merchant. Born in rural Queens, cabinet-maker Marinus Willett became a leader in the Sons of Liberty. Wealthy lawyers Gouverneur Morris and John Jay came from far more privileged backgrounds, while college student Alexander Hamilton shared Morris's and Jay's conservative social views.

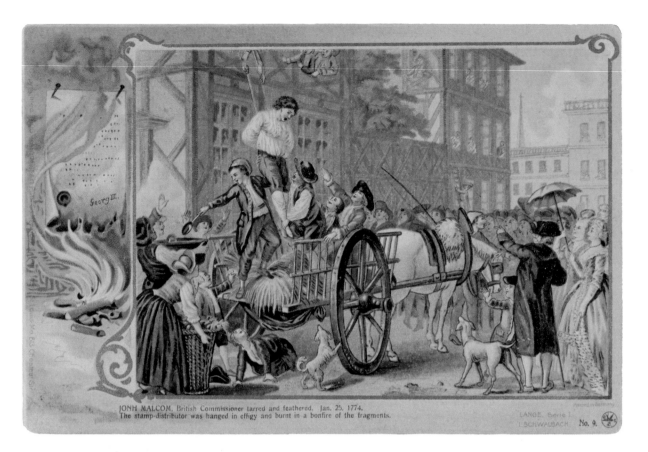

JONH MALCOM, British Commisioner tarred and feathered. Jan. 25, 1774.
The stamp-distributor was hanged in effigy and burnt in a bonfire of the fragments.

John Malcolm. British Commisioner tarred and feathered. Jan 2, 1774 c. 1903
American Historical Art Publishing Co., postcard

This 20th-century postcard envisions the rough treatment of a Boston loyalist in 1774, similar to incidents of crowd violence against Tories in New York City.

from the most extreme measures of the leather aprons, fearful that radical tactics were leading to a total breakdown in social and political order. Wealthier patriots were troubled by the assertiveness of leather-aproned radicals who sought to shape and guide decision-making as well as to intimidate "Tories" in the streets. "The mob begin to think and reason," Gouverneur Morris complained privately in May 1774 after Manhattan artisans formed a Mechanics Committee to counterbalance the Chamber of Commerce established by merchants. "They will bite, depend upon it," Morris added. "The gentry begin to fear this… we shall be under the worst of all possible dominions; we shall be under the domination of a riotous mob." Those New Yorkers who stayed loyal to the crown were even more outraged. Judge Thomas Jones, a conservative who became a loyalist, watched in disgust in 1775 as Liberty Boy Isaac Sears led a procession through the streets, which Jones denounced as "a mob of

negroes, boys, sailors, and pick-pockets" who were "inviting all mankind" to defend what they called "the 'injured rights and liberties of America.'"[10]

THE REVOLUTION

Despite the misgivings of gentlemen like Morris and the contempt of Tories like Jones, the more radical style of resistance—the willingness of common men and women to identify and rough up "enemies of the people" in public rituals— became even more open after the outbreak of the Revolutionary War at Lexington and Concord in Massachusetts in April 1775. That summer, a new revolutionary city government wrested power from the old colonial authorities in New York and created militia regiments loyal to the Continental Congress. Supporters of the King now became targets. By June 1776 crowds were seizing Tories, including "gentlemen," stripping them naked and riding them

New-York.

Statue of George III demolished

New York. Statue of George III demolished 19th century
Unknown artist, engraving

On July 9, 1776, New Yorkers tore down the statue of George III at Bowling Green, symbolizing their willingness to fight for independence from Great Britain.

on rails around New York City. A horrified Henry Brevoort watched as Theophilus Hardenbrook, a loyalist architect, was "taken from his house by a desperate mob, who tore all his clothes from his body, rode him round the city in a cart, pelted and beat him with sticks" until he was nearly dead.[11]

Despite their revulsion at such rough justice, numerous men and women of property stayed loyal to the rebel cause. Indeed it was affluent gentlemen from throughout the 13 colonies who drafted and signed a Declaration of Independence in Philadelphia in early July 1776. And though the events that unfolded at Bowling Green in front of Fort George five days later, on July 9, 1776, were the most radical of all, they drew the support of Jay, Morris, and other propertied patriots as well as of "the Mob." As copies of the Declaration of Independence were read aloud to Continental Army regiments guarding the city, a crowd pulled down the statue of George III on horseback that New Yorkers had erected in 1770 to celebrate Parliament's repeal of the Stamp Act. By symbolically toppling the king, patriots cut themselves free from over a century of British rule in New York, and from their identity as Britons that had shaped every aspect of their lives. The statue was shattered and hauled to Connecticut to be turned into musket balls for the Continental Army now fighting for the United States of America. One patriot noted that the king's troops might soon have "melted majesty fired at them."[12]

The revolution would continue to contain (if sometimes just barely) the tensions between leather aprons and silk stockings. After George Washington and the Continental Army suffered a disastrous defeat in the Battle of Brooklyn in September 1776, New York City became the command center and principal base for the British military and Tory sympathizers. Like other patriots across North America, the New Yorkers who now spent long years in the Continental Army, Navy, and state militias reflected the same social divisions that had shaped the emerging imperial crisis for over a decade. Artisans, farmers, seamen, laborers, and boys filled the ranks of Washington's fighting regiments as foot soldiers. On the other hand, with a few notable exceptions, Washington's officer corps was populated by propertied men including young New Yorkers such as Alexander Hamilton, a college student, and Aaron Burr, a law student. The affluent landholders Gouverneur Morris, John Jay, and Robert R. Livingston drafted New York's revolutionary State Constitution of 1777. That document freed Roman Catholics to worship openly in New York, but also confirmed that the poorest men would not be allowed to vote.

In November 1783 George Washington led his triumphant army into the streets of New York and the occupying redcoats sailed away to Britain and Canada (taking thousands of pro-English New Yorkers, and African Americans who had fought on the British side, with them). Some of the leather aprons found opportunity in this moment of transition, parlaying their roles as victorious revolutionaries into positions of stature. Isaac Sears invested in a venture that opened up Chinese trade to New York merchants, Alexander McDougall helped Alexander Hamilton found the Bank of New York, and Marinus Willett became a State Assemblyman, New York County Sheriff, and Mayor of New York City. Meanwhile, other men who had helped fill the ranks of the Continental Army and Navy returned to their homes and livelihoods in Manhattan's artisan and waterfront neighborhoods. Victory had been the shared accomplishment of leather aprons and silk stockings, even as they resumed life in a city where old social divisions remained intact and new ones arose. Those divisions would spark future conflicts and future activism in the name of the revolution's principles of liberty and independence.

Seaport City
1783–1865

New York emerged as the new nation's largest and richest city after the American Revolution. By 1810 its population of over 96,000 and its booming maritime trade enabled it to surpass Philadelphia as North America's leading urban and commercial center.

FIVE POINTS, 1827.

Five Points, 1827
c. 1850
McSpedon & Baker,
hand-colored lithograph

New York's exploding population, the growth of urban poverty, and the apparent disorder of neighborhoods like the racially mixed Five Points triggered responses from an array of 19th-century activists and reformers.

Cargo ships lined East River docks, merchants swarmed Manhattan auction rooms to buy and sell goods, and cart drivers, sailors, and pedestrians jostled each other in the city's streets. "Every thing was in motion," an English visitor observed in 1807, "all was life, bustle, and activity. The people were scampering in all directions to trade with each other."

Between the end of the Revolution and the mid-1820s, a series of innovations secured New York's dominance of the American economy. Manhattan merchants began trade with China, came to control much of the export of cotton from the American South to Europe and with other New Yorkers supported the construction of the Erie Canal, which opened the city to trade with the western frontier. In the 1830s the money accumulated by these merchants made the banks and insurance companies of Wall Street the financial hub of the Western Hemisphere. The nation's fanciest retail stores lined Broadway, while on nearby streets master craftsmen employed working men and women to mass produce an accelerating flow of goods for the city's and nation's growing populations of consumers. New residential neighborhoods spread steadily northward on Manhattan Island and across the East River in Brooklyn and Williamsburg as jobs drew waves of immigrants from Europe and migrants from American farms, towns, and other cities. As journalist and poet Walt Whitman proudly declared in 1842, New York City had become "the heart, the brain, the focus, the main spring, the pinnacle, the extremity, the no more beyond, of the New World."

New York also became the nation's most important city for activist movements for social and political reform. Members of the wealthy merchant elite,

Sons of Temperance apron and neck piece
1845
Satin and cotton with sequins, ribbon, sunburst, braid, tassel, and fringe

The Sons of Temperance, an all-male society founded in New York City in 1842, adopted these special aprons and neck pieces as marks of membership. With chapters across the nation, the Sons urged Americans to renounce alcohol and seek "virtue, morality, and sobriety." Female temperance activists worked in their own organizations such as the Martha Washington Temperance Society (founded in 1841).

poor working people, ex-slaves, and everyone in between took part in crusades against slavery, prostitution, illiteracy, irreligion, juvenile delinquency, poverty, the excessive use of alcohol, and other conditions they saw as social evils. These various movements were largely national in scope; New York City did not monopolize them. But the city's wealth, its dominance in communications and publishing, its central role in the exchange of people and new ideas between Europe and America, and its dense networks of social organizations all gave New York a lead position in what historians have called the "Benevolent Empire" of reform. By 1842, for instance, Nassau Street in lower Manhattan was the headquarters for 13 local and national antislavery, temperance, anti-prostitution, Sunday School, Bible, tract, and missionary societies. The same neighborhood, which had become the nation's most important printing district, churned out thousands of reform-minded books, tracts, pamphlets, circulars, leaflets, magazines, newspapers, and illustrations. The close proximity of the city's main post office in City Hall Park allowed such materials to be mailed across the country to reach the "unsaved" everywhere.

New York activists—whether working-class labor unionists, middle-class founders of Sunday Schools, or rich abolitionist merchants—shared an optimism and a zeal rooted in the belief that the American Revolution had created a republic pledged to ever-expanding virtue: a free people should and would choose to do right and reject wrong. Many activists, aflame with the evangelical religious faith kindled

by the nationwide Second Great Awakening (c. 1800–60), also shared the conviction that Protestant Christianity would be the means of purifying and perfecting American institutions while saving souls. "We are placed here as stewards for God," Gerard Hallock of the New York Tract Society declared in 1828, and many activists agreed with him that God expected the devout to rescue others from sin, vice, and hardship.

Inspired by that belief, evangelical Protestant and Quaker New Yorkers aided fugitive slaves, established Houses of Refuge for poor orphans and "fallen women," and personally went door to door in the city's slum districts distributing Bibles and religious tracts (pamphlets). In an urban society where new ideas about femininity kept most middle-class and wealthy women from meaningful careers, male abolitionists encouraged Protestant women to play a public role as volunteer activists—a role that by 1848 helped spark the women's rights movement in New York and across the country.

Activists, however, did not always interact harmoniously. As New York experienced explosive growth in population, business, and diversity, social change encouraged movements offering starkly conflicting responses to new urban tensions. Some Protestants, blaming Catholic immigrants for the miseries of poor neighborhoods like Manhattan's Five Points and Brooklyn's Kelsey's Alley, created nativist secret societies to reduce the political power of the foreign-born. Catholic activists responded by creating their own networks of self-help organizations and schools to

protect and nurture their community. Freed from the last legal bonds of slavery in 1827, the city's African Americans found themselves fighting local racism and discrimination in multiple forms, even as they worked to help free their enslaved brothers and sisters in the South. White workingmen (and some workingwomen), facing New York's ongoing industrial revolution and growing divides between employers and wage laborers, formed labor unions. At different times between the 1810s and 1860s, groups of working people also engaged in an array of other movements, ranging from evangelical revivals, temperance crusades, and party politics to experiments with socialist communes, dietary reform, and drives for an improved and expanded public school system.

By the Civil War (1861–65) New York City, with over 800,000 people the largest metropolis in the Americas and the nation's "capital" of commerce, finance, industry, immigration, media, and culture, was also one of the world's great incubators of reform and agitation. It would continue to play that role as Americans faced the growing conflicts and inequalities generated by an industrializing, urbanizing, and immigrant-driven economy— conditions that New Yorkers had already confronted during the first half of the 19th century.

CHAPTER FOUR

Workingmen & Aristocrats: New York's Labor Movement Takes Shape

View of Broadway, New-York from Hospital to Leonard Street, West-Side
1855
Frederick Heppenheimer, hand colored lithograph
(detail)

Throughout the early and mid-19th century, lower Manhattan was filled with tailors' shops like the one at left—battlegrounds in struggles between masters and journeymen over wages and advancement.

"The Rich against the Poor! Judge Edwards, the tool of the Aristocracy, against the People! Mechanics and workingmen! A deadly blow has been struck at your Liberty! The prize for which your fathers fought has been robbed from you! The Freemen of the North are now on a level with the slaves of the South!"[1]

These words were plastered in leaflets on New York City walls by angry laborers in June 1836. A jury had just found 20 tailors guilty of "riot and conspiracy injurious to trade and commerce." The men on trial were journeymen—trainees hoping to become master tailors. They were also members of the Association of Journeymen Tailors, a "trades union" they had formed to win higher wages from the master craftsmen they worked for.[2]

The Association demanded higher pay for its members and tried to block all journeymen—members or not—from accepting lower wages. This policy led to the jury's verdict: the men were guilty of illegally interfering with free transactions between employers and employees. In effect, the trial was about the very question of whether workers could band together to counterbalance the power held by employers who hired, fired, and paid them. Judge Ogden Edwards had openly sided with the prosecution, telling the jurors that trade unions were "illegal combinations" and that in his opinion the defendants were guilty.[3]

On June 11 Edwards handed down the sentences: Henry Faulkner, the Association's president, was fined $150 (over $3,000 today), a "ringleader" was fined $100, and the others had to pay $50 each. Many wealthy and middle-class New Yorkers breathed a sigh of relief. In their view, the journeymen's association had turned the city into a war zone. In the winter of 1835–36 unionists had called a strike and reportedly threatened to cut off the hands of—or even kill—workers who accepted lower wages. The *New York Enquirer* reported that strikers "assembled in front of those shops in Broadway, against the owners of which they have declared war" to identify the journeymen who were still going to work.[4]

Even more frightening was the fact that the union movement was spreading. And while most union members worked in skilled crafts, unskilled laborers also went on strike without having formed unions. In February 1836, for example, longshoremen, ship riggers, and construction laborers walked off their worksites, demanding higher pay. They scuffled with city watchmen until Mayor Cornelius Lawrence called in the National Guard, marking the first time that New York City's officials used military force to break up a strike. Later that year former Mayor Philip Hone wrote that unions were proof of a "spirit of faction and contempt of the laws" stirred up by "vile foreigners." The *New York Commercial Advertiser* agreed, denouncing the tailors' association as a "lawless combination" that could only bring "evil consequences."[5]

City Hall Park from the Northwest Corner of Chambers Street 1825
Arthur J. Stansbury, watercolor on paper

The open expanse of City Hall Park, officially completed in 1812, provided space for mass protests and rallies by working people, antislavery activists, and others.

The Tailor 1836
Edward Hazen, engraving from *The panorama of professions and trades; or Every man's book*

As master tailors measure a customer, journeymen sitting on the counter (right) stitch garments in this view of a traditional tailoring shop.

But other New Yorkers had a very different response to the trial. On June 13, 1836 at least 27,000 people crowded into City Hall Park in the largest protest meeting ever held in America to that date, echoing the outrage of the "Rich against the Poor" leaflet posted a few days earlier. Other unions—the Trade Society of Ladies Shoemakers and the Trade Society of Pianoforte Manufacturers—had already announced their support. Brooklyn's Union Society of Journeymen Tailors promised not to work for Manhattan workshops that refused to raise wages. The park was filled with thousands of union members pledging to pay the men's fines.

The protests showed that New York was becoming not only the nation's leading manufacturing city, but also a battleground between employers and laborers. At the end of the rally, some expressed their rage by setting an effigy of Judge Edwards on fire, although the thousands of protesters then went home peacefully. Their anger, their sheer numbers, and their willingness to organize were already making New York City a focal point of the nation's labor movement. The episode would prove to be just one shot in an ongoing, turbulent, decades-long confrontation between bosses and workers in New York City's workshops, factories, streets, and courtrooms.

A WORK-ROOM IN DOUGLAS & SHERWOOD'S SKIRT MANUFACTORY.

A Work-Room in Douglas & Sherwood's Skirt Manufactory 1859
Unknown artist,
line engraving

Increasingly, garment factories like Douglas & Sherwood's on White Street hired women and other relatively unskilled workers. They could be paid a lower wage than journeymen tailors expected to receive.

MECHANICS AND BOSSES

Going on strike (or "turning out") was a tactic that had been used by workers in New York long before the 1830s. More than 150 years earlier, in 1677 and 1684, cart drivers went on strike to protest city regulations; the city government punished them with fines. Strikes by bakers and others followed in the 18th century.

But it was the transformation of manufacturing after the American Revolution that fostered an activist labor movement in the city. Artisans, or "mechanics"—the master craftsmen, journeymen, and apprentices who built the city's houses, clothed its people, produced much of their food, printed their books, and put together their furniture and ships—made up at least 40 percent of the city's male work force in the early 19th century. Traditionally master artisans in small workshops trained apprentices who became journeymen and, in turn, masters themselves; all shared pride in their skill and their identity as "producers."

In the early 19th century, however, new canals and shipping lines, credit networks, and an influx of immigrant laborers began to change all that.

Now master artisans moved towards mass production aimed at expanding markets in New York, the western states and territories, and the coastal South. Rather than train apprentices and journeymen to become skilled masters themselves, employers cut costs and sped up production. They simplified tasks and divided them among undertrained apprentices, underemployed journeymen, women, children, or immigrants. Workshops increasingly looked like small factories; many masters also "put out" work to families to do at home in tenements and shanties nearby.

This industrial revolution helped New York City catch up with Philadelphia as the nation's manufacturing center (a race New York would win by 1850) but it also split the artisan community. It separated prosperous "bosses" from poor wage laborers, and both of them from the journeymen who were still hoping to become masters but feared sinking into "wage slavery" and poverty. Where they had once seen themselves as masters-in-training, journeymen now began identifying as "workingmen" in conflict with greedy "aristocrats"—a term they applied to artisan bosses as well as wealthy merchants, lawyers, and bankers.

POLITICAL ACTION

In response to these challenges, some New York journeymen turned to politics. In 1829 they came together to form the Workingmen's Party, dedicated to electing men to office who would support their agenda. "We have nothing to hope from the aristocratic orders of society," the party proclaimed. Party leaders used newspapers such as the *Working Man's Advocate* and *The Man* to spread radical new visions of how society could be reorganized. Robert Dale Owen argued for a state-run education system, in which children would be taken from their parents and given "equal food, clothing and instruction, at the public expense," as a way to remake America as a place of equal opportunity. Machinist Thomas Skidmore proposed a "General Division" of property every generation, so no American would own much more or less than any other—a true system of equality, as he saw it.[6]

Many Workingmen's Party members believed that the industrial revolution itself was hardening class divisions in New York. Printer George Henry Evans warned that the factory system could "destroy the dearest rights of freemen and convert their offspring into mere machines." Seeking new political allies, and torn between their sense of being "plain, practical mechanics" and their desire to become master artisans, the Workingmen's Party embraced a wide and somewhat vague definition of who could be counted as a "working man" ("small capitalists" were in, but wealthy bankers were out).[7]

The "Workies" (as contemporaries called them) managed to elect a carpenter to the State Assembly in 1829, a year when they won 6,000 out of 21,000 city votes. But the party was split by competing agendas and it soon splintered into rival factions. By 1836 it was dead. Still, its influence lived on within labor unions, as well as in the "Loco Foco" wing of the city's Democratic Party, which brought some of the "Worky" concerns about inequality into the mainstream of New York City politics. Democratic editors like the *Evening Post*'s William Cullen Bryant blasted the "injustice" of the verdict in the journeymen tailors' trial. At the same time, these same editors and party leaders ignored or ridiculed the more radical visions of Owen and Skidmore, helping to drive such ideas out of the mainstream of city politics.[8]

Agrarian Workingmen's Party of New York City c. 1830
Unknown artist, political cartoon

This Workingmen's Party cartoon contrasts a corrupt politician serving the devil (left) with an honest candidate (right) who addresses a figure of Liberty and vows to protect "the Poor" and "the Mechanic."

UNION MEN AND WOMEN

As the tailors' trial shows, in addition to political organizing workers also fought for their rights by organizing into labor unions. New York's first permanent union, a journeyman printers' society formed in 1794, had been quickly followed by others. The key weapon of unions was the strike, and New York journeymen launched over two dozen of them between 1795 and 1825. In 1833 New York unionists established the General Trades Union (GTU) as an umbrella organization to coordinate labor activism, and 50 new unions came into being. They launched nearly 40 strikes during the mid-1830s alone.

The union movement spread quickly. By 1834 about 11,500 men in New York City and Brooklyn had joined unions; about 25 percent of Manhattan's white male workforce had become union men. Union spokesmen were crafting a language of political and labor activism that painted conflict between masters and journeymen as the defining reality of workers' lives. As cabinetmaker and GTU leader John Commerford saw it in 1836, "organized bodies of journeymen should exist, to neutralize the schemes and effects of upstart mushrooms." By 1851 members of the Industrial Congress, another umbrella group, would declare that for laborers the very meaning of being American came down to "the right to Life, Liberty, and the fruits of their Labor."[9]

Unions frequently invoked the heritage of the American Revolution, but democracy went only so far in the early labor movement. Although African-American artisans formed a New York African Society for Mutual Relief in 1808, white journeymen barred them from joining their unions. Unskilled white workers formed their own unions and launched their own strikes, but they were accepted only gradually into the larger labor movement by more skilled craftsmen. The same held true for Irish and German workers, although they eventually overcame the anti-immigrant hostility of some native-born journeymen.

The city's female workers, increasingly concentrated in the garment trades, also faced enormous obstacles. Male unionists saw them as a threat, since bosses could replace skilled journeymen with lesser-skilled, lower-paid women and girls. The place for women, union spokesmen proclaimed, was in the home; the role of men was to fight for higher pay in order to spare their wives and daughters from the indignity and "slavery" of wage work. As one male labor activist described women in 1836,

Certificate of membership to the New York Mechanick Society 1787
Unknown artist, engraved certificate with wax seal

This membership certificate for the city's Mechanick Society—a master's organization—is topped by a hammer-wielding fist, a symbol the General Trades Union adopted as its own.

"the natural weakness of the sex—their modesty and bashfulness—their ignorance of the forms and conduct of public meetings" ill-prepared them to organize or strike.[10]

Yet organize and strike they did. In 1825 "tailoresses" struck for higher wages, and they continued to agitate over the following years. "If it is unfashionable for the men to bear the oppression in silence, why should it not also become unfashionable with the women?" asked tailoress Sarah Monroe during a strike meeting in 1831. In 1845 hundreds of women from six different trades organized the Ladies' Industrial Association as a citywide labor confederation against "tyrant employers." When a condescending male unionist offered to help them draft an address, "the women instantly rebuked his impertinence by saying that they were competent to manage their own affairs."[11]

LABOR WAR

On the other side, employers saw the labor movement as a violation of their freedom to hire whomever they wanted and to set wages without outside interference, and they fashioned their own tools in opposition. In the mid-1830s, New York masters established several trade associations including the Society of Master Tailors, which declared that unions were "subversive of the rights of individuals,

"Beware of Foreign Influence": Nativists & Catholics

"Here is a large body of ignorant men brought into our community… a body of men who servilely obey a set of priests imported from abroad." So declared artist, inventor, and New York University professor Samuel Morse in 1835. The objects of Morse's hostility were Roman Catholic immigrants arriving in the United States, most of whom landed in New York Harbor. The city's population more than doubled from 123,000 in 1820 to 270,000 in 1835, with much of the growth due to waves of Europeans fleeing poverty in their home countries. While many were Protestants, increasing numbers, especially from Ireland and Germany, were Catholics. Morse and other native-born Protestant activists believed that Catholics were part of a conspiracy hatched in the Vatican at Rome to end religious freedom and republican government in America and to increase "the number of their sect and the influence of the Pope in this country."[12]

"The Propagation Society. More Free than Welcome"
c. 1855
N. Currier, lithograph

This nativist cartoon imagines the Pope and five Catholic bishops (left) trying to land from a boat in order to take over America. They are confronted by native-born Americans (right), one of whom holds up a Protestant Bible to defeat the invaders.

"United American"
1849
N. Currier, hand colored
lithograph

In opposing foreign influence, nativists like this
member of the United Americans, a New York
fraternal order, played up patriotic imagery and
history while ignoring the role played by immigrants in the nation's past.

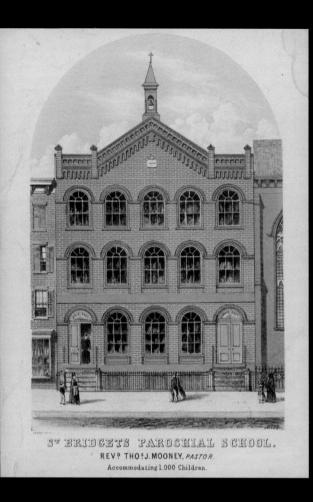

"St. Bridgets Parochial School" c. 1860
Keogh, color lithograph

Catholic immigrants fought back by creating their own citywide network of institutions—parish churches, charities, and parochial schools like this one—to insulate themselves from the hostility of Protestant nativists.

S.T BRIDGETS PAROCHIAL SCHOOL.
REVᴰ THOˢ J. MOONEY, *PASTOR*.
Accommodating 1,000 Children.

In response, Morse and his allies formed the nation's first openly nativist (anti-immigrant) political party, the North American Democratic Association, in Manhattan in 1835. For the next 20 years New York nativists would be key players in a nationwide movement to limit the influence and power of immigrants, especially Catholics. Another party, the American Republicans, rose to challenge a state law (1842) allowing Catholic voters to replace Protestant Bibles with Catholic ones in public schools attended by Catholic children. The American Republicans also pledged to keep foreigners out of office and wanted federal law changed so that immigrants could only gain citizenship (and voting rights) after 21 years, rather than after only five years.

In the early 1850s these positions were upheld by yet another nationwide party originating in New York City, the American Party or "Know Nothings," so-called because members replied "I know nothing" to questions about the organization's secrets. New York nativists enjoyed some short-term successes, electing James Harper as mayor in 1844 and seven congressmen statewide in 1855. But the growing immigrant vote, and the increasing centrality of the slavery issue in national politics, had greatly weakened the movement by the outbreak of the Civil War in 1861.[13]

1 **Frances Wright** 1881
John Chester Buttre, engraving

2 **Robert Dale Owen** undated
Unknown artist

3 **William Leggett** 1837–59
A. Sealey, engraving from a painting by
T.S. Cummings

4 **George Henry Evans** 1910
Unknown artist, from *A Documentary
History of American Industrial Society*

5 **Augusta Lewis Troup** 1894
Unknown artist, engraving from
*American Dictionary of Printing and
Bookmaking*

6 **Wilhelm Weitling** 19th century
Unknown artist, engraving

Radical visionaries helped shape
New York's labor movement. Feminist
and religious freethinker Frances
Wright challenged the inequalities
of an emerging class system. Robert
Dale Owen advocated a state-run
educational system for all, while
journalist William Leggett defended
journeymen's rights. George Henry
Evans warned against the factory
system and wanted the government to
grant free land to workingmen. Augusta
Lewis Troup founded the Women's
Typographical Union for female
printers after the Civil War, and Wilhelm
Weitling brought German socialist
ideas to New York's labor activism.

"Scene aus dem New-Yorker Turnerleben. Excursion of the New York Turners (Gymnastic Society)" 1854
Dumcke & Keil, hand colored lithograph

Immigrants played an increasingly central role in the city's labor movement. The Turners, a German-American athletic society espousing liberal and socialist views, influenced New York's unionists, as did clubs started by Irish and English workers.

detrimental to the public good... and oppressive towards industrious journeymen who are not members." Such associations created a way for employers to join together to fire or blacklist union organizers and pool resources to defeat strikes. Bosses also turned to the courts, filing charges with judges like Edwards who agreed that unions illegally interfered with free trade.[14]

Court convictions threatened to undermine the labor movement, but they also intensified the anger of workers who believed that employers were unfairly using the powers of the state to crush them. The sense of confrontation took a dramatic turn in August 1850 when some 300 striking tailors—most of them German immigrants—gathered outside a shop at 38th Street and Ninth Avenue that they accused of violating union wage rates. Police charged the crowd, killing two, injuring dozens, and arresting 40 more. For the first time in America, workers had been killed by government agents in a labor dispute.

Over the course of its first decades, New York's labor movement—like the nation's—scored numerous victories, persuading or forcing employers to raise wages, shorten hours, recognize the right to organize, and hire only union members. At the same time, bosses also succeeded in turning back various union efforts and using court injunctions to break strikes. Even more devastating for the entire labor movement were economic depressions triggered by financial meltdowns in 1837 and 1857, when wages plummeted and bosses laid off union-organizing "troublemakers," wiping out the gains of the movement and spelling the end of many unions.

Yet the era had also fostered a sense of group identity for many New York workers. For the most radical of them, the city had become a battleground between classes. In their eyes America had become a divided society, one that failed to deliver on the promises of the American Revolution, and workers themselves now had to seize those promises with their own hands. They would try to do so again during the Civil War, when over 90 city-wide strikes would erupt. Just as surely as New York had become the nation's unrivaled manufacturing metropolis, it had also become Labor's City—a role it would continue to play for decades to come.

—VOL. I. NO. 5.—

THE
AMERICAN
ANTI-SLAVERY
ALMANAC,
FOR
1840,

BEING BISSEXTILE OR LEAP-YEAR, AND THE 64TH OF AMERICAN
INDEPENDENCE.   CALCULATED FOR BOSTON; ADAPTED
TO THE NEW ENGLAND STATES.

NORTHERN HOSPITALITY—NEW YORK NINE MONTHS' LAW.

The slave steps out of the slave-state, and his chains fall.   A free state, with another
chain, stands ready to re-enslave him.

Thus saith the Lord, Deliver him that is spoiled out of the hands of the oppressor.

NEW YORK & BOSTON:
PUBLISHED BY THE AMERICAN ANTI-SLAVERY SOCIETY,
NO. 143 NASSAU STREET, NEW YORK;
AND BY J. A. COLLINS, 29 CORNHILL, BOSTON.

CHAPTER FIVE

Practical Abolitionists: David Ruggles and the New York Committee of Vigilance

**The American
Anti-Slavery
Almanac for 1840**
1840
American Anti-Slavery
Society

The American Anti-Slavery Almanac, published
jointly by abolitionists in New York City and
Boston, denounced a New York law that allowed
southerners to bring slaves into the state for up to
nine months.

On September 4, 1838 Frederick Bailey, a 20-year-old fugitive slave, stepped off a ferryboat onto Manhattan Island and began his first full day as a free man.

He had boarded a train in Baltimore the day before, armed with falsified papers that identified him as a free black sailor; his aim was to reach Canada or New England, beyond the reach of his Maryland masters. New York City was a temporary waystation, a place where he could disappear into the crowd. He was filled with joy at the urban spectacle: "I was walking amid the hurrying throng," he later recalled, "and gazing upon the dazzling wonders of Broadway. The dreams of my childhood and the purposes of my manhood were now fulfilled."[1]

Joy quickly turned to fear. By sheer luck, Bailey ran into someone he knew—another escapee, working as a whitewasher under a new name: William Dixon. Dixon warned Bailey that "the city was now full of southerners" returning home from their annual summer vacations in the north and that "there were hired men on the lookout for fugitives from slavery," including some black New Yorkers "who, for a few dollars, would betray me into the hands of the slave-catchers; that I must trust no man with my secret." Bailey realized that he was "an easy prey to the kidnappers, if any should happen to be on my track."[2]

After spending a lonely night on a deserted wharf, Bailey made his way to the bookstore and home of David Ruggles, secretary of the New York Committee of Vigilance, an organization founded in 1835 to confront slavery and racism head on. Born to free black parents in Connecticut in 1810, Ruggles had been a sailor, a grocer, and a printer before turning his home into a shop selling antislavery books and a meeting ground for the city's black and white abolitionists. By 1837 Ruggles and his comrades had already helped more than 335 African Americans escaping slavery.

A few days later, Bailey was joined by his fiancée, Anna Murray, a free black woman who had followed him from Baltimore. With David Ruggles as a witness, the two were married by another refugee from Maryland slavery. Within hours, the couple were on a steamboat on their way to Newport, Rhode Island, and from there to their final destination, the seaport of New Bedford, Massachusetts. Years later, after Frederick Bailey had changed his name to Frederick Douglass and become the nation's most prominent African-American activist, he remembered his New York host with appreciation: "Mr. Ruggles was the first officer on the underground railroad with whom I met after reaching the north... He was a whole-souled man, fully imbued with a love of his afflicted and hunted people..."[3]

"THE PRO-SLAVERY, NEGRO-HATING CITY OF NEW YORK"

By the time Bailey arrived on Ruggles's doorstep, the bookstore owner and a small band of other New Yorkers had been fighting slavery and racial discrimination for nearly a decade. Although New York State's remaining slaves had been freed in 1827, many white New Yorkers treated their free black neighbors with suspicion or open hostility. White artisans kept African-American workers out of many of the city's jobs and labor unions, while a growing population of Irish immigrants competed with black men and women for positions as servants, laundresses, seamstresses, waiters, barbers, and street vendors. Black children were limited to a small number of segregated schools. White business owners excluded "colored" people from equal treatment on the city's streetcar and steamboat lines, most boardinghouses and hotels, and many restaurants. The New York Zoological Institute refused to admit black New Yorkers as customers.

Nor did freedom bring political rights. New York State's 1821 Constitution required black men to

David Ruggles
undated
Unknown artist, charcoal print

"Frederick Douglass. The Colored Champion of Freedom"
c. 1873
Currier & Ives, lithograph

Frederick Douglass (right), who would become the century's most recognized abolitionist, remained a lifelong friend of Ruggles (left) after their meeting in New York.

own at least $250 in property in order to vote, and very few black New Yorkers had enough money to qualify; black women, like white women, were barred from voting completely. Even some of the white antislavery activists were unsympathetic to black people in their midst. For example, the American Colonization Society, founded in 1816 in Washington, DC with support from merchants, lawyers, and clergymen in New York and elsewhere, argued that the solution to the problem of slavery was gradually to send all African Americans—free and slave—back to Africa and rid America of their presence once and for all.

On top of all this, thousands of white New Yorkers were ardent defenders of southern slavery. The city's economy rested heavily on trade with the South: New York merchants and bankers shipped slave-grown cotton to England, extended loans to southern planters so they could plant their crops and buy new slaves, and insured their property. New York retailers, wholesale dealers, and working people profited when southern merchants and planters arrived in town to buy textiles and stay in Broadway hotels. Often those southerners brought their enslaved servants with them, which New York State law allowed them to do for up to nine months at a time.

Most New York City voters, moreover, were members of the Democratic Party, which actively supported slavery. When antislavery activists tried to hold an interracial meeting in the Chatham Street Chapel in July 1834, white mobs started three days of riots, driving some 500 African Americans out of their homes. In sum, New York often seemed to be as much a southern city as a northern one, a place whose economy and politics were bound

***The Disappointed
Abolitionists*** c. 1838
H. R. Robinson

Activists Isaac Hopper, David Ruggles, and Barney
Corse confront slave owner John P. Darg in New
York City in 1838. Unsympathetic to abolitionists,
the lithographer H. R. Robinson pictures Ruggles
as trying to extort money from Darg, saying, "I'm
afraid my pickings will not amount to much!"

up with slavery. No wonder that in 1839 the *Colored American*, the city's black newspaper, blasted what it called "the deep and damning thralldom which grinds to the dust the colored inhabitants of New York." Sixteen years later the black abolitionist William Wells Brown repeated the charge when he denounced "the pro-slavery, negro-hating city of New York."[4]

"PRACTICAL ABOLITION"

Facing such bleak circumstances, Ruggles and his colleagues dedicated themselves to bringing change through direct action. By the early 1830s Ruggles was a key member in a circle of activists based in the city's black church congregations and in black self-help organizations like the New York African Society for Mutual Relief. He identified strongly with William Lloyd Garrison's American Anti-Slavery Society, which called for interracial action to end American slavery immediately. But while Garrison advocated a course of nonviolence, Ruggles felt differently. He called for "practical abolition," meaning that black and white abolitionists must confront slave owners and their allies forcefully, even in the streets of New York City. "Whatever necessity requires, let that remedy be applied," he wrote in 1836. "Come what may, anything is better than slavery."[5]

Ruggles's solution was the Committee of Vigilance: a group of black and white New York anti-slavery activists he helped create in Manhattan in 1835. The committee's goal was to "protect unoffending, defenseless, and endangered persons of color, by securing their rights as far as practicable." Ruggles was the committee's secretary and lead actor, and New York, as the nation's major seaport, gave him plenty of opportunities to put theory into practice. In December 1836, for example, after the Portuguese slave ship *Brilliante* arrived in the harbor with five enslaved Africans on board, several men connected to Ruggles sprang into action. On Christmas Eve they stormed the *Brilliante* and escaped with two enslaved men. When a sailor tried to stop them, "one of the gang cocked a pistol at him, and threatened to blow his brains out." While the final fate of the two slaves is unclear, the raid demonstrated how activists close to Ruggles's committee were willing to risk their own safety to free others.[6]

The committee also used direct confrontation to fight for southern slaves whose masters brought them to New York but openly ignored the

The Butter and Milk Man 1840–44
Nicolino Calyo, watercolor and graphite pencil on paper

Along with African-American seamen, dock workers, and laborers, a small middle class of black clergymen, artisans, professionals, tradesmen (such as this vendor), and their families provided activists for the city's antislavery and anti-racist movements.

nine-month limit. Enslaved servants, both men and women, fought to use the law to escape or argue for their own freedom. Ruggles and his allies confronted slave owners face-to-face to try to force emancipations; the meetings sometimes became shouting or shoving matches. In one case in 1838 an enraged Virginian, John P. Darg, had Ruggles thrown into jail after he tried to negotiate freedom for Thomas Hughes, a slave of Darg's who had run away in New York with several thousand dollars of his master's money. Despite the setback, the abolitionists eventually won Hughes's freedom—after the master tried to sell him into the Deep South.

But most important to the committee was their crusade against the kidnappers who posed a threat to every black resident of New York City. Paid agents and bounty hunters roamed the city, seeking to capture runaways. They were aided by city officials who allowed black men, women, and children to be

jailed and shipped south with few questions asked, even though state law supposedly required they be granted trial by jury. The city's "kidnapping clubs," as Ruggles called them, went even further: city officials pounced on legally free black New Yorkers and dragged them south for sale on the flimsy assertion that they were runaways. Children as young as nine-year-old John Welch, lured from his Mulberry Street home, were caught up in this dragnet and were sometimes shipped hundreds of miles away before their parents could plead for their return.[7]

THWARTING THE "SLAVE-CATCHERS"

The committee fought back actively against the kidnappers and "slave-catchers." With funds provided by local white abolitionists and by a network of 100 black New Yorkers who raised cash from hundreds more, the Committee of Vigilance hired

Challenging Segregation in New York's Streets

In July 1854 Elizabeth Jennings, a young African-American teacher, boarded a horse-drawn streetcar at Pearl and Chatham Streets in Manhattan. When a conductor ordered her to leave the car because it was reserved for white passengers, she resisted, asserting that she "was a respectable person, born and raised in New-York." The conductor and a policeman pushed her from the car. Supported by New York abolitionists, including her father Thomas Jennings, a tailor and civil rights activist, she sued the Third Avenue Railway Company in order to demand "equal right to the accommodations of 'transit' in the cars." In 1855 Jennings won her case in the New York State Supreme Court, which found no legal basis for the whites-only policy, to the delight of Frederick Douglass and other black activists nationwide.[8]

Elizabeth Jennings Graham 1854–60
From "The Story of an Old Wrong," published in *The American Woman's Journal*, July 1895

Elizabeth Jennings remained a vigorous supporter of efforts to help New York's African-American community. In 1895 she founded the first kindergarten serving the city's black children.

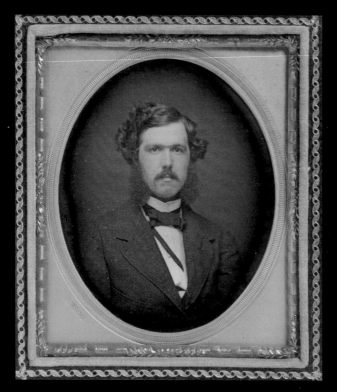

Portrait of Chester Alan Arthur c. 1858
Rufus P. Anson, sixth-plate Daguerreotype

Manhattan lawyer Chester A. Arthur successfully argued Elizabeth Jennings's lawsuit before the New York State Supreme Court. In 1881 he became the 21st president of the United States.

Old Storehouses, corner of Pearl and Chatham Street, 1861 1863
Sarony, Major & Knapp, New York, tinted lithograph

Elizabeth Jennings tried to board a Third Avenue Railway Company streetcar (right) at the intersection of Pearl and Chatham Streets (shown here in 1861).

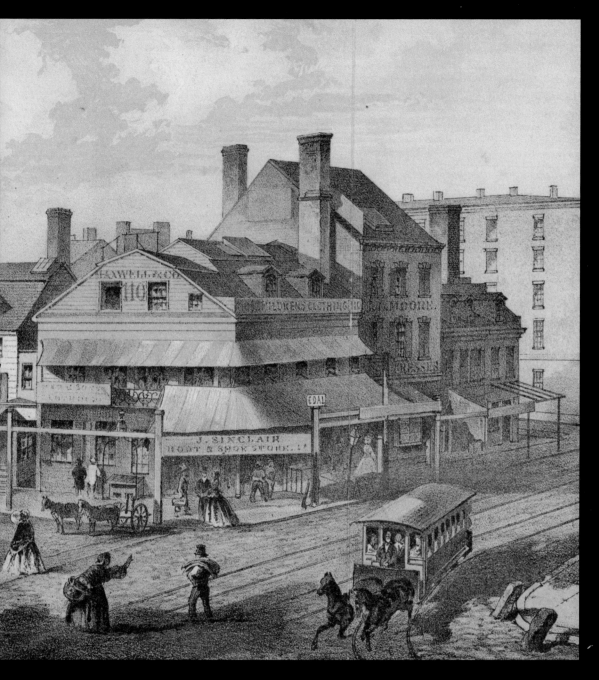

The segregation that Jennings fought was pervasive in mid-19th century New York City. A strict code of racial exclusion prevented African Americans from staying in most hotels, sitting where they liked in theaters and churches controlled by whites, or having equal access to the facilities of the all-important streetcars, horse-drawn buses, and ferries that enabled people to move across the growing urban region. Like Jennings, other activists, including David Ruggles, protested or resisted the inferior status imposed on black people by urban transit companies. In 1838, Samuel Cornish had urged readers of his newspaper, the *Colored American*, to "go by foot, Brethren," rather than endure segregation.[9]

skilled lawyers to help captives held in city jails or already deported to the South. Although the city's judges—many of them well-connected Democrats—sometimes refused to cooperate, by 1838 Ruggles and his committee had saved a reported 522 individuals from slavery. The committee counted on the influence and support of its white members, but black men and women were its troops on the ground, keeping an eye on potential kidnappers and mobilizing the city's African-American community to assist Ruggles.[10]

Ruggles also put together a network of safe houses and churches across the northeast that became stops on the "underground railroad" to freedom. He sent some refugees (like Frederick Douglass) along the East Coast to the black Quaker pharmacist Nathan Johnson and his wife Mary, a candy maker, in New Bedford. Others went to the Reverend J. W. C. Pennington in Hartford, Connecticut, and from there into western Massachusetts, New Hampshire, and Vermont. Another route ran up the Hudson River to Poughkeepsie or Albany. From there, fugitives could cross to Canada, or go into the Adirondacks.

By the 1840s, New York City's Committee of Vigilance had inspired the creation of similar groups in Philadelphia, Albany, Boston, Rochester, Cleveland, Detroit, and elsewhere, all bent on helping African Americans to flee from and resist slavery. Untold thousands of men, women, and children gained their freedom by "stealing themselves" from their owners and embarking on these secret routes.

PAYING A PRICE

Ruggles paid a price for his activism. After the *Brilliante* raid in 1836, an armed gang tried unsuccessfully to break into Ruggles's home, raising the fear that he could be seized and sent south to be sold. On another occasion, an enraged ship captain threw Ruggles down a flight of stairs when the abolitionist accused him of being a kidnapper. When Ruggles was told to make way for white passengers on a stagecoach in 1834, he refused, only to be beaten by the driver and several other whites.

Not only did Ruggles's health suffer from these assaults, but he lived a life of poverty. Despite support from abolitionists, the Committee of Vigilance was often short of money and in debt to creditors. He was also drawn into internal battles among abolitionists over the role of women in the movement and whether it was "appropriate" for women to speak publicly. Ruggles, who worked easily with

View of South Street, from Maiden Lane, New York City c. 1827
William James Bennett, watercolor on off-white wove paper

Slavery and antislavery jostled on New York's waterfront. Some New Yorkers secretly sent ships to buy slaves in Africa and sell them in the South, even though federal law prohibited such traffic after 1807. Legal slave-grown cargoes of cotton, sugar, and coffee crossed the docks daily. However, the harbor was also the scene of daring rescues of slaves from foreign ships.

David Ruggles worked with scores of abolitionists and influenced a younger generation of New York activists. Three black ministers—Samuel Cornish (co-founder of the nation's first black newspaper), Theodore S. Wright, and Charles B. Ray—were early mentors. Quaker activist Isaac Hopper was Ruggles's colleague on the Committee of Vigilance. With her husband, Mary Lyons carried forward Ruggles's legacy of aiding fugitive slaves who reached New York. Merchant Lewis Tappan helped fund the Committee of Vigilance. Lydia Maria Child, editor of the *National Anti-Slavery Standard*, also worked with Ruggles and Isaac Hopper. The Reverend J. W. C. Pennington and Stephen Myers helped move fugitive slaves along the underground railroad.

female activists in New York City, including the black abolitionists Hester Lane and Henrietta Ray and the white writer Lydia Maria Child, sided with the women. He also published a magazine, the *Mirror of Liberty*, in which a poem asked pointedly, "Was woman formed to be a slave... and Freedom never know!"[11]

Even more troubling to some of his comrades was Ruggles's lax bookkeeping and brash personality. In 1842 he resigned as secretary of the Committee of Vigilance and retired to an interracial community in Northampton, Massachusetts. There he opened a hospital featuring "hydrotherapy," seeking to cure patients with bathing and wrapping in wet towels. But he also continued his activism. In fact, Ruggles chaired the meeting where Sojourner Truth—his neighbor, patient, and fellow former New Yorker—made her first public address against slavery in 1844. But poor health caught up with Ruggles, and he died at age 39 in 1849, still fighting against slavery and racial discrimination.

THE STRUGGLE CONTINUES

Ruggles and his comrades left a complex legacy. In addition to the lives they saved through their direct activism, these abolitionists succeeded in keeping the issue of slavery in the public eye at a time when most Americans wanted to look away. By the late 1840s, slavery began to take center stage in the nation's politics, and in 1850 a federal Fugitive Slave Act aroused the anger of northerners by legally requiring them to do the dirty work of returning runaways to their masters. A new generation of activists in New York and across the North continued the struggle waged by Ruggles in lower Manhattan.

Around 1844, for example, the black abolitionist William Peter Powell managed to free two enslaved African men and a woman from a Brazilian coffee ship docked on the East River, much as Ruggles's companions had done on the *Brilliante* some eight years earlier. During the 1850s, Powell's acquaintances Albro and Mary Lyons passed hundreds of fugitive slaves through their boardinghouse near the South Street waterfront. Sidney Howard Gay, a white journalist, also maintained a Manhattan "station" for hundreds of escaping slaves. The Committee of Vigilance became a statewide body that by 1856 had reportedly helped 3,200 fugitives to freedom.

And yet New York remained a "pro-slavery, negro-hating city." Addressing a crowded hall in the Cooper Union on Astor Place in 1860, Alabama politician William Yancey told his listeners that the South demanded "that you will not allow anyone to steal away her niggers." "No, No!" New York Democrats roared back in agreement. The city's Democratic majority voted against Lincoln in 1860 and 1864, and in 1863 two of them, newspapermen David Goodman Croly and George Wakeman, invented a new word—"miscegenation"—to describe the "evil" sexual and social mixing of the races they alleged was the true goal of the Republican Party.[12]

While the Civil War (1861-65) finally fulfilled the abolitionist dream of ending slavery, it also brought racist violence to New York's streets. In July 1863 the federal draft law gave exemptions to any man wealthy enough to pay a $300 fee. This enraged immigrants who could not afford the fee, who blamed blacks for the war, and who feared job competition from freed slaves. Their anger exploded in the horrific Draft Riots of July 13-16, 1863, when thousands of white working men and women, many of them Irish immigrants, rampaged through Manhattan's streets, fighting with police, attacking abolitionists and Republicans, and lynching African Americans. At least 105 New Yorkers died (perhaps hundreds more), over 300 were wounded, and more than 100 buildings were burned down. Mobs attacked the homes of the Lyons family and William Peter Powell and they looted and tried to burn the West 29th Street townhouse of banker James Gibbons and Abigail Hopper Gibbons, daughter of Isaac Hopper. In the riots' aftermath, Manhattan's African-American population declined as blacks left and avoided the city.

The Committee of Vigilance was largely forgotten as historians in later decades focused on the efforts of white abolitionists or singled out just a few black antislavery activists such as Frederick Douglass and Harriet Tubman for attention. For most black New Yorkers and their white allies who struggled in later generations against racism, segregation, and discrimination in New York City as well as in the South, the name David Ruggles meant nothing. Yet in their efforts these later activists unknowingly echoed the defiance of the leader of the New York City Committee of Vigilance, who had once proclaimed, "I have tried to do my duty, and mean still to persevere, until the last fetter shall be broken, and the last sigh heard from the lips of a slave."[13]

Lieutenant Peter Vogelsang
1863–65
Copy photograph of carte de visite

New Yorker Peter Vogelsang, an activist colleague of Ruggles's during the 1830s, went on to fight against slavery in the Civil War.

Urban Crusaders

While abolitionists fought slavery and racism, other mid-19th-century New York reformers challenged conditions they viewed as evil byproducts of city life, including irreligion, intemperance (alcohol use), prostitution, gambling, begging, and crime. Sometimes ignoring the hard realities of a new industrial economy that left working people with few resources, these activists instead often blamed poverty on the "godlessness" and alleged moral flaws of the poor. In the city's emerging slum neighborhoods such as the Five Points in lower Manhattan, middle-class evangelical "home visitors" distributed Bibles and religious tracts to the working poor, and urged impoverished families to be "born again" by embracing Protestant Christianity.

"The Bible and Temperance" c. 1847
N. Currier, hand colored lithograph

Middle-class activists, like the Protestant minister pictured here reading aloud from the Bible, entered the homes of the city's poor to encourage them to give up evil habits (such as the intemperance of the drunken husband and father shown at right).

Convinced that the domestic life of the poor was itself a corrupting influence, some activists built alternative "homes," asylums, and reformatories to shelter, redeem, and isolate orphans, juvenile delinquents, prostitutes, and beggars whom they viewed as both vulnerable and dangerous. These sanctuaries were often built in the city's rural outskirts in northern Manhattan, isolating inmates from the supposedly harmful and tempting influences of urban slums, saloons, brothels, gambling dens, dance halls, and streets.

Children's Aid Society. Going West. Last party sent out by Mrs. John Jacob Astor before her death c. 1890
Jacob A. Riis, lantern slide

Boys prepare for their westward journey by "orphan train," paid for by the wealthy philanthropist Mrs. John Jacob Astor.

Still other activists invented a more dramatic solution for removing young New Yorkers from potential lives of crime, vice, and suffering: sending them to the west. An expanding transportation system, reformers argued, meant that city youths could be sent to distant rural areas where wholesome country life and farm labor would improve their moral and physical health. Between 1854 and 1929, New York's Children's Aid Society placed some 105,000 parentless or poor children on "orphan trains" that carried them across the country for adoption by farming families. Other urban agencies followed suit. By 1930 perhaps 250,000 American children, most from New York City, had been placed with families elsewhere.

Dining room, Orphan Asylum, 73rd Street, Riverside c. 1899
Byron Company,
gelatin silver print

As this late 19th-century photograph attests, institutions like the Orphan Asylum Society of the City of New York, founded by Mrs. Alexander Hamilton and other women in 1806, had long-lasting influence.

Gilded Ag

Progress

"It is so colossal…as to surpass the bounds of imagination," visitor Paul Bourget wrote of New York City in 1892.

Between the end of the Civil War in 1865 and the conclusion of World War I in 1918 New York did, indeed, become an urban giant. Politicians created a mega-city by merging the cities of New York and Brooklyn and consolidating outlying areas of the Bronx, Queens, and Staten Island into Greater New York, with Manhattan at its center. When this new five-borough city was born in 1898 the city's population jumped overnight from about 2 million to over 3.4 million people. By 1900 it was the world's second biggest city after London.

But redrawn boundaries were not the only reason for New York's phenomenal growth. Trade, finance, industry, and immigration continued to pump people, money, and new ideas into the city's densely packed neighborhoods and workplaces. So did a growing transit system—streetcars, elevated trains, ferryboats, new bridges, and, in 1904, a subway—that carried New Yorkers between their homes and jobs and allowed middle-class families to move out of lower Manhattan to newly developed neighborhoods uptown or across

the East and Harlem Rivers. Meanwhile, wealthy bankers, industrialists, and retailers built palatial mansions for themselves on Fifth Avenue.

At the same time, New York became the setting of contests between competing visions for the American labor movement. That movement had grown since the early days of the Workingmen's Party and the General Trades Union in the 1820s and '30s (see Chapter 4). During the 1880s Manhattan's and Brooklyn's 50,000-member Central Labor Union (many of

e to ive Era 1865–1918

"New York City— Grand Demonstration of Workingmen"
1882
Unknown artist, wood engraving from *Frank Leslie's Illustrated Newspaper*

New York's Central Labor Union (CLU) organized the nation's first Labor Day parade in 1882, shown here circling Union Square. Marching union members carried signs calling for a shorter (eight-hour) workday, and declaring "Labor Built This Republic and Labor Shall Rule It."

George's demands foreshadowed the aims of later New York progressive and socialist politicians, but, even though he earned 68,000 votes, he lost to the Democratic candidate. Many labor leaders, including cigar maker Samuel Gompers, concluded that electoral politics were a waste of time. Gompers's American Federation of Labor (AFL, 1886) replaced the CLU and Knights of Labor at the leading edge of the city's and nation's labor movement. By the early 20th century, the AFL was the most powerful American labor federation, negotiating with employers over "bread and butter" issues like pay and work hours. The AFL gained that power by focusing narrowly on the needs of skilled white male workers, and it rejected calls for radical political and economic change.

Less fortunate—and shut out of the AFL's unions of skilled workmen—were the laboring poor, most of them immigrants or the children of immigrants,

whose members also belonged to the Knights of Labor, a national organization) forged an inclusive movement open to skilled and unskilled workers, natives and newcomers, old and new immigrants, and men and women; some Knights of Labor local assemblies also had African-American members. The aim of the Central Labor Union (CLU) was to unite a broad working class against the power of wealthy

industrialists and corrupt politicians. In 1886 the CLU jumped into politics, backing the mayoral campaign of reformer Henry George, who called for taxes on landlords, government control of streetcar and elevated train lines, and the rights of "honest labor." Republican and Democratic politicians and journalists denounced George as a dangerous and radical "communist."

"The Ghetto, New York" c. 1915
Postcard

Filling with new immigrants like the eastern European Jews shown here, Manhattan's Lower East Side was the world's most densely populated place in the late 19th century.

Long Island City, Queens 1898
Byron Company, gelatin silver print

Spreading out into residential neighborhoods like this one in Queens, middle-class New Yorkers became an important force in the dawning Progressive Movement.

who toiled to make ends meet in workshops, factories, warehouses, docks, and streets. "The Other Half," reformer Jacob Riis called them—thousands of families crammed into airless and light-less tenement houses, shanties, and back alleys. For many men, women, and children these overcrowded homes were also their workplaces, as they labored long hours for low pay, mass-producing garments, cigars, paper flowers, or boxes for local manufacturers. Other men and boys worked in foundries and breweries, loaded and unloaded ships, built new streets, buildings, and

transit lines, or drove delivery carts. Many women and children laundered clothing, fed boarders who helped pay the rent, or scavenged the streets for castoff goods to use or sell.

By the 1880s this predominantly Irish and German immigrant workforce was changing. Poverty across eastern and southern Europe and anti-Semitism in Czarist Russia led Jews, Italians, and Slavs to steamship ports where they embarked for New York. These newcomers transformed the labor movement, forming new unions and locals both within and beyond the AFL. By the 1910s Jewish and Italian union members were sparking strikes that took so many thousands of workers out of the city's garment factories that observers called them "uprisings" and "revolts." They also turned women garment makers—considered unskilled workers on the bottom rung of the clothing industry—into central players in the city's labor politics. Sensing their zeal and potential power, even the conservative Samuel Gompers encouraged them to seize their rights in the workplace.

The new immigrant labor movement helped sustain New York's role as a city where radical ideas about reform and revolution were openly discussed and promoted. Like German labor organizers before them, many Jewish workers and some Italians had encountered social-ist and anarchist ideas in their homelands where poverty or persecution had led to membership in, or sympathy with, revolutionary groups. In New York these newcomers were further exposed to the crisscrossing influences of German, Russian, Italian, Spanish, Irish, English, and American radical thought available to them in a seemingly countless array of newspapers, lectures, debates, discussion groups, and alternative political parties. Chicago, San Francisco, Milwaukee, and other American cities also became centers for working-class radicals. But New York was indisputably the "capital" of the American left by the beginning of the 20th century, a place where men and women could drink deeply of the currents of anarchism, socialism, communism, atheism, feminism, "free love," and birth control—all of them calls to action.

Meanwhile, middle-class New Yorkers—and some wealthy ones—developed their own activist movements. Their outrage over corruption and misspent public funds, for example, toppled "Boss" William Tweed's political "machine" in 1871. Protestant zeal continued to shape middle-class reform and philanthropy in this era. But many educated New Yorkers—lawyers, doctors, teachers, journalists, social workers—increasingly believed that science was equal or even superior to religion as a guide to social action. The lessons of new or expanding fields—sociology, economics, public health, urban planning—pointed to the need for hard data, efficiency, and organization in order to make New York and the nation a better place. By 1900 New York was a hub of this rising Progressive Movement, in which investigative journalists such as Ida Tarbell and Lincoln Steffens (labeled "muckrakers" by President Theodore Roosevelt) exposed and challenged the immense power of Wall Street banker J. P. Morgan, oil tycoon John D. Rockefeller, and the city's Tammany Hall

political "machine." Progressive activists and voters would become a key bloc in shaping the city's 20th-century liberal politics—even as Morgan, Rockefeller, and Tammany remained symbols of the city's inequalities of power and wealth.

Middle-class and wealthy progressive women played a distinctive role in the city's late 19th-century and early 20th-century activism. They repeatedly sought to bridge the gulf that separated their own world from that of immigrant working women by ministering to them in settlement houses that provided much-needed social services, joining them in the campaign for woman suffrage, supporting the great garment workers' strike of 1909-10, and advocating

workplace safety following the Triangle Factory Fire (1911). The common cause made by women as different as future First Lady Eleanor Roosevelt and Polish Jewish labor organizer Rose Schneiderman would influence liberalism in America for half a century.

Other New Yorkers, less "visible" in this era of expansion and immigration, launched their own activist efforts. Largely ignored by white activists, the work of José Martí, Wong Chin Foo, Victoria Earle Matthews, and others on behalf of Latino, Asian, and black New Yorkers foreshadowed a later day when people of color would often be at the forefront of the city's movements for reform or revolution.

"The Central Bank"
1910
Frank A. Nankivell,
cover of *Puck*

New York journalists and illustrators fueled progressive reform movements when they criticized the vast power and wealth of Wall Street bankers such as J. P. Morgan, pictured here grasping for a child's piggy bank.

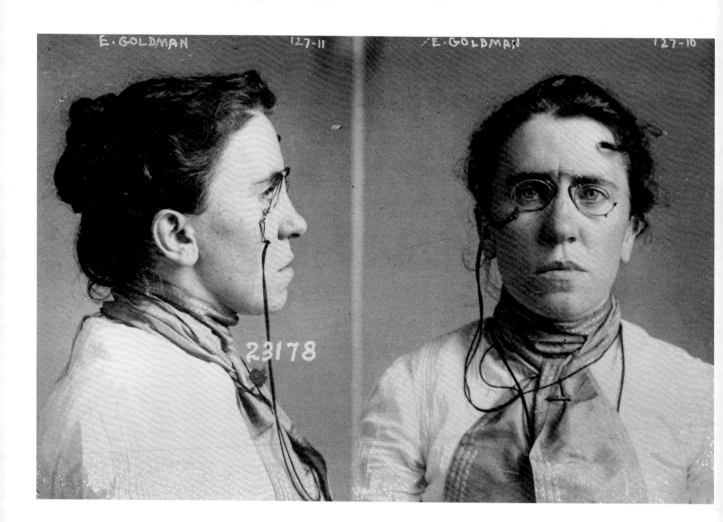

CHAPTER SIX

"Propaganda by Deed": New York City Anarchists

Emma Goldman
c. 1901
Unknown photographer

These "mugshots" of Emma Goldman were taken after one of her numerous arrests for radical agitation.

On August 21, 1893 a young Russian Jewish immigrant stood on a platform in Union Square before thousands gathered to hear her.

"**M**en and women," Emma Goldman began,

Do you not realize that the State is the worst enemy you have? It is a machine that crushes you in order to maintain the ruling class, your masters... Fifth Avenue is laid in gold, every mansion a citadel of money and power. Yet there you stand, a giant, starved and fettered, shorn of his strength... They will go on robbing you... unless you wake up, unless you become daring enough to demand your rights. Well, then, demonstrate before the palaces of the rich; demand work. If they do not give you work, demand bread. If they deny you both, take bread. It is your sacred right![1]

Her audience listened attentively. Many of them were workers fearful of losing their jobs in a nationwide depression that was just unfolding. At age 24 Goldman was already notorious, trailed by reporters and police detectives. The year before, she had helped her lover, fellow anarchist Alexander Berkman, plan an attack on industrialist Henry Clay Frick. Outraged by the killing of striking workers at Andrew Carnegie's steel plant in Homestead, Pennsylvania, Berkman had journeyed to Pittsburgh to try to assassinate Frick, who was Carnegie's manager, hoping to trigger a workers' uprising. Though the attack failed, Berkman was serving a 22-year prison term. Now, carrying a red flag, Goldman led marches through Manhattan's streets, urging workers to begin "the social revolution." After her speech she was arrested for inciting the crowd to riot. She spent 10 months in the penitentiary on Blackwell's Island in the East River.[2]

Anarchism was one of numerous radical movements that had emerged in 19th-century Europe as a response to the social upheaval of the industrial revolution. Anarchists believed that workers could only free themselves from poverty and oppression by abolishing government and creating a completely free and classless society of producers. Dismissing elections as a way to trick voters into accepting injustices, they argued that workers should take "direct action" by forming cooperative workshops and exchanging the fruits

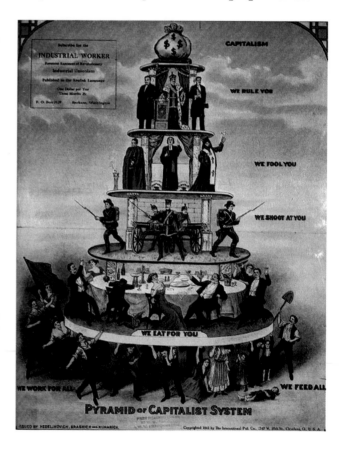

"Pyramid of Capitalist System" 1911
Nedeljkovich, Brashich and Kuharich, from *Industrial Worker* published by The International Publishing Company, Cleveland, Ohio

Although published in Ohio, this image captures the way many anarchists and socialists in late 19th-century New York viewed capitalism. The exploited working class (bottom) supports those above them in the social pyramid: the wealthy, the military, clergymen, and political rulers.

Bohemian Cigar Makers at Work in Their Tenement 1889-90
Jacob A. Riis, gelatin dry plate negative

Like this family of poor Czech cigar makers, many immigrants faced long work hours, low pay, and harsh conditions in New York, fueling the outrage and activism of anarchists.

of their own labor free from employers and politicians. Anarchists argued (and sometimes came to blows) with other leftists, especially socialists, who insisted that a government run by and for the working class had to come before any ideal classless society. In 1872 the hostility between the two groups had split their shared organization, the International Workingmen's Association. In New York, where most anarchists and socialists were European immigrants or their children, they often reserved their bitterest curses for each other rather than their shared enemy: capitalism.[3]

THE ANARCHISTS' CITY

By the 1880s New York City was home to a small but vigorous anarchist population of perhaps a few thousand. Its members were mostly European radicals who came to New York to escape police in their home nations. French anarchists clustered in Greenwich Village. Cuban anarchists made their home among a community of cigar makers on the Upper East Side. A growing number of Jewish radicals congregated in the tenements and cafés of the Lower East Side where they met fellow anarchists from Italy and Spain.

But the center of anarchism in New York was "Little Germany," a neighborhood that stretched over 400 city blocks in today's East Village and Lower East Side. By 1890 New York was the world's third largest German-speaking community: two out of seven New Yorkers had either been born in Germany or had at least one German-born parent. In New York many found conditions that seemed to rival

"New York City.— John Most, the anarchist, addressing a meeting of sympathizers at Cooper Institute, April 4th." 1887
Unknown artist, wood engraving from *Frank Leslie's Illustrated Newspaper*

Johann Most's fiery speaking style is on display in this contemporary newspaper illustration.

or surpass the misery of European cities. In 1865 an investigator noted that thousands of immigrant families were "literally submerged in filth, and half-stifled in an atmosphere charged with all the elements of death." In the city's tenement districts the infant mortality rate was over twice that in affluent Murray Hill uptown. Businessmen grew rich trading the stocks and bonds of railroads built and operated by workers, while cutthroat competition among the city's garment and cigar "sweatshops" kept small-scale employers and their laborers in poverty.[4]

Several events convinced some radicals that the government and workers were already at war. When 7,000 unionists and their families gathered in Tompkins Square Park in January 1874 to demand that the city government pay into a relief fund to feed the hungry, they were attacked by police. In 1877 a nationwide strike by railroad workers and coal miners was put down by soldiers, leaving about 100 dead. To many anarchists and socialists, a "social revolution" was needed in New York, Chicago, and Cincinnati as badly as in London, Paris, or St. Petersburg.

Late 19th-century Little Germany had its own anarchist geography for sharing such ideas: Justus Schwab's beerhall and lending library at 50 First Street, one of some 200 anarchist-affiliated saloons and clubhouses; the Cooper Institute on Astor Place, open to all, including radical speakers like Emma Goldman; and Harmony Park on Staten Island and Liberty Park in Ridgewood, Brooklyn, where anarchists gathered for summer picnics. And New York's role as the nation's printing and publishing center allowed German anarchists to launch 16 radical newspapers which they distributed across the country and the Atlantic between 1880 and 1914.

ANARCHIST IDEOLOGY

New York anarchists spread their ideas in print, via soapbox speeches, and in political gatherings. Among their many leaders, the most influential in crafting the movement's radical vision was Johann Most, the tireless editor of *Freiheit* (Freedom), a weekly paper with offices at 167 William Street. Most's radical career had begun at age 12 when he was expelled from school for organizing a "strike" against an abusive teacher. By the time he left Germany for London two decades later, he had spent five years in prison and been elected to the German

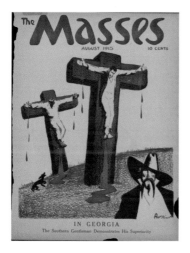

1 *Der Anarchist* July 15, 1893

2 *Freiheit* March 10, 1888

3 *The Pageant of the Paterson Strike* 1913
Unknown artist, program cover

4 *Mother Earth* August 1914
Cover illustration by Man Ray

5 *The Masses* August 1915
Cover illustration by Robert Minor

6 *Il Martello* August 27, 1927

For decades radicals made New York the information center of the American left. *Der Anarchist* and Johann Most's *Freiheit* reached German speakers on both sides of the Atlantic. The 1913 pageant for New Jersey strikers brought New York's anarchists and socialists together in support of workers' rights. Emma Goldman's *Mother Earth* and the Greenwich Village magazine *The Masses* aired controversial political views while also displaying work by Man Ray, Robert Minor, and other radical artists. Carlo Tresca's Italian-language *Il Martello* (The Hammer) lamented the 1927 execution of Nicola Sacco and Bartolomeo Vanzetti, Massachusetts anarchists many leftists believed to have been falsely convicted of murder.

Parliament. He moved to New York in 1882 when he was released from an English prison where he had been sent for celebrating the assassination of Russian Czar Alexander II.

Most spread the gospel of "Propaganda by Deed"—a call to commit acts of heroic revolutionary violence. In Goldman's words this would "strike terror in the enemy's ranks and make them realize that the proletariat [working class] of America had its avengers." Most's oratory stirred Lower East Side audiences. "It was but for Most to give the word," one observer noted, "and the audience would rush to build barricades and begin the revolution." Most briefly sought to turn words into action with a pamphlet on explosives, *Revolutionary War Science*, and he may have secretly sent dynamite to anarchists in Chicago. Months later, in May 1886, someone threw a dynamite bomb into a crowded labor rally at Haymarket Square, killing seven Chicago policemen and at least four others. Eight anarchists were convicted of the bombing on dubious evidence, and four were executed, furnishing the international anarchist movement with martyrs and the public with fuel for their fear of anarchists.[5]

"Propaganda by Deed" divided New York's

anarchists, as did a host of other tactical and philosophical questions. Was violence justified? Were labor unions vehicles for—or obstacles to—revolution? How much organization was appropriate in a movement dedicated to spontaneous action? And was it enough to mobilize immigrant radicals or did anarchists have also to convert native-born workers? Individual anarchists took different (and often evolving) positions on these questions. By 1887 Johann Most himself was questioning the usefulness of violence, as would Emma Goldman nearly 30 years later.

The appeal of anarchism went beyond the call for violent direct action. Emma Goldman, in particular, brought together different strands of thought and action—political, economic, cultural, and sexual—under the umbrella of anarchism. Goldman's eloquence in Yiddish, German, Russian, and English made her a popular speaker among the city's leftist audiences. Her monthly magazine *Mother Earth*, launched in 1906 from her apartment on East 13th Street, provided an intellectual forum for European and Greenwich Village writers. Repeatedly arrested and locked out of auditoriums on speaking tours across city and country, Goldman became one of the

Leonard Abbott speaking to anarchists in Union Square 1914
Unknown photographer

The ability of anarchists to draw crowds of supporters to sites like Union Square, now the city's main rallying point for leftists and labor unions, frightened many New Yorkers. Officials built a network of armories across the city to ready the city for putting down a possible armed revolution.

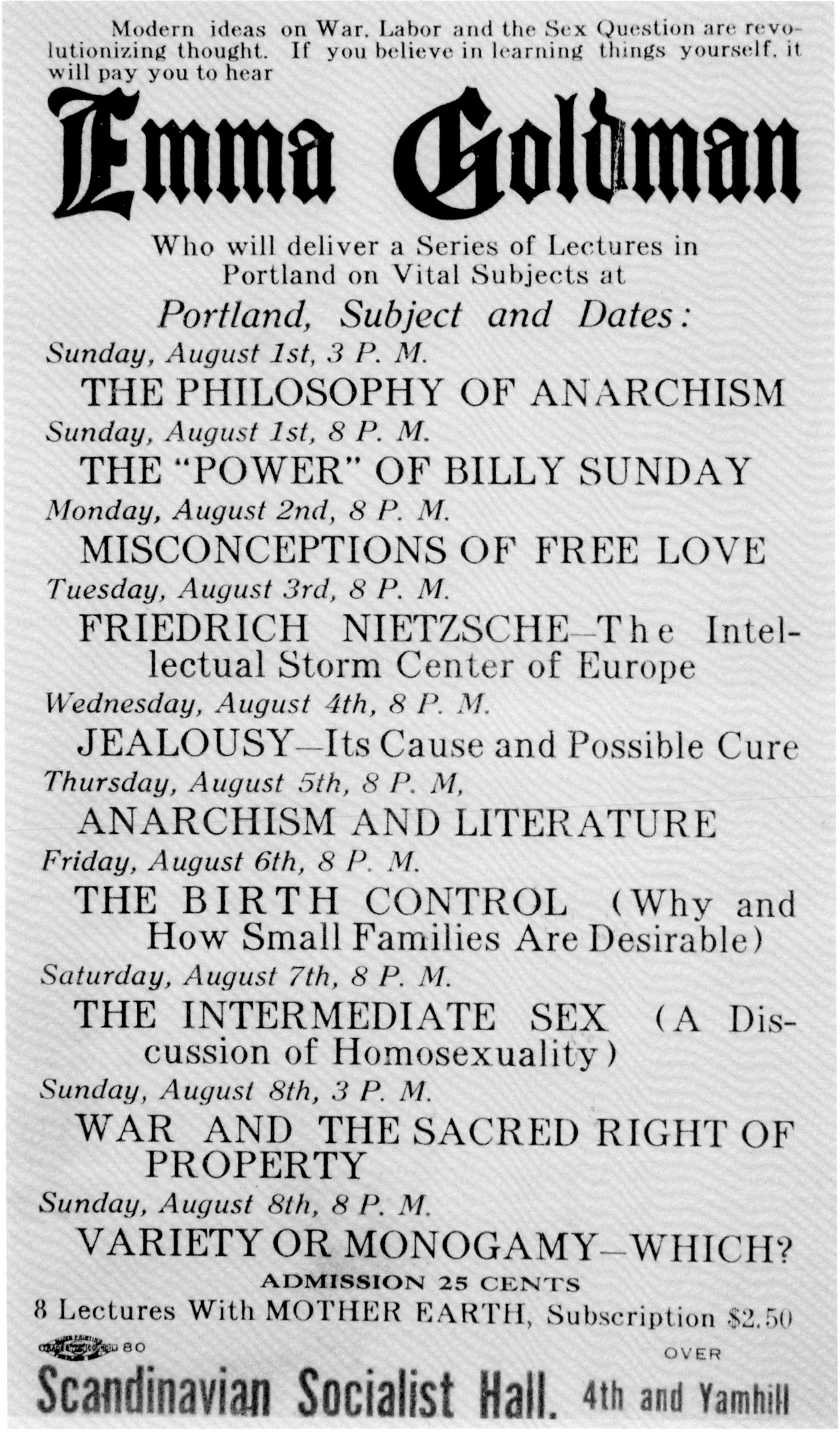

Modern ideas on War, Labor and the Sex Question are revolutionizing thought. If you believe in learning things yourself, it will pay you to hear

Emma Goldman

Who will deliver a Series of Lectures in
Portland on Vital Subjects at

Portland, Subject and Dates:

Sunday, August 1st, 3 P. M.

THE PHILOSOPHY OF ANARCHISM

Sunday, August 1st, 8 P. M.

THE "POWER" OF BILLY SUNDAY

Monday, August 2nd, 8 P. M.

MISCONCEPTIONS OF FREE LOVE

Tuesday, August 3rd, 8 P. M.

FRIEDRICH NIETZSCHE—The Intellectual Storm Center of Europe

Wednesday, August 4th, 8 P. M.

JEALOUSY—Its Cause and Possible Cure

Thursday, August 5th, 8 P. M,

ANARCHISM AND LITERATURE

Friday, August 6th, 8 P. M.

THE BIRTH CONTROL (Why and How Small Families Are Desirable)

Saturday, August 7th, 8 P. M.

THE INTERMEDIATE SEX (A Discussion of Homosexuality)

Sunday, August 8th, 3 P. M.

WAR AND THE SACRED RIGHT OF PROPERTY

Sunday, August 8th, 8 P. M.

VARIETY OR MONOGAMY—WHICH?

ADMISSION 25 CENTS

8 Lectures With MOTHER EARTH, Subscription $2.50

80

OVER

Scandinavian Socialist Hall. 4th and Yamhill

Handbill advertising a lecture series by American anarchist Emma Goldman in Portland, Oregon
1919

In one of her last nationwide speaking tours before being deported Emma Goldman discussed anarchism, birth control, homosexuality, free love, and other controversial topics.

Organizers of the Silk Strike in Paterson, New Jersey 1913
Unknown photographer

Leftists who rallied to support the 1913 Paterson strike included (front row, left to right) socialist Hubert Harrison, soon to be a major figure in Harlem activism, and Elizabeth Gurley Flynn and William "Big Bill" Haywood, both of the Industrial Workers of the World (IWW).

nation's most dogged activists for free speech and a free press—rights she expected to be central to the coming anarchist society.

Goldman brought together the causes of freedom of speech, improving the lives of the poor, feminism, and sexual liberation in ways that challenged authorities while stimulating her listeners and readers to think and act in new ways. Arguing that contraceptives allowed working-class women to limit the number of their children, control family expenses, and lead better lives, she defied official bans on publicly discussing birth control. Like other anarchists, Goldman renounced marriage as a form of slavery: "I did not propose to forge chains for myself." Goldman was also one of the only public speakers in America to address homosexuality as a reality worthy of open discussion rather than censorship and repression. Freedom to love, she argued, had to be liberated from outmoded rules, the financial drain of uncontrolled pregnancy, and sexual double standards. A future anarchist society, she believed, would ensure these freedoms; frank discussion of them was a step in the direction of creating that society.[6]

"THERE GO THE FILTHY ANARCHISTS!"

But to most Americans, Goldman's controversial ideas—combined with news of anarchist violence—discredited the movement as a threat to both decency and safety. Between 1881 and 1906 European anarchists and other leftists tried to assassinate monarchs and heads of state in Russia, France, Austria, Italy, and Spain; they succeeded in killing five of them. Most horrifying for Americans, in 1901 anarchist Leon Czolgosz fatally shot US President William McKinley. In response, New York State enacted a Criminal Anarchy law, which became a model for a 1903 federal act that sought to prevent anarchists from entering the country. Many labor leaders, including Samuel Gompers of the American Federation of Labor, distanced themselves from anarchists. In Manhattan Johann Most's son, John Jr., later recalled that "the neighbors threw insults—and sometimes rocks at us: 'There go the filthy anarchists!'"[7]

Even before the McKinley shooting New York officials and businessmen had made it clear how much they feared radicals. Especially after 1886, when labor unions and unionized voters flocked to support radical mayoral candidate Henry George, the city's police and judges increased efforts to crack down on leftists. Goldman was not the only anarchist who spent time in the Blackwell's Island penitentiary; Johann Most was sent there three times between 1886 and 1901.

More broadly, the threat of radicalism reshaped the social geography of the city. After moving his main factory from Manhattan to Long Island City, Queens, during the 1870s, piano manufacturer William Steinway admitted that he had relocated partly because "we wished to escape the anarchists and socialists who even at that time were continually breeding discontent among our workmen and inciting them to strike." As labor militancy grew so did fears. Some 20 fortress-like armories were built across the city to house National Guard regiments that could be used to put down uprisings by the city's growing immigrant working class. Inspecting the new armory at Columbus Avenue and 61st Street in 1887 a reporter noted that guardsmen could defend it against workers "in the mediaeval manner with boiling oil and melted lead, or even in the modern manner with musketry fire."[8]

A NEW CENTURY

Despite the opposition, New York's anarchists persevered, and their ranks grew in the new century. Jewish anarchists played important roles in the city's garment workers' unions. Italian anarchists, some of whom had fought in uprisings against the Italian government during the 1890s, flocked to the metropolitan region's factories. In Greenwich Village, native-born, college-educated Americans created a "Bohemia" where they could be free to embrace unconventional ideas. They were attracted to the Industrial Workers of the World (IWW), which was founded in 1905 to spread the idea that workers should form one big union and launch a general strike to paralyze capitalism and bring about a classless and stateless society. In 1913 Village socialists and anarchists journeyed to Paterson, New Jersey, to join an IWW-supported strike by 25,000 silk workers for an eight-hour day and better work conditions. Villagers John Reed, Mabel Dodge, John Sloan, and others mounted an elaborate theatrical pageant in Madison Square Garden to raise funds and public awareness for the struggle. But the grand spectacle lost money and the strike itself ultimately failed.

World War I and its aftermath shattered the anarchist movement. In 1917 Goldman and Berkman (who had been released from prison in 1906) came out vocally against America's entry into the war, but new federal laws outlawed dissent. The US Post Office denied mailing privileges to *Mother Earth* and other radical publications, effectively shutting them down. Because they opposed the war, anarchists were depicted as German sympathizers or even agents.

Tensions rose after the war as a wave of strikes and bombings across the country further inflamed public opinion against radicalism. The terrorism culminated in a blast on September 16, 1920 that indiscriminately killed 38 and seriously wounded 143 pedestrians on Wall Street—the deed of anonymous anarchists inspired by the ideas of Luigi Galleani, who had been an activist in the Paterson silk mills.

Nine months earlier Emma Goldman, Alexander Berkman, and 247 other Russian-born anarchists and communists found themselves leaving New York harbor, deported as dangerous aliens. They were welcomed by the government of the new Soviet Union, but their enthusiasm evaporated in the face of arrests and executions of Russian anarchists and the violent suppression of a strike launched by anarchist workers and sailors in 1921. Embittered at what she called "that cold monster the Communist State," Goldman left Russia that year, moving first to Germany and then France. She lived long enough to become an ardent supporter of the anarchists fighting for the Spanish Republic during the Spanish Civil War (1936–39) before dying in Canada in 1940.[9]

Lamenting the failure of anarchists to bring social revolution in America, Johann Most complained that "we resemble voices crying in the wilderness, kept unheard… anarchism [is] a violet that blooms unnoticed." Goldman agreed that "the people are asleep; they remain indifferent." In truth anarchists, rooted in foreign-language clubs and newspapers, never reached most English-speaking workers. Their call for "Propaganda by Deed" alienated and frightened potential supporters. For many immigrants anarchism was a phase that they or their children left behind as they adapted to life in New York City.[10]

The Modern School, New York City c. 1911
Unknown photographer

The teaching staff of the Modern School included Will Durant (top row, center), who later became a prominent writer and historian.

ANARCHIST LEGACIES

Yet the anarchist tradition enjoyed an influential afterlife, shaping the city's and nation's activism in future decades. Inspired by European anarchists who believed true freedom required an overhaul of education, New Yorkers founded the Ferrer Center and its Modern School on St. Mark's Place in 1911. The school and others across the country became cradles of innovative ideas for children, helping to spread the "Montessori Method" (despite the opposition of some anarchists who viewed Montessori as "authoritarian") and shaping educational reform in 20th-century America.[11]

Meanwhile, immigrants found inspiration in the feminism of Goldman and other anarchist writers and speakers. Women in the city's Italian anarchist community challenged the authority of fathers, husbands, priests, bosses, and male anarchists over their own lives. Parents and teachers "have made us into cooking and sewing machines," one wrote in 1906. "In a short time we will create a new society, where men's supremacy over women will cease to exist and human solidarity will reign supreme," predicted another in 1901.[12]

Indeed, anarchist ideas about gender and sexuality provided a seedbed for later feminists. Goldman and Berkman, for example, were among the early collaborators of fellow New Yorker Margaret Sanger in her campaign for legal birth control during the 1910s. Sanger went on to win court victories legalizing contraceptives, establish the American Birth Control League in 1921, and cofound the International Planned Parenthood Federation in 1952.

Goldman and her anarchist comrades had helped turn New York into a global incubator for new ideas about freedom, sex, the family, and the rights of women in modern industrial society. Their part in helping to bring about this revolution in "manners and morals" would be, perhaps, their most lasting victory. And small numbers of New Yorkers—members of the Catholic Worker movement, Judith Malina and Julian Beck of the Living Theatre, and others—carried forward a faith in anarchism that would flare up again during the 1980s in efforts by squatters to resist East Village gentrification, in Occupy Wall Street in 2011, and at other unfolding moments of activist resistance.

Battling the Slums: Housing Investigation and Reform

"We know now that there is no way out; that the 'system' that was the evil offspring of public neglect and private greed has come to stay," wrote journalist Jacob Riis in 1890 as he described the plight of New York's tenement dwellers. By Riis's own estimate 75 percent of the city's people lived in tenements—multi-storied houses containing multiple apartments with shared hallways, stairs, and toilets. By the 1880s, when Riis began investigating, thousands of these tenements were filthy, overcrowded, dangerous places lacking light, fresh air, or clean water. Riis used words to reach New York's reading public, but he also relied on photographs he and others took on journeys into the slums. In slide lectures he delivered and in published versions of his pictures, Riis unfolded "How the Other Half Lives"—and demanded change.[13]

Riis sought to arouse the consciences of officials and middle-class readers and voters by describing how tenement conditions brought illness and misery to the city's poor families. He also tried to frighten his audiences into action by arguing that the disorder and squalor of tenement life caused crime, mob violence, sexual vice, and most of the city's other social ills. Himself a Danish immigrant, Riis readily used negative stereotypes, common in his era, to describe the Lower East

"The Battle with the Slum" advertisement for a lecture by Jacob A. Riis 1905
Jacob A. Riis, lantern slide

A determined Jacob Riis stares out from this advertisement for one of his slide lectures, in which he showed photographs of tenement conditions to arouse public action for better housing.

Ludlow Street Cellar Habitation 1895
Jacob A. Riis, gelatin dry plate negative

Riis sought to capture the bleakness of tenement life with his camera, as in this photograph of a Lower East Side basement dwelling.

Living Room in Riverside Buildings, Brooklyn c. 1895
Unknown photographer, hand-colored lantern slide

In contrast to tenement living, Riis championed the tidy, airy, low-rent "model" apartments built in Brooklyn by Alfred Tredway White.

Side's Italian, Jewish, Chinese, and African-American slum dwellers. But he also argued that these New Yorkers deserved "a clean and comfortable home" in order to be good citizens.[14]

Unlike anarchists seeking a classless society, Riis's goal was far more modest. He wanted tenement landlords to settle for lower rents and to plow more of their revenues into improvements—"Philanthropy and five per cent.," he called it. He applauded reformers like Brooklyn's Alfred Tredway White who built five "model" apartment houses for working families in 1877-79. Riis's writings and pictures also influenced New York State's 1901 Tenement House Act, which required ample space, light, air, and private toilets in all new apartments. Beyond that, Riis produced a body of pictures foreshadowing the "documentary" photography of later New Yorkers who also used searing images to spur social activism.[15]

CHAPTER SEVEN

"Inside the Monster": Latino Activism in 19th-Century New York

South Street and Brooklyn Bridge, New York c. 1890
Published by Detroit Photographic Company, photochrome postcard

José Martí's Front Street office was only one block from these East River piers and ships that connected New York's Cuban exiles to their homeland.

On the stormy night of April 11, 1895, six exhausted men dragged a rowboat and several thousand rounds of ammunition onto a beach on Cuba's southern coast.

Five of the men were bent on helping to lead a revolution that had broken out against the island's Spanish rulers. The sixth man, José Martí, had spent 15 years—more than a third of his life—organizing that revolution from a small office at 120 Front Street in lower Manhattan and from boardinghouses and hotel rooms scattered across New York City and the neighboring city of Brooklyn. Now, Martí hoped, the moment had arrived when Cuban patriots would free their country from 400 years of Spanish autocracy, slavery, and economic exploitation.

The twists and turns of Martí's life had taken him from Havana, where his Spanish immigrant parents met and married, to a Cuban prison where Spanish authorities put him to hard labor at age 17 for treasonous activities, then to periods of exile in Spain, Mexico, Guatemala, and Venezuela, and finally to New York, where he settled in 1881.

By 1895 much of Latin America knew Martí as an important poet, playwright, journalist, teacher, and diplomat. But Martí's main work in New York was to collaborate with other émigrés in planning a revolution that would make Cuba an independent nation. He and his comrades were also in the thick of the movement to free Puerto Rico, Spain's other remaining American colony. (The two causes, indeed, were intertwined in a common effort: "Cuba and Puerto Rico are the two wings of one bird," wrote Martí's New York colleague, Puerto Rican-born Lola Rodríguez de Tió.)[1]

Martí's experience in New York embodies an important aspect of New York's activist history. Like generations of other insurgents, he and his fellow 19th-century Latino activists found in the Western Hemisphere's largest, richest, and most international city a refuge, a base of operations, and a center for raising money and buying arms. In fact,

revolutionaries came to New York from the world over. The Italian Giuseppe Garibaldi in 1850-51; Margarita Maza de Juárez, the wife of Mexican President-in-exile Benito Juárez, in 1864-66; the young Vietnamese radical Ho Chi Minh and Korean nationalists during the 1910s; the Polish Zionist David Ben-Gurion in 1915-17; the Russian Communist Leon Trotsky in 1917; and the Irish nationalist Eamon de Valera in 1919-20—for all of them New York was a safe haven and sometimes served as a cradle for revolutions fought hundreds or thousands of miles away.

Yet, for Martí and others, New York could prove a double-edged sword. The city was a base for planning freedom struggles, but it was also a place whose businessmen were spreading American economic and political influence abroad, especially in Latin America—often in ways that made freedom struggles more difficult. The sanctuary, it seemed, was also a very real threat. Martí expressed his mixed feelings about New York and the United States when he wrote in 1895 that "I lived inside the monster, and know its entrails—and my sling is David's."[2]

LATINO NEW YORK

When Martí first visited New York in 1880 he found a small but vibrant community of Spanish speakers. Due in part to a long history of trade with Spain's colonies—which included traffic in enslaved Africans, American-made textiles, New York grain and flour, Mexican and Peruvian silver, Honduran dye woods, and especially Caribbean sugar, molasses, rum, coffee, and cigars—many Spanish-speaking businessmen, diplomats, and workers moved to the city. The connections between New York and Cuba were particularly close. By 1870

1

2

1 **José Martí** undated
Unknown photographer

2 **Giuseppe Garibaldi**
c. 1870
Unknown photographer,
albumen print

3 **Ho Chi Minh** 1921
Unknown photographer

4 **Leon Trotsky** c. 1920
Bain News Service,
glass negative

José Martí made New York his base for organizing an international Cuban insurrectionary movement. Other revolutionaries who found temporary homes in New York included the Italian Giuseppe Garibaldi on Staten Island in the 1850s; the Vietnamese Ho Chi Minh, who claimed to have lived in Harlem and Brooklyn during the 1910s; and the Russian Leon Trotsky in the Bronx in 1917.

3

4

CUBAN DRILL-ROOM IN NEW YORK CITY.—Sketched by Theo. R. Davis.—[See Double Page.]

over 2,700 Cubans—out of a total of about 3,600 Caribbean and Spanish-speaking residents—made their homes in the area of the future five-borough New York City, and by the mid-1890s, 94 percent of Cuban sugar was bound for the United States, where most of it was unloaded on Brooklyn's docks. A Cuban joked in 1864 that "it appears as if New York is a neighborhood of Havana."[3]

In reality, Cuba and Puerto Rico were becoming economic colonies for New York shippers, refiners, and financiers, even as their peoples struggled against Spanish political control. At the same time, for Latin Americans (and some native New Yorkers) inspired by the ideals of the American and French Revolutions, New York itself became a base for plots dedicated to liberating Latin America from Spanish rule. This was especially true after Francisco de Miranda recruited 180 New York volunteers in 1806 for a foiled attempt to free Venezuela, and after Simón Bolívar (who visited New York in 1807) and José de San Martín launched successful wars of independence throughout South America during the 1810s. Cuban intellectuals fleeing Spanish punishment, most notably the priest Félix Varela in 1823, made New York their home. Varela became a seminal figure in the rise of Manhattan's Catholic

Diocese as a home for immigrants, while penning pro-independence and antislavery tracts for Cuban and North American readers.

As the North American city in most frequent and profuse maritime contact with Latin America, New York quickly took the lead over New Orleans, Philadelphia, and other ports as the launch point for revolutionary activism. In 1868, after conferring with allies in New York, a doctor named Ramón Betances launched an anti-Spanish revolt in Puerto Rico. Two weeks later a Cuban planter, Carlos Manuel de Céspedes, freed his slaves, armed them, and launched what became known as the Ten Years' War (1868-78) for Cuban independence. The dual revolutions galvanized New York Latinos. Merchants, lawyers, journalists, and their wives and daughters used the Republican Society of Cuba and Puerto Rico, founded in Manhattan in 1865, to raise funds and supplies for the insurgents, publicize their cause, and serve as a temporary government-in-exile.

The Puerto Rican uprising was quickly crushed by Spanish troops, and some 200,000 Cubans perished in the Ten Year's War. That war ended in defeat for the rebels and ill feeling among émigrés alienated by the internal bickering that the war had

exposed, both in Cuba and in their own Manhattan meeting halls. But the wars also brought a new wave of diverse Cuban and Puerto Rican refugees to New York—artisans, professional families, and free black cigar makers. These newcomers would play a vital role in New York's revolutionary agitation for the rest of the century.

ENTER MARTÍ

When José Martí settled among these activists in 1881, New York's role as an international city and media center provided him with opportunities. In Manhattan Martí found paying work as official Consul for Uruguay (1884) and then Paraguay and Argentina (1890). He also supported himself translating books into Spanish for New York publishers who exported their wares to Latin America; worked as an American correspondent for Argentinian, Mexican, and Venezuelan newspapers; and wrote for Spanish-language periodicals published in New York, including *La America, El Latino-Americano,* and *La Revista Ilustrada* (which reached 9,000 readers across Latin America).

By the 1880s New York was already home-in-exile to such Cuban insurgent leaders as Miguel Fernandez Ledesma and the Ten Years' War veteran General Calixto García. Working with and among them, Martí came to play a special role as master organizer. A man of "frail" build and almost constant ill health, he was nevertheless an electrifying speaker. A Pinkerton detective working for Spain, reporting on a speech by Martí at Steck Hall on East 14th Street in 1883, noted the presence of "nearly 300 people of various races and ages." Martí's plea for perseverance in the cause of Cuban freedom, the spy observed, "received an immense ovation from those present."[4]

Working with the Puerto Rican exile Lola Rodríguez de Tió and others, Martí also organized several revolutionary organizations, including the New York Cuban Revolutionary Committee (1880). Most importantly, he founded the Cuban Revolutionary Party (1892), which united émigrés throughout the Cuban diaspora, and its New York-based newspaper, *Patria,* which Martí arranged to have smuggled into Cuba. Many Cubans, both on and off the island, presumed that Martí, the Party's official "Delegate," would become the first president of a future free Cuban republic.

For the 15 years he lived and worked in New York Martí struggled to maintain the unity of the

Ticket to a benefit "In Aid of Cuban Liberty" 1870

Brooklyn had its own community of Cuban nationalists, although this fund-raising event held during the Ten Year's War seems directed at sympathizers among non-Cuban Brooklynites.

extremes of poverty and wealth drove Martí to fill his journalism with pointed morals for Latino readers, reinforcing his message that Caribbean revolutions must create democratic governments empowering "the former slave, the oppressed campesino [peasant], and the urchin of the city streets" as well as the island's middle and upper classes. He spoke out on behalf of others whose plight he saw playing out in New York City's streets—socialists and anarchists, tenement dwellers, Jewish refugees from Russia, and striking Knights of Labor protesting the "ill-gotten wealth" of streetcar companies. For all his bitterness about the greed and bigotry he encountered, Martí also understood the city as a refuge for the oppressed. "New York is becoming a kind of vortex," he reported, "whatever boils over anywhere else in the world spills into New York. Elsewhere they make men flee, but here they welcome the fleeing man with a smile."[6]

FIGHTING RACISM IN NEW YORK AND BEYOND

In New York, Caribbean expatriates also faced the problem of racism head on. Indeed, Martí recognized the issue as a potentially fatal stumbling block for Cuban and Puerto Rican nationalism. Like other white Cuban New Yorkers, Martí had grown up in a slave society. His father briefly owned two slaves, and as a boy Martí witnessed the whipping of enslaved plantation workers. "I saw it when I was a child, and still my cheeks burn with shame," he later

diverse coalition of exiled Cuban revolutionaries that stretched from New York to Florida, Mexico, and throughout the Caribbean. And his own struggles in New York City became a symbol, for Martí, of the conflict between Latino freedom and increasing US economic dominion in Latin America. In his angrier moments he saw New Yorkers—people "disturbed only by their eagerness to possess wealth"—as the embodiment of the "brutal North that despises us." When a servant at the Murray Hill Hotel treated him brusquely, Martí brooded: "These people speak as if they were brandishing their fists before your eyes."[5]

Although he did not offer a systematic critique of the American (or any other) economy, New York's

Casanova Mansion c. 1915
Unknown photographer, gelatin silver print

Casanova Mansion, subterranean passage c. 1910
Unknown photographer, gelatin silver print

The exiled Cuban writer Cirilo Villaverde and his wife Emilia Casanova de Villaverde used their waterfront mansion in rural Mott Haven in the Bronx as a supply depot for the Ten Years' War (1868-78). The mansion's underground vaults stored weapons and ammunition that the couple bought in New York and then shipped to Cuba via Long Island Sound.

recalled. Spain finally freed Puerto Rico's slaves in 1873 and Cuba's in 1886, partly to diminish the appeal of the revolutionary movements to black residents. Attempting to divide and conquer those movements, Spain also encouraged white islanders to fear the possible political ambitions of the freed slaves. In New York Martí denounced such tactics and crossed racial lines himself. He relied on his friend, the black Havana journalist Juan Gualberto Gómez, as a trusted intermediary who enabled him to direct revolutionary proceedings from New York.[7]

The bigotry of white New Yorkers, and the need to enlist black Latino immigrants in the revolutionary cause, confirmed the view of Martí and other activists that racial discrimination was an evil to be defeated. A generation after the Civil War, New York remained a deeply segregated city, a place where economic and educational opportunities, civil rights, and equal treatment remained elusive for nearly all African Americans. In New York Martí lamented privately in 1888, "blacks are considered little more than beasts." Yet as early as the 1860s black and white Cuban New Yorkers had been working together in the city's Cuban independence movement, making the insurgency one of New York's few institutions in which any racial integration took place.[8]

For Martí integration was necessary not only because justice demanded it, but also because it was the way to mobilize Afro-Cubans and Afro-Puerto Ricans in the city, in Florida, and in the islands to support the cause of liberation. Writing in 1893 Martí appealed to the transnational émigré community: "No man has any special rights because he belongs to one race or another: say 'man' and all rights have been stated." He worked alongside an array of Caribbean New Yorkers of African descent, including Sotero Figueroa, a printer who became managing editor of *Patria*, and Arturo Schomburg, a young Puerto Rican intent on forming revolutionary clubs and raising money from scattered émigré neighborhoods in Manhattan and Brooklyn. (Schomburg's collection of Afro-Americana later became the nucleus of the New York Public Library's Schomburg Center for Research in Black Culture).[9]

Believing that educating New York's growing community of working-class Afro-Cubans and Afro-Puerto Ricans would prepare them for political equality, Martí and others took direct action. In 1890 they co-founded a school, *La Liga de Instrucción* (The League of Instruction), at 178 Bleecker Street; a second school was later opened in Tampa, Florida. Martí himself taught night classes at La Liga, and

Señoras de la Liga
1899
Unknown photographer

This page from a Spanish-language book published in New York in 1899 suggests the role played by women of African descent in the Cuban and Puerto Rican independence movements both on the islands and in New York City.

brought his daughter, Maria Mantilla, to play piano at the school on Monday evenings.

Martí's outspoken activism against racism—at a time when few native white New Yorkers challenged it—earned him the support of black Latinos in New York's cigar factories. According to Bernardo Vega, a later Puerto Rican émigré who knew some of Martí's former comrades during the 1910s, the city's Latino cigar makers, black, white, and of mixed race, declared December 24, 1893 "The Day of the Homeland" and each worker set aside one day's pay. They then presented $12,000 to Martí for the revolutionary cause.[10]

Emilia C. de Villaverde.
(DURANTE EL PERIODO REVOLUCIONARIO.)

Señor Sotero Figueroa.

INSPIRADO POETA PUERTORRIQUEÑO; DISTINGUIDO PERIODISTA; COM-
PAÑERO INFATIGABLE DE JOSÉ MARTÍ, EN LOS DÍAS DE MAS
CRUDA LABOR, Y MIEMBRO PROMINENTE DEL CONSEJO
CUBANO DE NUEVA YORK.

Rafael Serra.

1   **Emilia Casanova de Villaverde**
    1874
    Unknown photographer

2   **Señor Sotero Figueroa** 1899
    Unknown photographer

3   **Calixto García Iñiquez** 1898
    Unknown photographer

4   **Lola Rodríguez de Tió** 1898
    Unknown photographer

5   **Rafael Serra** 1899
    Unknown photographer

5   **Arthur Alfonso Schomburg**
    1900-35
    Unknown photographer

The revolutionary movement included Cuban and Puerto Rican New Yorkers of both sexes and of European, African, and mixed ancestries in important positions. Emilia Casanova de Villaverde founded *La Hijas de Cuba* (the Daughters of Cuba, 1869) for New York women supporting the Ten Year's War. Puerto Rican printer and writer Sotero Figueroa was described as José Martí's "right hand." Calixto García led troops in both the Ten Year's War and the 1895 Cuban revolution. Martí's collaborator Lola Rodríguez de Tió championed both the Puerto Rican and Cuban independence movements. Rafael Serra sought to sustain those movements among Latino New Yorkers following Martí's death, as did historian and book collector Arthur Schomburg.

"Cuba's heroes and their flag" 1896
J. Weisenback Lith., chromolithograph

New Yorkers celebrated Martí and other Cuban heroes as the island's war for independence continued in 1896. The Cuban flag had been designed by political exiles in New York City in 1850; other exiles would use it as inspiration for the Puerto Rican flag, which they designed in New York in 1892.

"THIS POISONED CUP"

"Everything binds me to New York, at least for the next few years of my life," Martí had written a friend in 1887, "everything binds me to this poisoned cup." The dual nature of New York confronted Martí and his comrades daily. Strategically situated near a Western Union office and the piers of steamship lines that traded with the Caribbean, even the location of Martí's Front Street office captured the contradictions. It symbolized both the centrality of New York to his revolution and the ever-growing ambitions of New York telegraph and shipping magnates to shape Latin American affairs for their own benefit.[11]

Between 1892 and 1894, New York became Martí's home base for multiple journeys aimed at bringing the revolution to fruition. His meetings with Cubans in the Dominican Republic, Haiti, Costa Rica, Jamaica, Panama, New Orleans, and Philadelphia forged a strategy for invading the home island, while his ecstatic reception by thousands of cigar makers in Key West and Tampa gave him the popular mandate and funding that sometimes eluded him among New York's faction-alized exiles. On January 29, 1895, Martí and two colleagues officially urged the Cuban people to revolt, and nine weeks later he joined the uprising in his homeland. Thirty-eight days after landing, while fighting in a skirmish at Dos Rios in south-eastern Cuba, José Martí was shot and killed by Spanish troops.

The revolution he organized continued for three years, but ultimately fulfilled Martí's anxieties. In 1898, following the pro-rebel frenzy stirred up by William Randolph Hearst's *New York Journal* and Joseph Pulitzer's *New York World*, the United States declared war on Spain and quickly seized Cuba, Puerto Rico, Guam, and the Philippines. Almost overnight, Americans—and New York busi-nessmen who hastened to buy up sugar plantations and consolidate their operations—had acquired from Spain the islands' economic "empire" just as Martí had feared.

Puerto Ricans acquired US citizenship (but not statehood) in 1917, facilitating the waves of migra-tion to New York City that followed. Cuba gained formal independence in 1902, but, under the federal Platt Amendment, the United States reserved the right to intervene in the island's political and eco-nomic affairs. During the 1930s Martí was celebrated as a national hero by the conservative military

elite that ruled the island. In the 1950s a new and successful revolution, led by the Communist Fidel Castro, also embraced Martí as modern Cuba's founding father.

But memories of José Martí also persisted in New York. "We come from the school of Martí," declared Afro-Cuban activist Rafael Serra in a Spanish-language New York newspaper in 1896. "In it our soul was softened and our character was formed." Martí's commitment to racial equality and Caribbean independence lingered, notably among the city's Latino cigar makers, whose clubs and union locals attracted new immigrants in the early 20th century, including the Puerto Rican socialists and nationalists Bernardo Vega and Jesús Colón. New York City remained the off-island center of the Puerto Rican independence movement.[12]

A century later, Martí's Pan-Latin activism and poetry remain vital to many in New York's Latino population of over 2.3 million (now over 28 per-cent of the city) and to millions of people across "Our America." Meanwhile, each day thousands of pedestrians stroll along the southern boundary of Central Park, largely oblivious to the statue of a man on horseback who faces down the Avenue of the Americas much as he faced Spanish bullets on a Cuban battlefield in 1895.

Group portrait of Club Cubano Inter-Americano officials and guests 1957
Unknown photographer, gelatin silver print

A continuing presence: A bust of José Martí takes center stage at a gathering of a Cuban-American organization in New York in 1957.

Advocating for Migrants of Color

"I never knew that rats and puppies were good to eat until I was told by American people," Wong Chin Foo (王清福 Huang Qingfu) informed an audience at Manhattan's Steinway Hall, attempting to dispel stereotypes about the Chinese diet. Educated in Shanghai and Pennsylvania and fluent in English, Wong arrived in New York in 1877 eager to defend his countrymen against American ignorance and prejudice. By 1890 Chinatown was home to some 2,000 immigrants, mostly men who worked as laundry workers and laborers. White New Yorkers consumed racist images of Chinatown residents as opium addicts, seducers of white women, and inscrutable aliens. Wong used English-language newspaper articles to present his fellow Chinese as worthy of respect and sympathy. Disputing that laundry work was "natural" to them, he explained that "they become laundrymen here simply because there is no other occupation by which they can make money as surely... The prejudice against the race has much to do with it." While his words often fell on deaf ears, Wong continued to fight the hostility and suspicion his people faced in New York.[13]

WONG CHING FOO.—[Photographed by Rockwood.]

Wong Chin Foo 1877
Engraving after a photograph by Rockwood from *Harper's Weekly*

Wong Chin Foo (王清福 Huang Qingfu) published New York's first Chinese-language newspaper, *The Chinese American*, in 1883.

ENTHUSIASTIC THOUSANDS OF NEW YORK'
SPECIAL ENVOY OF THE NEW CHIN

Another newcomer, Victoria Earle Matthews, worked to protect her fellow African Americans arriving in New York from the South in search of a better life. Born in slavery in Georgia in 1861, Matthews educated herself while working as a domestic after migrating to New York in 1873. As white reformers established settlement houses to aid European immigrants, Matthews saw a need for similar institutions in the black community, especially for single women arriving with little money and scant knowledge of how to avoid city dangers such as prostitution. Her White Rose Mission (1897) on East 97th Street provided temporary lodging, vocational classes, and training in "practical self-help and right living," as New York's black population grew from 60,666 in 1900 to 91,709 in 1910.[14]

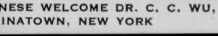

NESE WELCOME DR. C. C. WU,
INATOWN, NEW YORK

"Enthusiastic Thousands of New York's Chinese Welcome Dr. C. C. Wu, Special Envoy of the New China, Chinatown, New York" c. 1920
E. C. Kropp Co., postcard

Following Wong's death in 1898 new generations of Chinatown activists championed political movements in their homeland. Here marchers celebrate a visit by a diplomat of the revolutionary government that had overthrown the emperor and established the Republic of China in 1912.

Victoria Earle Matthews 1903
Unknown photographer, gelatin silver print

Like Wong Chin Foo, Matthews worked as a journalist as well as an activist in New York. Although so light-skinned that she could "pass" as white, Matthews affirmed that "there is no one so black that is not akin to me."

CHAPTER EIGHT

"I Am a Working Girl": Upheaval in the Garment Trades

"I am a working girl. One of those who are on strike against intolerable conditions... I offer a resolution that a general strike be declared—now."

Clara Lemlich c. 1910
Unknown photographer

Clara Lemlich insisted that a strike vote be called in 1909. She later became a Communist and an activist in the movement for consumer rights.

So proclaimed Clara Lemlich, a 23-year-old garment worker, from the stage of the Great Hall in Cooper Union in lower Manhattan. Lemlich spoke in Yiddish, the native language of most of the hundreds of men and women assembled on the evening of November 22, 1909. She was a founding member of Local 25 of the International Ladies' Garment Workers Union (ILGWU), many of whose members were young immigrant women. They worked in hundreds of garment-making factory lofts, often for as little as three dollars for a 56- or 58-hour work week. Impatient after two hours of speeches, Lemlich was calling for action.[1]

The audience roared back its agreement. The meeting's presiding officer, Samuel Gompers, one of the nation's most powerful labor leaders, supported Lemlich's call. "Strike and let them know it," he told the crowd. The 1909 garment workers' strike, soon known as the "Uprising of 20,000," was underway. The strike and its aftermath would reverberate for decades and help make New York City the standard bearer of 20th-century urban reform. As Gompers told male cloakmakers in 1910 when they prepared to launch their own strike inspired by the women, "this is more than a strike... it is an industrial revolution."[2]

GARMENT CITY

By 1909 garment production was the largest manufacturing business in America's largest industrial city. The city's workshops produced 70 percent of all the women's clothing and 40 percent of all the men's clothing sold in the United States. Thousands of immigrants flooded into the needle trades. Some workers who managed to accumulate savings turned employer, setting up shops where they "sweated" the labor of fellow immigrants. Their own

"Union Special Trade Mark" industrial sewing machine
c. 1920
Singer Manufacturing Company

By the early 20th century sewing machines like this one enabled employers to hire women to perform quick, repetitive, and low-paid garment work.

take-home earnings were often only slightly higher than that of their employees; a bad season could easily drive them back into the ranks of workers. The fierce competition for profit encouraged them to force down workers' earnings by lowering pay rates, demanding a faster pace of work, or firing those who dared to ask for more.

Not every workplace was a sweatshop. By the turn of the century the city's garment factories ranged from tenement workshops to spacious modern lofts occupied by successful firms such as the largest, Max Blanck's and Isaac Harris's Triangle Waist Company. Still, low pay, long hours, unclean and unsafe working conditions, and abusive owners were standard in the needle trades. So was employer resistance to unions.

Nevertheless, by the 1880s immigrant Jewish workers from Czarist Russia, Ukraine, Poland, and Lithuania—many of them exposed to revolutionary socialism, anarchism, and labor activism in the "old country"—were forming new unions that built on the earlier traditions of New York's native, Irish, and German tailors (see Chapter 4). Initially many of these unions welcomed only men, and many male workers believed that women had no place in manufacturing and that they drove down wages. Still, women had come to play a role in the labor protests of their husbands, sons, brothers, and fathers, and sometimes they went on strike themselves. On picket lines in the late 19th century, Jewish women shamed "scabs" (non-striking workers) by reciting a Hebrew invocation, "Righteousness delivers from death," and carrying black candles, symbols of the plague. They also learned tactics from other movements. For example, in 1880 nationalists in Ireland had socially shunned an Englishman, Charles Boycott, when he tried to collect rents from protesting farm tenants. The technique crossed the Atlantic, where workers were soon "boycotting" anti-union shops. In New York, Jewish men and women also felt a new freedom to express themselves: "In Russia for the mass gathering one had to go to a forest, one had to be on the lookout for the police, but in the United States we sang the Marseillaise

Necktie Workshop in a Division Street Tenement c. 1890
Jacob A. Riis, gelatin dry plate negative

Workers at a small bench hand finish garments while managers look on 1910
Unknown photographer

Tenement sweatshops (like the necktie shop at left) were increasingly joined by more factory-like settings (above) in New York's booming garment industry.

[the French revolutionary song] when we walked the streets…," tailor Julius Gershin later recalled. "And when we walked in the street and sang the Marseillaise, we felt in heaven."[3]

THE UPRISING

A dispute over piece rates (wages paid for the number of garments produced) triggered women workers to stand up for themselves in 1909, as 20,000 young garment workers picketed hundreds of shops. But once on the picket lines they faced daunting challenges. Owners argued that they alone had the right to determine pay rates and that union demands for closed (all-union) shops were "un-American." Employers hired prostitutes and male criminals to provoke and rough up picketers; Clara Lemlich suffered several broken ribs during an attack, although she returned to the picket line. Police arrested over 700 strikers for disorderly conduct, obstructing traffic, and other infractions.[4]

But something unexpected happened. Women wearing expensive clothing began appearing on picket lines alongside the workers. Charity worker Mary Dreier was among those arrested, although she was quickly released when police realized that she was not a Jewish or Italian "girl." Alva Belmont, one of the nation's wealthiest women, attended night court at the Jefferson Market courthouse to monitor the sentencing of arrested strikers. Anne Morgan, daughter of banker J.P. Morgan, walked the

picket line and donated funds to underwrite mass rallies in the city's premier concert halls. Realizing that garment firms hired African Americans as strikebreakers, inflaming racial tensions, woman suffragist Elizabeth Dutcher took strikers to speak in a Brooklyn African-American church to persuade sister workers not to "scab." (On the other hand, however, the ILGWU did little or nothing to recruit black workers into its own ranks.)

Many of these allies belonged to the Women's Trade Union League (WTUL), an organization that united wealthy, middle-class, and working-class women in efforts to unionize female workers and to win the vote for women (see Chapter 9). The city's newspapers mocked the strikers' new friends, calling them the "Mink Brigade," but WTUL members successfully grabbed the headlines, using publicity techniques they had learned in the woman suffrage movement. When arrestees were released from being jailed in the city workhouse on Blackwell's Island, activists presented them on stage at Carnegie Hall under a banner reading "The workhouse is no answer to a demand for justice," ensuring press coverage. Some working-class WTUL socialists did not trust the "Mink Brigade," fearing that rich and middle-class women might seek to control the strike and blunt the edge of the workers' demands. But Belmont, Morgan, Dutcher, and others proved to be useful—if sometimes uneasy—allies for the duration of the strike.[5]

Strike Pickets
February 5, 1910
Bain News Service,
photograph

Striking shirtwaist
workers pose proudly
during the 1909-10
"Uprising."

THE PROTOCOLS OF PEACE

In February 1910 shirtwaist workers and employers reached a settlement. Local 25 won higher wages and shorter hours in 320 shops, most of which recognized the union. Some of the largest employers, however, including the Triangle Waist Company, refused to do so, and many other workshops were not covered at all by the new contracts. Even so, the strike energized the city's labor movement; over the next four years, the ranks of the city's unions mushroomed from 30,000 to 250,000.

Impressed by the shirtwaist strikers' militancy, the ILGWU's cloakmakers' locals, whose membership was largely male, launched their own general strike, the "Great Revolt," in July 1910, when 75,000 cloakmakers walked off the job. Once again a coalition of supporters crossed lines of class, education, and birth. Boston lawyer (and future Supreme Court justice) Louis D. Brandeis arrived in New York to advise the strikers and to try to persuade workers and employers to compromise with each other for mutual advantage. He negotiated an accord between the bosses and the workers—the "Protocols of Peace"—under which union members and employers agreed to work together to set wages, hours, and other conditions for each factory. Brandeis also established a compromise called "the preferential shop": owners would have to hire union workers, but they could also hire non-members if they were better-skilled or more efficient.[6]

Brandeis and other professionals believed that economic and legal expertise could bring rationality and justice to the notoriously chaotic garment industry and that collaboration between workers

Women's Trade Union League 1910
Byron Company, gelatin silver print

In the offices of the Women's Trade Union League, women of different classes and ethnicities came together to work for the labor movement and woman suffrage.

Women who were arrested on the picket lines and sent to Blackwell's Island wear "Workhouse Prisoner" signs
c. 1910
Unknown photographer

Arrested shirtwaist strikers used their jail experience to arouse public sympathy.

"Protocols of Peace" cartoon 1910
Leon Israel

Even under the Protocols of Peace, garment employers and unions never fully trusted each other, as this contemporary newspaper cartoon suggests.

and businessmen would bring shared benefits. Unions had an important role to play in this: As lawyer Julius Henry Cohen put it, "the enlightened employer needs his organization. The worker needs his union. The public needs both, and each needs each other." Many progressive thinkers saw in this idea the possibility for a new era in labor relations. The garment lofts of lower Manhattan were to be laboratories of progress.[7]

Brandeis used the idea that successful collaboration required a strong union to convince hundreds of New York garment shops to accept and even encourage their workers to join ILGWU locals. But by 1914 the Protocols were unraveling. Workers in some factories accused employers of twisting or ignoring the new work codes, and they launched unauthorized "wildcat" strikes. Meanwhile, some employers, large and small, refused to sign on to the Protocols at all.

The Protocols' problems reflected the ongoing weaknesses of New York's needle trades activism. Working women had energized the city's unions in the 1909 strike and put themselves at the center of the American labor movement for the first time; unskilled and semiskilled workers now stood at the labor movement's leading edge. But many young women who flocked into the ILGWU left it as bosses resumed a hard line after the 1909 contracts expired. The successful strikes had generated a coalition with overlapping but widely differing agendas, from wealthy feminists to Columbia University economists, from socialists to banker Jacob Schiff, who worried that labor unrest could encourage

Houses of Welcome: The Settlement House Movement

In 1893 two young nurses, Lillian Wald and Mary Brewster, decided to bring medical care into Lower East Side tenements. As payment they took whatever the patient could afford—which sometimes meant nothing. Wald and Brewster began building two institutions, the Visiting Nurse Service and Henry Street Settlement. Today, both continue as agencies providing social services in New York City's neighborhoods.

Wald and Brewster belonged to a generation of young reformers from middle-class or wealthy families swept up in the "social settlement" movement, which started in London when college students and charity workers inhabited a building in that city's slums in 1884. American settlement workers moved into houses in poor urban areas and turned them into neighborhood centers for tackling problems ranging from sickness and illiteracy to juvenile delinquency and prostitution. Jane Addams's Hull House in Chicago became the most famous, but in New York, the nation's largest city, there were over 70 settlement houses by 1911.

Lillian Wald c. 1890
Hargrave & Gubelman,
photograph mounted
on board

Lillian Wald in her
early twenties, as a
student nurse in New
York City.

"Getting Books" at 48 Henry Street
c. 1900
Jacob A. Riis, gelatin dry plate negative

Neighborhood children using the library in the King's Daughters Settlement House on the Lower East Side.

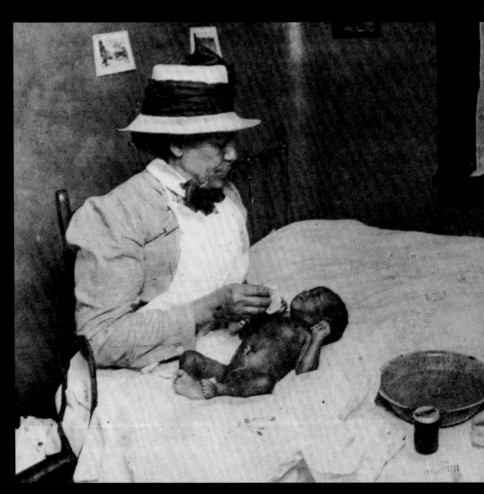

Settlements offered English-language classes, vocational training, aid to new mothers, and cultural and athletic clubs for neighborhood residents. Like other progressives, settlement workers sought to bridge the gap between classes and ethnic groups, while also encouraging immigrants to be proud of the cultural "gifts" they brought from Europe. In emerging black communities, settlement workers Victoria Earle Matthews and Verina Morton Jones provided services to the city's most neglected population.

Anarchists and other leftists criticized settlement houses for not going far enough to bring economic change. "Teaching the poor to eat with a fork is all very well," Emma Goldman commented, "but what good does it do if they have not the food?" Even so, Goldman knew and admired Wald, whose passion for justice and equality led her to co-found the National Association for the Advancement of Colored People, work for woman suffrage, and espouse pacifism in the Woman's Peace Party during World War I. Wald and other settlement workers became a driving force for change, persuading lawmakers to oppose child labor and slum housing, and advocating government protections for workers, families, the jobless, and the disabled. Today, 38 settlement houses remain crucial providers of healthcare, education, and social services in New York neighborhoods.[8]

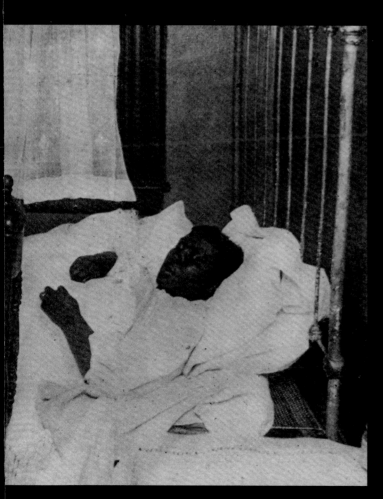

African-American Nurse from Henry Street Settlement visits mother and baby c. 1910
Unknown photographer

An advocate of black civil rights and racial integration, Lillian Wald accepted New York's prevailing racial norms when she created a segregated all-black nursing corps to visit African-American families.

anti-Semitism. As early as 1911 it was uncertain where that coalition was headed, and what could hold it together.

FIRE

"I turned back into the shop. Rose Feibush, my beautiful, dear friend, jumped from a window."[9]

Half a century later, shirtwaist maker Sylvia Riegler remembered as if it were yesterday the horror of March 25, 1911 at the Triangle Waist Company in Greenwich Village. A cigarette or match carelessly dropped started a fire in the firm's eighth floor workshop. As flames raced through the top three stories of the loft building, hundreds of frantic workers —mostly young immigrant women—boarded elevators or climbed stairs to safety on the rooftop. But others, blocked by a locked exit door and trapped on a collapsing fire escape, could not flee. Firetruck ladders reached only to the building's sixth floor. "People had just begun to jump as we got there," a young social worker named Frances Perkins recalled. Within half an hour 146 women and men were dead or dying. A reporter wrote, "I remembered their great strike of last year in which these same girls had demanded more sanitary conditions and more safety precautions in the shops. These dead bodies were the answer."[10]

The ILGWU turned the funerals of the victims into acts of protest that quickly exposed tensions simmering within the reform coalition. At a mass meeting in the Metropolitan Opera House eight days after the fire, the ILGWU's Rose Schneiderman voiced the outrage of her fellow workers as she addressed the well-to-do audience in the best seats:

Members of Local 25 and United Hebrew Trades march in the streets after the Triangle Fire 1911
Unknown photographer

Grief-stricken garment workers marched through New York streets to honor the fire's victims and protest the conditions that produced the tragedy.

"Who Is Guilty? To the 140 Victims of the Asch Building Fire, March 25, 1911"
1911
Boardman Robinson, oil, pen, and ink on board

This cartoon for the *New York Tribune* urged middle-class readers to ask hard questions and take action to ensure that disasters like the Triangle Fire never happened again.

"We have tried you good people of the public—and you have been found wanting... Every year thousands of us are maimed. The life of men and women is so cheap and property is so sacred!"[11]

But the fire ultimately strengthened New York's progressive-labor coalition, as middle-class and working-class activists came together to promote change. They were empowered by a new, surprising ally. By 1911 Tammany Hall, the city's notoriously cynical Democratic Party machine, was reading the writing on the political wall: the growing population of left-leaning immigrant voters was the key to winning elections. Tammany boss Charles F. Murphy allowed two young protégés, State Assembly leader Alfred E. (Al) Smith and State Senate leader Robert F. Wagner, to create the New York State Factory Investigating Commission (FIC) to examine the conditions behind the Triangle tragedy.

The FIC quickly became a center of activism, bringing together ILGWU and WTUL crusaders, investigators, and social scientists. Between 1911 and 1915, the FIC became a "traveling road show

1 **Louis Brandeis**
undated
Bain News Service,
photograph

2 **Mrs. O.H.P.
(Alva) Belmont
(left) and Inez
Milholland** 1913
Harris & Ewing, glass
plate negative

3 **C. F. Murphy
(center) and
Alfred E. Smith
(right)** 1916
Bain News Service,
photograph

4 **Rose
Schneiderman**
1915
Unknown
photographer

5 **Frances Perkins**
c. 1912
Unknown
photographer

The struggles of
New York garment
workers brought
together an unlikely
coalition of activists.
Lawyer Louis Brandeis
spearheaded the
Protocols of Peace.
Wealthy socialite Alva
Belmont and attorney
Inez Milholland, both
woman suffragists,
aided the shirtwaist
strikers in 1909-10.
Tammany Hall's
Charles Murphy and
Al Smith committed
the city's Democratic
Party to labor
reform. Immigrant
labor organizer
Rose Schneiderman
worked with wealthy
and middle-class
reformers after the
Triangle Fire, while
social worker Frances
Perkins investigated
factory conditions
for the FIC.

of reform," investigating conditions in over 3,000 workplaces. Like other progressives, the FIC staff relied on data, first-hand investigation, and the power of publicity to shock the public into supporting change. When a skeptic questioned FIC allegations concerning bleak conditions in canneries, Al Smith, who had toured factories across the state with the Commission, shot back, "You can't tell me. I've seen these women. I've seen their faces. I've seen them."[12]

The result was dozens of laws and ordinances that regulated safety, hours, and conditions in thousands of workplaces. Inspections and enforcement were also strengthened, and child labor was more strictly regulated. By expanding the power of government to investigate, enact, and enforce, New York took the national lead in making the industrial worksite a safer place for working people.

TOWARD THE NEW DEAL

The long-term repercussions of New York City's 1909 strike, the Protocols of Peace, and the Triangle Fire would help reshape the meaning of liberalism in 20th-century America. The new laws defined government as a force to regulate businesses and safeguard the health, wellbeing, and earning abilities of workers. They also created a strong ongoing relationship between government officials and labor unions.

Over the next 40 years men and women who had been activists in the events of the 1910s would fashion new roles for themselves in Albany and Washington. As governor of New York, Al Smith enacted an array of reforms (although he failed in his bid to become the nation's first Roman Catholic president in 1928); his chief political advisor was FIC and Protocols veteran Belle Moskowitz. Labor activists, including Rose Schneiderman and Sidney Hillman (briefly chief clerk under the Protocols), made organized labor a central lobbying group within the Democratic Party, a role that bore fruit at the national level after the election of New Yorker Franklin Roosevelt to the White House in 1932. Frances Perkins became FDR's Secretary of Labor, and in 1936 another FIC veteran, US Senator Robert Wagner, crusaded successfully to get Congress to enact the National Labor Relations Act (the "Wagner Act"), which committed the federal government to supporting the right of unions to bring employers to the bargaining table. This New Deal vision of an expanding government seeking to readjust the balance between "haves" and "have-nots" would shape American politics for over 50 years.

There were other long-term repercussions, too. As the ILGWU and other unions became important in politics, their central offices expected members to follow orders from above. Little room was left for the kind of thrilling self-empowerment "working girls" had felt on the shop floors in 1909. Moreover, women were largely excluded from top leadership positions in the ILGWU.

In the 1960s and 1970s, to escape the costs of union contracts and work regulations, many New York companies moved their factories to southern and western states or overseas. Manufacturers blamed unions for keeping labor costs high, while unions faulted companies for sidestepping organized workers. The aging union leadership was increasingly disconnected from younger, mostly black, Puerto Rican, and new immigrant workers. Still, as the American labor movement declined in power in the late 20th and 21st centuries, New York remained the nation's most unionized state. In 2008, 24.9% of working New York State residents were union members, more than twice the national average (12.4%); in the city, most union members worked for municipal departments or in service work, rather than in manufacturing.

Major figures in American reform continued to look back on events in early 20th-century Manhattan as the turning point in their activist careers. Frances Perkins, for one, never forgot what she witnessed at the intersection of Washington Place and Greene Street on March 25, 1911. "The New Deal," she reminisced over 40 years later, "was based really upon the experiences that we had had in New York State and upon the sacrifices of those who, we faithfully remember with affection and respect, died in that terrible fire… they did not die in vain and we will never forget them."[13]

President Roosevelt signs Wagner Peyser Act June 6, 1933
Unknown photographer

Veterans of New York's workplace reform movement attained national power during Franklin D. Roosevelt's presidency. Here Secretary of Labor Frances Perkins (center), Senator Robert F. Wagner (right), and Congressman Theodore Peyser (left) watch as the president signs a bill to aid unemployed workers during the Great Depression.

Socialist Legacies: Housing Cooperatives and the Amalgamated Bank

In 1920 Eugene V. Debs, a federal prisoner for allegedly urging draft resistance during World War I, won 919,000 votes nationwide as the Socialist Party of America's presidential candidate. Some 132,000 of those votes came from New York City, where immigrant Jewish labor unions gave the party, founded in 1901, an electoral base. During the 1910s city socialists had elected lawyer Meyer London to Congress and 10 others to the state assembly, and in 1917 they cast 145,000 votes for their mayoral candidate, Morris Hillquit. Most socialists hoped for a peaceful transformation of the American economy when working-class voters embraced their agenda: public works projects for the jobless, minimum-wage laws, old age pensions, votes for women, taxes on the wealthy, and government or workers' ownership of "all large-scale industries."[14]

Amalgamated Housing Inc. Broome Street entrance gates and arch 1931
Samuel H. Gottscho, acetate negative

In 1930 the Amalgamated Clothing Workers union built their second cooperative housing project, offering desirable, affordable apartments to garment workers moving out of tenements on the Lower East Side.

Amalgamated Clothing Workers Apartments, Sedgwick Avenue and Gun Hill Road, Bronx 1929
Wurts Bros.,
acetate negative

Cooperative housing projects offered varied services to shareholders and their families. Here, Freda Kazan teaches nursery school in the Bronx Amalgamated houses.

During the 1920s, facing a conservative backlash against leftists, socialists turned to institution-building to safeguard the gains their unions had secured for workers. In New York, the socialist-leaning Amalgamated Clothing Workers of America built the nation's first limited-equity residential cooperative, the Amalgamated Housing Cooperative, in the Bronx (1927). Under "limited equity," residents who bought shares (rather than paying rent) could only re-sell those shares at set prices, guaranteeing that apartments stayed affordable. Made possible by legislation passed under progressive governor Al Smith, the cooperative idea was popular with Jewish activists: Communists built the United Workers Houses, Yiddish-speaking activists founded the Sholem Aleichem Houses, and Zionists created the Farband Houses, all in the rapidly developing Bronx. Comfortable apartments, attractive grounds, and affordable prices allowed garment workers' families to attain a middle-class way of life.

Another legacy was the Amalgamated Bank of New York (1923), also founded by the clothing workers' union. The first city bank to offer free checking accounts with no minimum balance, it also eased requirements for workers seeking personal loans. Although two private equity firms became part owners in 2011, the Amalgamated Bank's connection to activism remained: it became an unofficial repository for funds of the Occupy Wall Street movement.

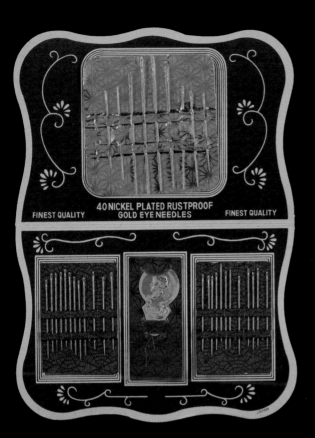

Set of sewing needles advertising the Bronx Amalgamated housing cooperative supermarket 1955-70

Another convenience of the Bronx Amalgamated housing was its cooperative supermarket, where member families could buy goods at cheaper prices than at for-profit grocery stores.

CHAPTER NINE

"New York is the Battleground": The Campaign for Woman Suffrage

Members of the National American Woman Suffrage Association gather at Midland Beach, Staten Island, prior to their liberty flight
1916
Unknown photographer

Woman suffragists gathered to cheer Leda Richberg-Hornsby and Ida Blair (seated, fourth and fifth from right) as they prepared to fly over New York harbor. Their plane towed a banner reading "Women Want Liberty Too."

On December 2, 1916, a two-seat airplane took off from Staten Island and headed north over New York harbor.

Planes were still a new sight in the city's skies, and this flight was especially unusual: both its pilot and passenger were women, and they had a political purpose for taking to the air. Leda Richberg-Hornsby, the eighth American woman to earn a pilot's license, and Ida Blair were both woman suffragists, activists determined to win the vote for women. Despite angry resistance from millions of men (and some women) who viewed politics and government as exclusively male preserves, New York suffragists could take heart from the fact that by 1916 women had won the vote in eleven states—though all were in the west—and they wanted New York to be next.

Richberg-Hornsby and Blair announced that their aim was to disrupt a grand extravaganza unfolding in the harbor below. With thousands looking on, President Woodrow Wilson was arriving on his yacht *Mayflower* to turn on a new electric light in the Statue of Liberty's torch. Richberg-Hornsby and Blair intended to "bomb" the yacht with leaflets and petitions supporting a constitutional amendment to allow American women to vote. "This is war for woman's rights," Richberg-Hornsby declared.[1]

The plane took off but stiff winds blew it off course, and Richberg-Hornsby had to crash-land in a Staten Island marsh before the "bombs" could be dropped. The pilot and her passenger were unhurt, and they remained unshaken in their resolve to continue the struggle.

The airborne gesture was neither the first nor the last time that woman suffragists used New York City as a stage for bold spectacles to gain attention for their cause. As the nation's financial and media center, New York provided activists with priceless opportunities for raising money and public awareness. The city was the birthplace of a brand-new field called "public relations," pioneered by New Yorkers Ivy Lee, Edward Bernays, and others. Like these male publicists, suffragists proved brilliant at seizing attention. Their goal was to jolt, inform, and persuade other American women as well as male voters and politicians. "New York is the battleground of the whole nation," suffragist leader Carrie Chapman Catt declared in 1909, and suffragists sought to turn that battleground to their advantage.[2]

THE BATTLEGROUND

New York City had long been a center in the struggle for woman suffrage. During the 1860s the national movement's two most well-known leaders, Susan B. Anthony and Elizabeth Cady Stanton, moved from upstate New York to a house on West 45th Street, when Stanton's husband was appointed to a post in the US Customhouse downtown. In 1866 Stanton became the first woman to run for Congress (she won fewer than 30 votes). Her campaign foreshadowed that of another New Yorker, journalist and

"The woman-suffrage movement in New York City" 1894
B. West Clinedinst, cover of *Frank Leslie's Illustrated Weekly*

By the 1890s feminists were turning New York into an important center of activism for woman suffrage.

Wall Street stockbroker Victoria Woodhull, the first woman to run for the presidency in 1872, who similarly received only a handful of votes.

New York City was also one of the nation's prime centers for the "New Woman"—a popular phrase in the late 19th century. By the 1880s increasing numbers of young middle-class and wealthy American women were going to college (including Manhattan's Cooper Institute and Barnard College) and embarking on careers as teachers, nurses, social workers, journalists, artists, and even doctors and lawyers. Most of their mothers, confined to the household as wives and caregivers, had lacked such opportunities. New York became home to many "New Women," both single and married, who felt their education and achievements entitled them to vote and play a role in political decision-making.

In 1890 the National American Woman Suffrage Association (NAWSA) became the country's leading organization advocating votes for women. New York became its headquarters in 1909 when the wealthy Manhattan socialite Alva Belmont supported NAWSA's relocation from Warren, Ohio, to 505 Fifth Avenue at 42nd Street. By placing NAWSA in the nation's business and intellectual capital, the move brought immediate benefits. In 1909–10 sales of NAWSA literature jumped tenfold, from $1,300 to almost $14,000. NAWSA's national membership increased from about 5,000 in 1900 to 100,000 in 1915 to over one million by 1918, a reflection of the growing popularity of the cause, but also of the effectiveness of New York as a base for mobilizing mass support.

NEW BEGINNINGS

From their new headquarters, New York City's suffrage activists worked on two fronts. On one hand, they tried to get the New York State legislature (and other statehouses) to hold referendum votes so that male voters could choose to enable women to vote, state by state. Simultaneously, they sought to convince Congress to ratify the "Susan B. Anthony Amendment" to the Constitution, first proposed by Anthony in 1878, to give all American women the vote. Under its upper middle-class leaders Anna Howard Shaw and Carrie Chapman Catt, NAWSA tended to emphasize the respectable, "ladylike" nature of the cause. Winning the vote for women, they argued, would allow American females to strengthen their traditional role as wives and mothers, helping to protect their families through

the law-making process. NAWSA's conservative tactics—collecting petition signatures, testifying before legislative committees, holding annual conventions—reinforced the message that "femininity" and activism could be reconciled without threatening the men who ultimately would decide the issue.

Even before NAWSA's move to Manhattan, New York City suffragists were inventing edgier tactics for pushing the cause forward. Harriot Stanton Blatch, Elizabeth Cady Stanton's daughter and founder of the Equality League of Self-Supporting Women (1907), emphasized "the value of publicity or rather the harm of the lack of it." But hand-in-hand with organizing public spectacles, Blatch believed suffragists had to immerse themselves in the

"Votes for Women"
1909
New York State Woman Suffrage Association, postcard

This postcard showcased the soon-to-be-opened national headquarters of NAWSA and its New York State division. In 1910 they would share an entire floor in this building at Fifth Avenue between 42nd and 43rd Streets.

1 **Elizabeth Cady Stanton (left) and Susan B. Anthony** 1866–71
Sarony & Co., carte-de-visite albumen print

2 **Harriot Stanton Blatch (left) and Rose Schneiderman** 1910–11
Unknown photographer

3 **Dr. Anna Howard Shaw (left) and Carrie Chapman Catt at a suffrage parade** 1917
Bain News Service, glass negative

4 **Verina Morton Jones** 1912
Unknown photographer, from *The Crisis*

5 **Alice Paul (left) & Mrs. O. H. P. (Alva) Belmont** November 17, 1923
Unknown photographer, glass negative

6 **Dorothy Day** 1916
Unknown photographer

7 **Mabel Lee** 1916
Unknown photographer, from the Barnard College yearbook

Four generations of women activists fought for the vote in New York. Elizabeth Cady Stanton and Susan B. Anthony lived and strategized in Manhattan during the late 1860s. Stanton's daughter Harriot Stanton Blatch collaborated with immigrant workers such as Rose Schneiderman to win the vote in a new century. NAWSA's Anna Howard Shaw and Carrie Chapman Catt combined street tactics with conservative strategies during the 1910s. Physician Verina Morton Jones led the Equal Suffrage League for the city's African-American women. New Jerseyan Alice Paul headed the National Woman's Party (NWP) with financial help from Alva Belmont. Dorothy Day began her long activist career as an antiwar protester and NWP picket during World War I. Chinese immigrant Mabel Lee led other Asian-American New York suffragists in a suffrage parade in 1917.

Mabel Lee
"Oh, what may man within him hide!"

Emmeline Pankhurst on Wall St. 1911
Bain News Service, glass negative

London's "suffragettes" exerted a strong influence on New York's movement. Here Emmeline Pankhurst, legendary founder of England's WSPU, makes a pro-woman suffrage speech on Wall Street during a visit to New York.

coldblooded world of politics, to think and plan the way male political strategists did. Women needed to cultivate legislators and party leaders and bargain with them for concrete gains, such as getting suffrage referendums included on election ballots. New allies had to be found; traditional "feminine" behavior and avoidance of "corrupt" politicians would not do.[3]

Blatch was inspired by the new militancy of the British suffrage movement, centered in London's Women's Social and Political Union (WSPU). Known as "suffragettes," WSPU members were increasingly visible in public, questioning and even heckling members of Parliament. By 1908 and 1909 some, in carefully staged acts, were also throwing rocks through windows and chaining themselves to government buildings to protest their lack of the vote. The London influence was soon felt in New York—although without the rock-throwing. "We must eliminate that abominable word ladylike from our vocabularies," English WSPU member Bettina Wells told New York suffragists. "We must get out and fight."[4]

On May 21, 1910, with organizational support from Blatch and her allies, 10,000 New Yorkers, mostly women, marched to Union Square where speakers demanded that women be granted the vote. The rally, the largest suffrage demonstration yet held in the country, signaled New York City's increasingly central role in the national movement.

BRIDGING SOCIAL DIVIDES

Blatch and her allies greatly broadened the suffrage activists' ranks, enlisting the immigrant garment workers and laundresses of the city's Women's Trade Union League (WTUL), an organization that bridged the social gap between wealthy, middle-class, and working-class women in a joint effort to advance women's economic rights. "It is the women of the industrial class, the wage-earners, reckoned by the hundreds of thousands," Blatch maintained, who would win the vote by influencing male voters in their own communities. Blatch and her colleagues brought suffrage into the political arena, lobbying politicians and laying extensive behind-the-scenes groundwork for public spectacles.[5]

Women with links to WTUL and also to the city's Socialist Party became the Equality League's most effective orators and mobilizers. Leaders included Leonora O'Reilly, the daughter of Irish-American Brooklyn labor unionists, and Polish

Jewish immigrant capmaker Rose Schneiderman. Irish-born Equality League speaker and laundress Margaret Hinchey revealed her limited formal education, but also her determination, when she wrote to O'Reilly about her suffrage work:

> Spoke outside of 3 factories at noon hour, and when I got through the men took of there hats and hurray votes for women... We hat a street meeting last night when we got there were 2 people... Mrs. Cammons and myself laughed at the way I collected people she said I could be herd 1/2 mile away we got 14 signitures all voters.[6]

These women distributed Yiddish, German, and Italian leaflets in their home neighborhoods, and won over immigrant laborers building the subway on Varick Street by waving Irish, Italian, and Greek flags while lecturing the men on women's rights. In one parade, Mrs. Loo Lin of Chinatown carried a flag reading "WOMEN VOTE IN CHINA, WHY NOT HERE?"[7]

Yet the suffragists never really bridged the "color line" in New York. African-American women worked for the vote, but they were often excluded from suffrage organizations and demonstrations. Members of the city's chapter of the National Association of Colored Women sought to mobilize the black community for woman suffrage, and the NAACP journal *The Crisis* devoted two special issues to the subject. Victoria Earle Matthews and Sarah J.S. Tompkins Garnet fought for woman suffrage alongside racial equality in late 19th-century New York. In 1915 and 1917 Annie K. Lewis of the Colored Women's Suffrage Club of New York, Helen Holman, Irene Moorman, and Lyda Newman worked to get black male voters to support the cause, as did physician Verina Morton Jones. But despite such efforts, leading white suffragists (most notably Alice Paul, but also Carrie Chapman Catt) condoned a segregated, inferior place for black women. They argued that this was necessary politically to attract white southern voters to the movement, but the attitude also sometimes reflected their personal prejudice.

Initially, public "stunts," parades, and street speeches offended some NAWSA members as undignified and unfeminine. But after Catt and Shaw traveled to London in 1909 and met with WSPU activists, they also increasingly welcomed public demonstrations. Soon, riding on Fifth Avenue parade floats or appearing on Broadway stages (where actresses Ethel Barrymore, Lillian Russell, and others promoted the cause), suffragists were performing elaborate pageants. Suffrage marchers chanted catchy, easily remembered slogans, much

Margaret Hinchey
1914
Bain News Service, glass negative

In marches, Margaret Hinchey (far right) and other working-class New York suffragists stressed the movement's links to the labor movement and the fight against child labor. The figure third from left may be Barnard College student and Chinese-American suffragist Mabel Lee.

1 **"Votes for Women"** 1900–20
Celluloid button

2 **"Vote 'Yes' on Woman Suffrage"**
1900–20
Celluloid button

3 **"I March for Full Suffrage June 7th. Will you?"** c. 1900–20
Celluloid button

4 **"Women Should Vote"**
c. 1900–20
Celluloid button

5 **"Votes for Women"** c. 1917
playing cards

6 **Women's Political Union Pennant** c. 1917
Langrock Bros. Co. N.Y., wool felt with celluloid and metal badges

Woman suffragists used New York City's manufacturing and commercial resources to order a wide range of symbols and souvenirs publicizing their cause. The buttons shown here belonged to NAWSA leader Carrie Chapman Catt.

like the ads for consumer products being concocted by Manhattan's advertisers:

> For the long work day,
> For the taxes we pay,
> For the laws we obey,
> We want something to say.[8]

Extensive planning went into these public displays. In the nation's largest, busiest, and most distracting city, suffragists had learned the first lesson of urban activism: Eye-catching and ear-catching street theater was a powerful tool—and a necessity—for winning the attention of the passing crowd.

OPPOSITION

Yet suffragists in the streets faced challenges as well. Women asserting themselves in public places—in open-air rallies, male worksites, or on street corners—were still controversial in the 1910s. Blatch was even refused service in a Manhattan restaurant when she arrived to dine with a working-class woman, unescorted by a man. Amused or hostile street crowds, usually dominated by men, found suffragist speeches to be threatening or even scandalous. Future US President Woodrow Wilson echoed other American men when he described the "chilled, scandalized feeling that always comes over me when I see and hear women speak in public." Listeners interrupted suffrage speakers with catcalls, jokes, and rude comments. On Wall Street in 1908 hostile men bombarded suffrage speakers with "apple-cores, wet sponges, coils of ticker tape, and bags of water dropped from upper windows."[9]

Yet suffragists turned hostility to their own advantage. In March 1913 Alice Paul of NAWSA's Congressional Committee organized a mass march of 8,000 suffrage activists in Washington, DC, the day before president-elect Wilson's inauguration. Tens of thousands of men surrounded and jostled the marchers, jeering and shouting obscenities. The suffrage spokeswomen turned the tables by using their own newspapers and statements to the mainstream press to publicize their mistreatment, thus making the point that they needed the vote to counterbalance the political power of such "low" men.

THE FINAL PUSH

New York's suffragists returned regularly to the city's streets to prod all-male legislators and voters to extend votes to women east of the Mississippi. They also organized on a

"Election-Day" 1909
Dunston-Weiler Lithograph Co., New York, postcard

New York was also headquarters for groups like the National Association Opposed to Woman Suffrage (1911), whose female leaders held that gaining the vote was unnecessary "if men will stand fast and protect us." City publishers also issued anti-suffrage postcards like this one warning that wives and mothers would abandon their family responsibilities if they gained political rights.

"Washington Hikers"
c. 1913–14
Bain News Service, glass negative

In addition to airplanes, woman suffragists used other new technologies, such as cars and motorized trucks, to promote their cause. Here a group on Manhattan's 34th Street publicizes an upcoming Carnegie Hall rally and a protest "hike" to Washington, DC.

neighborhood-by-neighborhood basis. Carrie Chapman Catt received regular reports from suffrage leaders recruited in each of the city's 63 assembly districts and 2,127 election districts.

Activists mobilized their forces in 1915, when woman suffrage was on the ballot in New York and three other states. In Queens suffragists launched a 200-car automobile parade through the borough. Suffrage publicist Rose Young organized a one-day "strike" in which women refused to do their families' cooking, cleaning, and other unpaid chores. Twenty-five thousand marchers along with 74 horseback riders, 57 bands, and 145 automobiles proceeded up Fifth Avenue. But the 1915 referendum lost by 195,000 votes, even though 553,000 male voters across New York State had supported it.

Two years later, when woman suffrage was again on the state ballot, activists marched 20,000 strong up Fifth Avenue from Washington Square to 62nd Street, carrying petitions with a million pro-suffrage signatures and patriotic World War I banners proclaiming that "Our sons are fighting for democracy. In the name of democracy give us the vote." This time, the measure carried statewide, with a margin of some 80,000 votes. New York's suffragists had won over a majority of the city's and state's male voters. On November 6, 1917 woman suffrage became the law of New York State, the first eastern state to gain it.[10]

THE CAMPAIGN SHIFTS

Meanwhile, a new campaign to enfranchise all American women took shape in the nation's capital. In 1916 Alice Paul, who had briefly been a social worker on the Lower East Side, and her Brooklyn-born collaborator Lucy Burns launched the National Woman's Party (NWP). Paul had decided that NAWSA, with its tactic of politely persuading politicians, was merely "an immense debating society." She argued that confrontation was needed to push President Wilson to support the Susan B. Anthony Amendment.[11]

Paul opened the NWP headquarters in Washington with financial and tactical support from formidable New York City suffragists, including Blatch, Belmont, lawyer Crystal Eastman, and

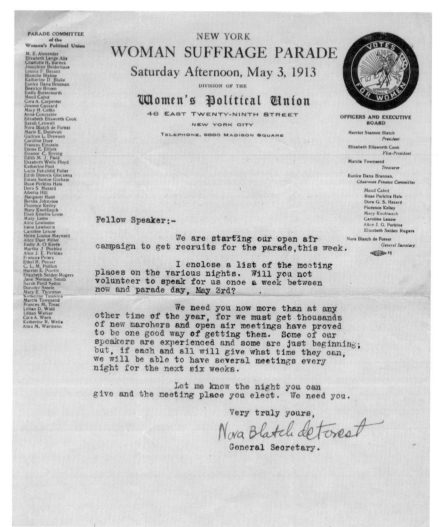

Letter to Julie Reinhardt from Nora Blatch de Forest 1913

Like other progressive reformers, woman suffragists relied on efficient organization and discipline to maximize their impact. In this letter, Nora de Forest, Harriot Stanton Blatch's daughter, urges a fellow New York activist to make public speeches for the cause.

Woman Suffrage pickets at the White House 1917
Harris & Ewing, glass negative

The NWP's "silent sentinels" picketing outside the White House.

factory reformer Florence Kelley. She rallied them to oppose NAWSA's Catt, who viewed Paul's aggressive tactics as "a stupendous stupidity" that would only alienate Wilson. Paul and Burns countered that suffragists needed to hold Wilson and Congress accountable for the fate of woman suffrage.[12]

Like London's suffragettes, these militants also decided to provoke the president and national public opinion in the most direct ways possible. In January 1917 "silent sentinels" carrying suffrage banners began a picket line in front of the White House that gathered six days a week for over a year. Their demonstrations embarrassed Wilson. The picketers—including Paul, Burns, and Greenwich Village writer Dorothy Day—were repeatedly arrested for obstructing traffic and sent to the Occoquan Workhouse in Virginia. In late 1917 jailers brutally force-fed some of the prisoners when they went on a hunger strike; their treatment became a public scandal.[13]

President Wilson realized that the women had attained their propaganda goal of "arrest and martyrdom." Caught between NAWSA's friendly support for his wartime policies and NWP's aggressive civil disobedience, in 1918 the president advised Congress to pass the Anthony Amendment. On June 4, 1919 the Nineteenth Amendment was passed by the Senate and was ratified by the required 36 states a year later.[14]

In the 1920s suffrage veterans continued crusading to expand women's rights, but competing philosophies now widened their differences. Under Catt's leadership, NAWSA transformed itself into the nonpartisan League of Women Voters (1920), devoted to expanding women's influence in public policy. Meanwhile, in 1923 Alice Paul proposed another constitutional amendment guaranteeing that "men and women shall have equal rights throughout the United States," without legal inequalities and discrimination. Labor activists and working-class feminists made up a third group. Arguing that mothers and future mothers needed special protection, they pressed for state and federal laws shortening work hours for women. Paul, who believed that men and women needed absolute legal equality without special privileges for either sex, rejected this approach.[15]

Alice Paul lived to the age of 92, dying in 1977 just when it seemed her Equal Rights Amendment might win ratification by the states. But in the 1970s and early 1980s, conservatives campaigned to stop the amendment and it died one state short of ratification. By then, however, a new women's liberation movement, again with New Yorkers among its leaders and combatants, was transforming American workplaces, schools, and homes.

Battles over Sexuality and Birth Control

In 1873 a New Yorker named Anthony Comstock scored two victories in his unfolding crusade to save his fellow Americans: He founded the New York Society for the Suppression of Vice (NYSSV), and he persuaded Congress to pass the "Comstock Law," making it illegal to trade or circulate "Obscene Literature and Articles of Immoral Use." Comstock meant to stamp out activities he denounced as dangerous to the morals of those who fell victim to them: prostitution, masturbation, contraception, abortion, and consumption of pornography and literature advocating sexual freedom outside of marriage. Authorized by New York State to search and seize "obscene" material and arrest its producers, Comstock claimed to have destroyed 15 tons of books during his 37-year career.[16]

In the 1910s, however, "Comstockery" (as critics called it) met its match in a young Irish-American New Yorker named Margaret Higgins Sanger, who worked to make what she labeled "birth control" safe and available. Sanger viewed contraception as a class and feminist issue:

"St. Anthony Comstock, the Village nuisance" 1906 Louis M. Glackens, from *Puck*

By 1906 New Yorkers like artist Louis Glackens were tired of Comstock's repressive attitude toward any public display of sexuality or nudity. Glackens's cartoon exaggerates "St. Anthony's" prudery by showing him disturbed by "nude" animals and lingerie in shop windows.

Mrs. Margaret Sanger 1916
Bain News Service, glass negative

Margaret Sanger (right) and her colleague Fania Mindell (left) in their Brownsville, Brooklyn, birth control clinic.

She believed unwanted pregnancies, multiple children, and illegal, dangerous "back alley" abortions disproportionately threatened the health, freedom, and happiness of working-class women and families.

In 1914, when her newsletter *The Woman Rebel* was outlawed as obscene, Sanger fled to England. But in 1916 she opened a birth control clinic—the nation's first—in Brownsville, Brooklyn, for immigrant Jewish and Italian mothers. Tried again for violating state anti-contraception laws, Sanger rejected the judge's offer of leniency in exchange for her promise to obey the law: "I cannot promise to obey a law I do not respect." Although the NYSSV continued to bring charges against "obscene" books and plays into the 1920s and '30s, Sanger's American Birth Control League (1921, renamed Planned Parenthood Federation of America in 1942) made her a leader in the long campaign to legitimize birth control. Sanger became an inspiration to later feminists who embraced her view that the American woman must be the "absolute mistress of her own body."[17]

Flyer for 46 Amboy St. birth control clinic, Brownsville, Brooklyn 1916

Sanger used English, Yiddish, and Italian to inform Brownsville women about her clinic.

Midcentu
Metropol

The years between the end of World War I in 1918 and the dawn of the 1960s made New York the world's most influential city. Manhattan-based banks, exchanges, and corporations had furnished the financial muscle that enabled Allied armies to win World War I.

ry
is 1918–1960

During the "Roaring Twenties," a decade of expanding prosperity and booming optimism, these same businesses—many housed in new midtown or Wall Street skyscrapers—increased their dominance in national and global markets. Wall Street, in fact, replaced the City of London as the world's leading lender, reflecting New York's new role as the ultimate symbol of American ascendancy while Europe's great cities sought to recover from the war. Writing in 1930 the Russian revolutionary Leon Trotsky, who had once lived in the Bronx, noted that "New York impressed me tremendously because, more than any other city, it is the fullest expression of our modern age." By the time Trotsky wrote, the city—with nearly 7 million inhabitants—was the most populous place on earth.

In these interwar years many New York activists faced an onslaught of hostility from newly empowered adversaries. A conservative mood sparked by the war, fueled by fears of

Rent Strike in New York 1932
Sueddeutsche Zeitung Photo, photograph

Police round up demonstrators and evict Bronx tenants who "struck" against rents they could not afford during the Great Depression.

Clothing factory
1946
Brown Brothers, gelatin silver print

New York City's post-World War II industrial economy provided employment for well over half a million men and women, including these garment workers, even as labor unions were torn apart by accusations of Communist influence.

radical change and a dedication to preserving capitalism, had emerged across the country. With a successful Communist revolution in Russia (1917) raising the possibility of global working-class revolt, labor unions were labeled "un-American." In 1919 and 1920 federal agents deported hundreds of foreign-born leftists who had never become US citizens. Congress passed laws that drastically limited the number of southern and eastern European immigrants who could arrive at Ellis Island—a policy designed to keep Jews, Catholics, and radicals from entering the United States. For the next 40 years, with the influx of European newcomers slowed, New York would increasingly be a city of aging white immigrants and their American-born children and grandchildren, joined by growing communities of African Americans and Puerto Ricans.

Yet the 1920s also saw the continuation, sometimes in altered form, of "progressive" movements that had unfolded earlier in the century. New York City was home to a multitude of organizations that fought for controversial causes, ranging from free speech and birth control to public housing and economic planning. Meanwhile in the state capital in Albany, Democratic governors Al Smith and Franklin Roosevelt continued the drive for social welfare legislation and government oversight of industry first launched in the wake of the Triangle Fire (1911). By the early 1920s African-American and Caribbean newcomers to Harlem were once again transforming New York into a hub of activism on racial civil rights issues.

But it was the Great Depression (1929–41) that ignited a broad, passionate new era of activism as millions of Americans lost their jobs, their savings, and their homes, and capitalism's promise for a secure and prosperous future seemed to dissolve. New York during the 1930s was home to the national headquarters of the Communist Party, various socialist parties and organizations, labor unions, and the Catholic Worker movement, as well as right-wing militants like the German American Bund (the American version of the Nazi Party). The city was alive with street rallies, picket lines, mass meetings, and violent brawls. The economic desperation of the time inspired hopeful visions of a radically transformed world, though activists disagreed furiously over what precise form this better world would take. New Yorkers expressed these visions in speech, print, song, drama, and art as they worked to make them a reality.

United States entry into World War II (1941–45) revived the city's economy. Government spending brought workers in record numbers back to factories, shipyards, offices, and shops across the five boroughs. This revival of prosperity, and of New York's primacy as the world's most influential city, continued into the 1950s. As home to the United Nations and hub of cultural sophistication, Manhattan lived up to its reputation as the informal capital of the "American Century," publisher Henry Luce's term for an era of rising American world power. At the same time, the "outer boroughs" hummed with busy factories, businesses, and the homes of tens of thousands of working-class and middle-class families, many of whose breadwinners were union members. In this era of renewed prosperity, a set of Depression and World War II era institutions—free public universities, a municipal healthcare system, new parks, rent control—continued to offer a model of urban liberalism and "big government" not fully matched anywhere else in the United States.

The postwar years, however, were not free of conflict and tension. While some in New York's growing African-American and Puerto Rican communities attained middle-class status, and

Demonstrators protesting housing discrimination 1950
Unknown photographer

Post-World War II protests against discrimination in new public housing projects foreshadowed future conflicts over the "Jim Crow" policies of New York landlords, banks, and federal agencies.

black and Latino artists were key innovators in the city's cultural life, most faced racist discrimination, poverty, and limited opportunities. Despite the general liberalism of President Franklin Roosevelt's New Deal during the 1930s, a new federal policy (1938) quietly discouraged banks from making mortgage loans to people of color. This policy, known as "redlining," helped maintain slum conditions in segregated minority neighborhoods in New York and across urban America until the 1970s. In an era of postwar abundance for white working and middle-class families, black and Puerto Rican New Yorkers faced separate and inferior schools, job discrimination, and police brutality. But they also achieved victories: Brooklyn Dodger Jackie Robinson's racial integration of major league baseball (1947), and successful campaigns to gain

city and state laws (1950–51), the first in the nation, outlawing racial discrimination in government-funded housing. As black, white, and Puerto Rican New York activists threw themselves into the new civil rights movement of the late 1950s, many did so with the angry conviction that racism was a powerful reality to be fought at home as well as in the "Jim Crow" South.

Other local tensions mirrored global confrontations. The Cold War between the United States and the Communist Soviet Union left New Yorkers facing the harsh reality that their city would be a prime target of Russian atomic bombs and missiles if World War III ever erupted. For many, the Cold War also brought the fear that one's political views and activities might be recorded and used to take away opportunities for travel, security clearance,

residency, or employment. For thousands of New Yorkers who had been Communists during the 1930s and '40s, who merely knew Communists, or held liberal and leftist views shared by Communists, the recent past became a threat to their livelihoods and freedom. The result was a "chilling" of free thought and speech in the nation's most dynamic urban incubator of ideas. Years later young activists throughout the country would lament the absence of a "missing generation" of radicals who had not been able to develop as leaders and role models during this era of fear and conformity.

Yet New York activism never truly died, even in the worst years of the anti-Communist "witch hunts." Leftist labor unions and organizations fought back to defend their First Amendment rights. Even as Communism became taboo, New York dissenters fashioned new tools of resistance. They risked arrest to protest government-ordered nuclear war drills, handed out leaflets denouncing atomic radiation's environmental impact, and asserted women's right to oppose Cold War policies threatening their children's futures. The seeds of a coming era of activism and turbulence were planted in New York even before the 1960s dawned.

CHAPTER TEN

"The New Negro": Activist Harlem

Silent protest parade in New York City 1917
Underwood & Underwood, photograph

African-American New Yorkers march in protest against the East St. Louis riots on Fifth Avenue from 57th Street to 24th Street.

Ten thousand strong, the protesters marched silently down Fifth Avenue. Almost all of them—men, women, and children—were black.

Some 20,000 other African-American New Yorkers watched from the sidewalks. The date was July 28, 1917 and the marchers were protesting events that had taken place almost 1,000 miles away. In early July a white mob in East St. Louis, Illinois, had rampaged for three days, killing between 100 and 200 black people and driving 6,000 from their homes. The riot was part of a nationwide pattern: White urbanites were attacking black newcomers, enraged by growing migration of African Americans from the rural South into cities across the country. Black workers had been flocking to jobs in urban factories that produced war goods for the Allies fighting World War I in Europe. In the North, they faced racism from white laborers, and white fears about racially changing neighborhoods.

"The world must be made safe for democracy," President Woodrow Wilson had proclaimed the previous April, when the United States had joined the war on the side of the Allies. Now, on Fifth Avenue, marchers carried a banner reading, "Mr. President, why not make America safe for democracy?" Others held placards declaring, "We are maligned as lazy and murdered when we work," and "We have fought for the liberty of white Americans in six wars; our reward is East St. Louis."[1]

HARLEM, "NEGRO MECCA"

Organizers of the silent march included James Weldon Johnson, field secretary of the National Association for the Advancement of Colored People (NAACP), and W.E.B. Du Bois, the NAACP's publicity and research director, editor of its magazine *The Crisis*, and a man considered by many to be the nation's leading black intellectual. Their work reflected the growing centrality of Harlem in the nation's African-American affairs.

Between 1910 and 1930, New York City's black population jumped from 91,709 to 327,700, making

Marcus Garvey 1924
Unknown photographer

it the world's largest black urban center. Harlem, in particular, became a magnet for black southerners fleeing rural poverty and racist discrimination for a freer, hopefully more prosperous, life in the North. They were joined by Caribbean immigrants seeking opportunities they could not find in their home islands.

The neighborhood became a gathering point for what Du Bois called the "Talented Tenth"—a generation of educated, self-educated, and fiercely ambitious black men and women bent on making a better life for themselves. Many also dedicated themselves to improving conditions for black people as a whole. They included Du Bois himself, born in Massachusetts and educated at Harvard and the University of Berlin, and Marcus Garvey, a Jamaican printer who settled in Harlem in 1916 after living in South and Central America and London. These activists and others created their own cityscape in Harlem, ranging from "Speaker's Corner" at 135th Street and Lenox Avenue, where speakers standing on top of soapboxes harangued curious crowds, to the dignified lecture rooms of the Colored Branch of the YWCA on 137th Street. Writers, artists, and performers participated as well, using their movement, later known as the Harlem Renaissance, to assert a new black culture that defied bigotry. They created the image of a "New Negro"—independent, proud, and willing to fight against racism.

Harlem intellectuals and agitators faced a set of persistent questions. Should the answer to racism be nationalism—the creation of a separate black world with its own institutions, either in America or Africa? Or was the fight for full integration into the American mainstream the true solution to their people's plight? How much should black people depend on aid and collaboration from white sympathizers,

W. E. B. Du Bois in the office of *The Crisis* undated
Unknown photographer, gelatin silver print

Marcus Garvey and W. E. B. Du Bois were two very different activist leaders of the 1910s and '20s.

UNIA Parade, organized in Harlem 1920
Unknown photographer

By 1920, when UNIA members carried a placard proclaiming "The New Negro Has No Fear" in this parade, Harlem was black America's most populous and politically vibrant neighborhood.

as opposed to relying solely on their own efforts? Two New York-based organizations—Garvey's Universal Negro Improvement Association (UNIA) and Du Bois's NAACP—offered sharply different answers, shaping African-American activism for a century to come.

AFRICA FOR THE AFRICANS

"Let the world understand that 400,000,000 Negroes are determined to die for liberty. If we must die we shall die nobly. We shall die gallantly fighting on the battle heights of Africa to plant the standard that represents liberty."[2] .

By July 1921 when Marcus Garvey spoke these words in Harlem's Liberty Hall, he had already sparked the enthusiasm of millions of black men and women. His goal was to unite "all the Negro peoples of the world into one great body to establish a country and Government absolutely their own," via black-owned businesses and a homeland in Africa

free from white control, all to be orchestrated by his organization, the Universal Negro Improvement Association (UNIA).[3]

Garvey's vision ignited imaginations and passions across both hemispheres. His weekly newspaper, the *Negro World*, circulated among activists in the Caribbean and Africa. Nearly 400 UNIA chapters sprouted across the American South; others opened in Philadelphia, Boston, Chicago, Detroit, and Denver. But Garvey created his single largest audience in New York City, where he claimed 30,000 followers.

After arriving in New York in 1916, Garvey had taken his message to the streets. A compelling speaker, he quickly commanded attention and loyalty. In 1920, when Garvey's International Conference drew 20,000 delegates to a mass rally in Madison Square Garden, 121 of his key supporters (including 20 women) signed his "Declaration of the Rights of the Negro Peoples of the World." The manifesto declared "our most solemn determination to reclaim... the vast continent of our forefathers." The conferees also elected Garvey the "Provisional President of Africa."[4]

Garvey demanded "Africa for the Africans," free from the control of European powers. He argued that moving to Africa was the only way for black Americans to prevail over white racism. "Our children are forced to attend inferior schools...," the UNIA Declaration asserted, "[blacks] are refused admission into labor unions, and nearly everywhere are paid smaller wages than white men." As Garvey put it, black Americans should "give up the vain desire of having a seat in the White House" in exchange for governing "a country of our own."[5]

Garveyism also provided a set of loyalties and celebrations aimed at transforming black consciousness in America. The UNIA pointed proudly to the black-owned restaurant and grocery stores it helped to sponsor in Harlem. Garvey also stressed the need for black students to learn black history, a subject that was ignored by white educators. His aide Henrietta Vinton Davis promoted the sale of a black doll for children to instill "a spirit of race pride in the Negro race."[6]

The UNIA's focal point was its shipping fleet, the Black Star Line. Garvey proposed to use steamships to raise money for the movement by carrying cargo and passengers, a plan that he promised would eventually enable large numbers of black Americans to move to Africa. By late 1919

Garveyite Family, Harlem 1924
James Van Der Zee, gelatin silver print

A member of the African Legion, a paramilitary organization that was part of Garvey's UNIA, poses proudly with his wife and son.

Stock certificate for one share (five dollars) of the Black Star Line, Inc.
November 21, 1919
Issued by the Universal Negro Improvement Association

The UNIA sold stock shares like this one to launch its Black Star shipping line in 1919.

UNIA agents in New York and elsewhere had sold $188,000 in Black Star Line stock to eager black buyers. UNIA used the funds to buy four old steamships. Manned by an all-black crew, the *Frederick Douglass* carried cargo between New York, the Caribbean, and Gulf Coast ports. Garvey planned to use the *Shadyside* to transport paying passengers on Hudson River day excursions.

Garvey also became convinced that the Republic of Liberia in West Africa would be the nucleus of his African homeland. "If we had twenty ships…," Garvey argued, "every day in the week… a ship of the Black Star Line would sail out of New York port with at least a thousand unemployed from New York to Liberia." By 1921 many of his followers, beset by postwar layoffs of black workers, eagerly awaited the mass exodus to their promised homeland.[7]

NEW ABOLITIONISTS

While the UNIA prepared for migration, another New York City organization fought prejudice on the ground at home. After racist workers burned down a black neighborhood in Springfield, Illinois—Abraham Lincoln's home city—an interracial group of civil rights activists gathered in New York in 1909 and 1910 to found the National Association for the Advancement of Colored People. Many of the founders were inspired by W. E. B. Du Bois's Niagara Movement, started in 1905 to press for "every single right that belongs to a freeborn American—political, civil, and social." Du Bois rejected the prevailing views of the era's most influential black leader, Alabama's Booker T. Washington. Where Washington counseled black Americans to become economically self-reliant as farmers and small tradesmen before they asked for political and civil rights, Du Bois defiantly urged them to fight for those rights, due them as citizens and human beings.[8]

Du Bois became a key leader of the NAACP, leaving his professorship at the all-black Atlanta University to become the organization's publications and research director in "the metropolis of the nation." Harlem-based black activists—James

To Drink or Not to Drink: Prohibition, Pro and Con

On January 17, 1920, Congress enacted the 18th Amendment to the Constitution making intoxicating liquors illegal throughout the United States. For decades, organizations such as the Prohibition Party (1869), the Women's Christian Temperance Union (1874), and the Anti-Saloon League (1893) had lobbied to restrict alcohol consumption across the country. To these activists alcohol was a corrupting evil: it mocked Christian values, set young drinkers on a path of vice, and destroyed families. Because Irish Catholics, Germans, Italians, and other immigrants in large cities like New York traditionally drank alcohol, prohibitionists often voiced views that were nativist, anti-Catholic, and anti-urban.

Although Prohibition reduced alcohol use in America, many New Yorkers and other Americans resisted the law. The comedian Groucho Marx, for example, previously a non-drinker, decided that if drinking was illegal there must be something to it that I had never discovered." By 1925 the city had 35,000 illegal saloons and gangsters were making fortunes smuggling and selling alcohol.[9]

Untitled [Anti-Prohibition Parade] July 4, 1921
Paul Thompson, gelatin silver print

New York anti-prohibitionists ride a parade float adorned with a Biblical quotation countering the claim by prohibitionists that drinking was "unchristian."

Women's Organization for National Prohibition Reform reply card 1929–33

Pauline Sabin and other WONPR leaders proved to be effective organizers. Sabin drew on the political skills she had learned in the woman suffrage movement of the 1910s.

DO NOT WRITE IN THIS SPACE

OFFICERS	WOMEN'S ORGANIZATION FOR

OFFICERS

MRS. JOHN S. SHEPPARD
Chairman

MRS. EDWARD K. McCAGG
Secretary

MRS. JOSÉ M. FERRER
Treasurer

WOMEN'S ORGANIZATION FOR NATIONAL PROHIBITION REFORM

MRS. CHARLES H. SABIN, Chairman

NEW YORK STATE DIVISION
485 MADISON AVENUE, New York City

BECAUSE *I believe* that National Prohibition has increased lawlessness, h
AND BECAUSE I believe that the cause of real temperance has been ret
I ENROLL as a member of this Organization which is pledged to wo
18th Amendment and to return to each state its power to re
sale and transportation of intoxicating beverages.

Please Write Clearly

(Miss
or
Mrs.)
Occupation

Permanent Address ....Town...........

The work of the organization is financed by voluntary contributi
ever small, will be gratefully received. Checks should be made pa
José M. Ferrer, Treasurer, at 485 Madison Avenue, New York City,

"Repeal 18th Amendment" thimble 1918–33

Like women suffragists earlier, WONPR activists used public relations techniques, including the distribution of souvenirs, such as this "Repeal" thimble, to reach a wide audience.

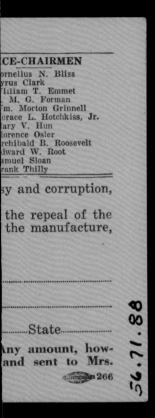

sy and corruption,

the repeal of the
the manufacture,

State

ny amount, how-
and sent to Mrs.
266

56.71.88

**Thunder Storm
Extinguished Light
in Torch of Statue
of Liberty** 1930
Rollin Kirby, graphite on
illustration board

New York World
cartoonist Rollin Kirby
reached thousands
of newspaper readers
with anti-Prohibition
cartoons like this one,
which used the Statue
of Liberty to symbolize
Prohibition's negative
impact on personal
freedom in America.

An activist opposition to the law also emerged. On July 4, 1921,
Mayor John Hylan and thousands of other New Yorkers marched
up Fifth Avenue in an anti-Prohibition parade promoted by an organization called the American Liberties League. By the late 1920s, a
mix of arguments—anger at the bigotry associated with the temperance movement, outrage at crimes sparked by the law, and the idea
that Prohibition infringed on personal liberty—brought together a
coalition of groups calling for the 18th Amendment's repeal. In 1929 a
wealthy New Yorker, Pauline Sabin, cofounded the bipartisan Women's
Organization for National Prohibition Reform. By 1932 WONPR
had over a million members nationwide. The Great Depression added
another argument for repeal: legalizing breweries, distilleries, and
bars would provide jobs for the jobless. New York Governor Franklin
Roosevelt backed repeal during his successful 1932 presidential
bid. On December 5, 1933, the 21st Amendment—with New York the
ninth of 36 ratifying states—ended the nation's 14-year experiment
with Prohibition.

Weldon Johnson, Walter White, and others—eventually joined him on the staff. But white New York progressives were also instrumental; they included social worker Mary White Ovington, philosopher John Dewey, anthropologist Franz Boas, publisher Oswald Garrison Villard, and Henry Street Settlement's Lillian Wald. Joel Spingarn, a wealthy writer and son of German Jewish immigrants, became one of Du Bois's closest allies. The American Fund for Public Service, a foundation established by a wealthy white leftist, Charles Garland, provided money for the financially struggling organization during the 1920s. Invoking the glories of an activist past, Du Bois's monthly *Crisis* urged both whites and blacks to "enroll with us as a new abolitionist... and do it now."[10]

By 1919, 55,000 Americans—mostly black—were members of NAACP branches established in 34 states. The organization promoted an ambitious agenda of demands: "abolition of lynching... the Negro's untrammeled right to the ballot... the abolishment of 'Jim-Crow' [railroad and street] cars; equal educational and industrial opportunities; and the abolition of all forms of enforced segregation." These goals focused on the South, where nearly 90 percent of African Americans still lived. Under discriminatory state and local governments most black southerners lacked equal access to public facilities and decent housing, attended segregated and inferior schools, and were barred from voting. Meanwhile the southern black community was subject to a campaign of terror: between 1890 and 1919 nearly 2,500 black Americans were lynched by white mobs.[11]

The NAACP turned to the courts to defeat racist legislation and defend victims of discrimination. In 1917, for example, NAACP lawyers achieved a major victory when the US Supreme Court agreed with them in the case of *Buchanan v. Warley* that a Louisville, Kentucky, law—and by extension, similar laws across the country—violated the 14th Amendment by preventing black people from buying property in "white" neighborhoods. Lawsuits, many of them directed from New York headquarters but mounted by lawyers educated at Washington's all-black Howard University, chipped away at discrimination across the South, the region that future NAACP president Walter White called "our first line trenches in the fight on prejudice."[12]

As residents of Harlem and other northern communities knew, however, racism was not limited to the South. White urbanites in postwar Chicago,

12th Annual Conference of the NAACP, Detroit, Michigan June 1921
Unknown photographer

From its New York headquarters, the NAACP organized a nationwide civil rights network. New Yorkers in attendance at the 12th national conference included James Weldon Johnson (standing with briefcase below first step, at right) and Walter White (third from left in the same row).

1 **Henrietta Vinton Davis** 1893
Unknown photographer

2 **Madam C.J. Walker (driving) with (left to right) her niece Anjetta Breedlove, Madam C.J. Walker Manufacturing Company factory manager Alice Kelly, and bookkeeper Lucy Flint** c. 1911
Unknown photographer

3 **Dr. George Edmund Haynes** 1919
Unknown photographer

4 **A. Philip Randolph** 1920
Unknown photographer

5 **Hubert Henry Harrison** undated
Unknown photographer

6 **Williana Burroughs** 1933
From *The Daily Worker*, October 1933

In addition to Du Bois and Garvey, numerous black men and women engaged in Harlem-based activism. Henrietta Vinton Davis became the UNIA's first international organizer and a Black Star Line director. After making a fortune selling hair care products to black women, Louisiana-born Madam C. J. Walker worked in hopes of ensuring that people of color could play a role in the post-World War I affairs of Africa. Social worker George Edmund Haynes cofounded the National Urban League (1911) to help southern migrants find work and adjust to life in northern cities. Born in Florida, A. Philip Randolph became a Socialist Party organizer in New York and cofounded the Brotherhood of Sleeping Car Porters (1925), later the nation's most powerful black labor union. Hubert Harrison from St. Croix combined leftist radicalism and black nationalism as a Harlem orator, writer, and agitator. Williana Burroughs became an important American Communist after joining the party in New York in 1926.

Detroit, Indianapolis, Atlantic City, and other towns resisted black newcomers using tactics ranging from school segregation to beatings and firebombs. Activists fought back. In 1911—the same year in which Booker T. Washington was beaten by an angry white man while visiting Manhattan—Joel Spingarn set up a local Vigilance Committee to monitor the "insult" and exclusion the city's black men and women daily endured in the city's shops and eateries. In 1913 New York State passed a law prohibiting racial discrimination in "all public resorts, places of amusement, and public accommodations," although the statute was often ignored by business owners who continued to segregate black customers or kept them out altogether. The NAACP fought back with lawsuits that won court decisions or out-of-court settlements forcing businesses to obey the law.[13]

In neighborhoods across the city black New Yorkers hoped to escape the overcrowding and high rents of Harlem, but white residents formed associations to keep them out. The NAACP provided legal aid to people like Samuel and Catherine Browne, a mail carrier and public school teacher, who, in 1925, moved into a white Staten Island neighborhood only to confront death threats from local Ku Klux Klansmen and stone-throwing mobs. The Brownes resisted the attacks and Samuel Browne became a leader of a Staten Island NAACP branch. But occasional victories did not offset the struggles of residents of slums who could find nowhere else to live. The emergence of other black neighborhoods—especially Bedford-Stuyvesant in Brooklyn—often replicated Harlem's problems, even as these communities provided comfortable homes for middle-class African Americans alongside crowded tenements for the poor. "Rather die now, than live one hundred years in a ghetto," Joel Spingarn told a midwestern audience in 1914. By the 1920s his sentiment echoed grimly in New York despite the NAACP's efforts to combat segregation there as elsewhere.[14]

GARVEY'S FALL

As for black Americans hoping to go to Africa with Marcus Garvey, their dream came to an end during the same era. The UNIA lost momentum as money troubles surfaced, key aides challenged Garvey's leadership, and rival black activists criticized his movement. Garvey hurt the UNIA in 1922 when he met with Edward Clarke, a leader of the Ku Klux Klan, in Atlanta. America "is a white man's country," Garvey declared in defending the meeting. This statement was consistent with his message that different races needed their own territories, but his willingness to "accept segregation with a lover's kiss," as a black Indiana newspaper put it, outraged African Americans across the country. Meanwhile Garvey's plan to use the Black Star Line to carry cargo and passengers ended up losing rather than making money.[15]

Most damaging of all, in 1922, the Justice Department charged Garvey with mail fraud in an open attempt to control the "pro-negro agitator" in an era of racial unrest and fears of radical insurrection. Convicted and imprisoned in 1925, Garvey had his sentence reduced by President Coolidge in 1927 on condition that he leave the country. Garvey returned to Jamaica and then moved to London, where he died in 1940 a largely forgotten figure.[16]

Yet, in the years that followed, Garvey's message of black self-determination and separatism continued to inspire people in the Caribbean and Africa, as well as among New York's black thinkers and doers. One of them, Malcolm Little, came to suspect that white racists had murdered his father, a Michigan UNIA organizer, in 1931. As Malcolm X, he would later take his own stand in Harlem, counseling African Americans to defend themselves "by any means necessary." Garvey's views would be rediscovered by other Black Power militants in New York, the United States, and across the so-called Third World during the 1960s and '70s.[17]

RACE CONSCIOUSNESS

As the UNIA waned, the NAACP emerged as the nation's most influential organization for championing the message not only of integration but of "race consciousness" as well. From its Fifth Avenue office, the organization forged a nationwide network of black men and women whose financial contributions—often measured in coins and single dollar bills—helped keep it alive. NAACP branch leaders and field workers across the South truly were the front line. They reported local conditions to New York, provided the information necessary for lawsuits and legal defenses, and sustained the organization on the ground. The Fifth Avenue headquarters became a lifeline for black activists across the country. "We are calling on you up there because we can't get there to ask for ourselves," a group of Arkansas sharecroppers protesting brutal labor conditions wrote to the New York office in 1921.

Flag announcing a lynching flown from the window of the NAACP headquarters at 69 Fifth Avenue, New York
1936
Unknown photographer, gelatin silver print

Continuing its anti-lynching campaign, the national NAACP headquarters hung this banner from its window every time a lynching occurred during the 1930s. The offices on lower Fifth Avenue were a meeting ground for Harlem activists and white civil libertarians.

As the NAACP faced the onset of the Great Depression of the 1930s, its members in Harlem and across the country adapted whatever tactics and strategies they could—self-assertion, self-defense, interracial cooperation—to keep fighting what Du Bois had urged in 1919: "a sterner, longer, more unbending battle against the forces of hell in our own land." Other NAACP activists, including Rosa Parks, E.D. Nixon, Martin Luther King Jr.'s grandfather A. D. Williams, and New Yorker Ella Baker, would plant the seeds of the civil rights movement of the 1950s and '60s. All relied on the New York office for support, just as the New York office depended on them.[18]

Defending Civil Liberties: The ACLU

In 1920 social worker Roger Baldwin founded the American Civil Liberties Union (ACLU) in New York, an organization that has played an important—and controversial—role in American law and life ever since. Baldwin's own, earlier experience with government infringement of personal liberties played a key role in the ACLU's creation. In 1917, during World War I, he had cofounded the National Civil Liberties Bureau to defend the legal rights of pacifists, including draft resisters, who refused to serve in the military. In August 1918 federal agents raided the NCLB's Union Square offices and confiscated its records; Baldwin himself served a nine-month jail term for refusing to be drafted. In an atmosphere of continued wartime and postwar government suppression of free speech, Baldwin decided to create a broad-based organization to defend the rights of dissenters and radicals nationwide.

"Political Prisoners in Federal Military Prisons"
November 21, 1918
National Civil Liberties Bureau, pamphlet

Founded by Crystal Eastman and Roger Baldwin as an arm of the pacifist American Union Against Militarism in 1917, the National Civil Liberties Bureau was the forerunner of the ACLU.

ACLU leaders celebrate a labor victory in the Supreme Court case *Hague v. CIO* 1939
Unknown photographer

ACLU lawyer Arthur Garfield Hays and Socialist Party leader Norman Thomas (second and third from left) celebrate the 1939 US Supreme Court decision protecting the free assembly rights of labor organizers in Jersey City, New Jersey.

He named the new organization the American Civil Liberties Union.

During the 1920s and '30s Baldwin's ACLU assembled committees of lawyers and activists in New York to target laws and government actions they believed violated the Bill of Rights. Attorneys working for the organization's state offices joined the cause. In courtrooms and legislatures across the country, the ACLU championed the First Amendment rights of birth control advocates to speak and publish, launched one of the earliest discussions of police brutality, and defended the right of striking workers to picket their workplaces. During World War II the organization challenged the US government's internment of 110,000 Japanese Americans as racist and unjustified, while also helping to spearhead the movement that ended racial segregation in the US Armed Forces in 1948.

"[E]very view, no matter how ignorant or harmful... has a legal and moral right to be heard," the ACLU declared in 1921. The organization prided itself on defending the free speech and assembly rights of all Americans, from Communists and labor activists to racist Ku Klux Klansmen. Behind the scenes, however, factions within the ACLU argued bitterly over how closely to associate with radicals. In 1940 ACLU anti-Communists "purged" Communist (and former IWW activist) Elizabeth Gurley Flynn from its Executive Committee. Denounced by conservatives as a "Communist Front," the ACLU challenged Cold War measures that limited free speech and political choice, but also held back from scrutinizing the FBI's campaign against alleged leftists.[19]

From the mid-1950s onward, as the black civil rights movement, the Vietnam War, and the women's and gay rights movements erupted, the ACLU played a key role in causes that expanded the meaning of civil liberties. In cases involving school prayer, pornography, abortion rights, sexual privacy, flag burning, and the right of neo-Nazis to march, ACLU lawyers helped convince judges—including those sitting on the US Supreme Court—to defend the liberties of individuals against the state and powerful interest groups. With over 1.75 million members and affiliated offices in every state, Puerto Rico, and Washington DC, the ACLU continues to provoke strong emotions while actively shaping American society.

"No More Monkey Business" 1975
American Civil Liberties Union, poster

The ACLU was a key player in the so-called Scopes "Monkey Trial" (1925), sending New Yorker Arthur Garfield Hays to aid lawyer Clarence Darrow in defending the right of a Tennessee teacher to teach Darwin's theory of evolution. This ACLU poster celebrates the trial's 50th anniversary.

CHAPTER ELEVEN

"Art Is a Weapon": Activist Theater in the Great Depression

Marc Blitzstein with cast of *The Cradle Will Rock* 1937
Unknown photographer

Composer-lyricist Marc Blitzstein (center, holding score) and cast members during a rehearsal of *The Cradle Will Rock*.

The ticketholders stood glaring at the locked doors that kept them from entering the playhouse.

It was the evening of June 16, 1937 and the cast of Marc Blitzstein's new musical, *The Cradle Will Rock*, was supposed to be readying the show's first public preview in the Maxine Elliott Theatre on 39th Street and Broadway. A young director named Orson Welles was staging the play, which focused on a steelworkers' strike in a fictional Midwestern city. Welles was working under the supervision of the Federal Theatre Project (FTP), the US government agency tasked with funding plays as a way to help theater workers survive the hard times of the Great Depression. But tonight the FTP had locked the theater: supposedly, government budget cuts meant that the production had run out of money.

The cast of *The Cradle Will Rock*, however, had another explanation for the lock-out. Across the country, steelworkers and others were challenging companies for the right to unionize. They were emboldened by the organizing drive of the new Congress of Industrial Organizations (CIO), and by the Wagner Act of 1935, which placed federal support behind such efforts. But resistance to the union movement from businessmen and conservative politicians was growing as well.

The Cradle Will Rock spelled out a strong message of support for workers in their struggles against what the playwright portrayed as greedy, callous, and corrupt capitalists. But because of that message the play might embarrass Franklin Delano Roosevelt's White House, busy fighting hostile Republican and southern Democratic congressmen who claimed that Roosevelt's policies—including support for labor unions and "radical" artists—were un-American and even communistic. Cast members believed that the liberal presidential administration was bowing to the pressure of conservatives for political reasons and censoring free expression of pro-labor, "radical" views.

But Welles, Blitzstein, and their producer, another young New Yorker named John Houseman, were not giving up so easily. Working frantically, they arranged to have the play open that same night at another theater, the Venice, 19 blocks uptown on 58th Street. Here they could perform on their own, outside of government control.

Cast and audience trekked uptown, but once there, they had to overcome another hurdle. Ironically, given the play's pro-union stance, the actors' union—Actors' Equity— refused to allow its members to appear on stage without the FTP's permission. To sidestep the union and the FTP, Welles and Houseman improvised, scattering their actors in audience seats rather than on stage. "There is nothing to prevent you... getting up from your seats, as US citizens, and speaking or singing your piece when the cue comes," they told their cast.[1]

At 9:05 an expectant audience of 2,000 watched as the curtain lifted to reveal a bare stage, with Marc Blitzstein banging away on a rented, beat-up piano. One by one, actors—some of them professionals, others amateurs drawn to the troupe by the promise of weekly government paychecks—stood up around the theater. They unfolded the tale of Steeltown, U.S.A., where the workers under Larry Foreman (actor Howard da Silva) went on strike to confront Mr. Mister (Will Geer), the town's malignant, all-powerful company owner. With actors popping up everywhere, "the audience found itself 'turning, as at a tennis match' from one character to another...," Houseman later recalled. When the curtain went down, "there was a second's silence—then all hell broke loose" as the audience roared its approval.[2]

The "runaway opera" played to full, enthusiastic houses for two weeks. But its triumph also marked a high tide for the era's outpouring of activist art. In 1939 the entire FTP was disbanded when a hostile Congress cut its funding. By then, as worries about an impending world war distracted New Yorkers and other Americans, a decade of "socially conscious" theater had reached its end.[3]

THE WEAPON

"Art is a weapon" became the rallying cry for many young New York artists during the 1930s. The Great

First National Workers Theatre and Spartakiade Conference poster 1932
Hugo Gellert

By 1932, when this poster advertised a workers' theater conference, New York was a center for left-wing dramatic troupes. The title "Sparta-kiade" was inspired by Spartacus who was leader of a slave revolt in ancient Rome and a hero to 20th-century Marxists.

Rebel Arts Group banner 1936–39
Unknown artist

Visual as well as performing artists made New York a hotbed of leftist creativity during the Depression. This banner, with its message of gender and racial equality and working-class solidarity, was designed by members of the Rebel Arts Group, a Socialist Party organization that included painter Fairfield Porter and poster designer Harry Herzog.

Depression had spurred members of a new generation to question the very ground rules of life in New York City and America. Following the Wall Street stock market crash of 1929, the American economy slowed drastically as banks closed and employers laid off workers. By 1935 one-third of all employable New Yorkers—about one million people—were jobless. The Depression hit the arts especially hard. At least 8,000 actors and 4,000 chorus "girls" and "boys" were out of work in New York City. Capitalism, the economic system through which the United States had risen to world power—with New York as its largest metropolis and business command center—seemed to be collapsing, leaving millions of Americans to scrounge for work, money, food, and survival.[4]

Still, the city continued to serve as a refuge for artists and an incubator for their work. For a century New York had been the nation's cultural capital drawing generations of ambitious creators to its schools, studios, galleries, newspapers, magazines, and to Broadway, the nation's largest, most influential theater district. Now, with the economy collapsing, many young New Yorkers looked for radical alternatives, turning to the Communist Party and the Soviet Union as lifelines to the future. Among them were Jews whose immigrant parents had been active in the socialist and labor movements, and African Americans weary of Harlem's poverty. By the mid-1930s probably half of the party's 65,000 American members (and many thousands more non-member sympathizers) lived in New York City.

1 **Orson Welles** 1937
Carl Van Vechten, gelatin silver print

2 **Lee Strasberg** c. 1946
Unknown photographer, gelatin silver print (detail)

3 **Rose McClendon as Serena in *Porgy*** 1927
Vandamm, gelatin silver print

4 **Hallie Flanagan, national director of the Federal Theatre Project, speaking on CBS Radio** 1936
Unknown photographer

5 **John Garfield (left) and Will Lee (right) during rehearsals for *Heavenly Express*** 1940
Talbot Studio, photograph (detail)

6 **Will Geer as Ed Tilden in *On Whitman Avenue*** 1946
Lucas-Monroe/Lucas-Pritchard, gelatin silver print

Hundreds of theater folk created left-leaning plays in 1930s New York; many would later face hardships for their activism. Director Orson Welles courted controversy with *The Cradle Will Rock* and other plays. Group Theatre co-founder Lee Strasberg would become one of the nation's most influential acting teachers. The Players' Theatre Workshop's Rose McClendon gave voice to African-American talents. From a Manhattan office, Hallie Flanagan ran the Federal Theatre Project. The Workers Laboratory Theatre's Will Lee would go on to play "Mr. Hooper" on the television series *Sesame Street*. Actor Will Geer, later a star on television's *The Waltons*, helped spark the early gay rights movement when he introduced Californian Harry Hay to Marxism.

From their national headquarters facing Union Square, Communists urged Americans to reject a failed system for a hopeful, exhilarating model: the Soviet Union, where poverty and want were supposedly vanishing and artists were allegedly free to express the values of universal human dignity, rather than those of self-interest and class privilege. Even for the vast majority of young New Yorkers (including artists) who did not join the party, its stated positions—support for labor unions, resistance to racism and war, equality between the sexes, the need to pressure officials to provide housing and jobs for the masses—often fueled hopes for a better world. At the same time, New York leftists outside the Communist Party—including Socialists, anarchists, and independent Marxists—were scathing

in their denunciations of Soviet realities such as the purging of political dissidents in Russia.

A LIVING STAGE

In the early 1930s leftist hopes and energies spurred the emergence of scores of workers' theaters and dance troupes throughout the city, more than anywhere else in the nation. Some of these efforts, such as the German Workers Club's Prolet-Buhne (Worker's Stage) and the Yiddish-language Artef (the Arbeiter Teater Verband/ Workers Theatrical Alliance), had started in the 1920s. Others, such as the Pro-Lab, the Workers Laboratory Theatre (WLT), the Theatre Union, the Theatre of Action, the New Dance Group, and the

Untitled [Protest]
c. 1940
Alexander Alland,
acetate negative

Young Depression-era New York leftists march in an antiwar parade. They carry a "scale" from which the figure of a man hangs sacrificed to the greed of capitalism (symbolized by bags of money).

Workers Dance League, were brand new. Many were affiliated with the Communist Party. All dedicated themselves to the goal of art by and for working people—a "living stage" from which young writers and performers could turn audiences into an aware, militant, unified working class fighting for its rights.

Over coffee in the all-night Stewart's Cafeterias on Sheridan Square and Union Square, actors, directors, and playwrights argued over their goals. Should they simply be working to forge a strong labor movement, or should they try to spur a revolution to create a Communist United States? In either case, they thrilled at the opportunity to pool their individual talents into a collective project for social change. To save scarce money as well as to experiment in communal living many actors and actresses shared apartments. A group of male and female WLT members, for example, rented an East 13th Street apartment; over 20 members later moved into a house on East 27th Street. As John Houseman

put it, the theater offered "an escape from the anxiety and squalor of their own lives and a direct participation in that 'joyous fervor' that accompanies the creation of a brave new world."[5]

How to build that brave new world? The troupes reached out to the city's numerous labor unions and leftist workers' clubs, which bought blocks of tickets and invited the troupes to perform in union halls, at fund-raising benefits, and at May Day rallies. When employees in a University Place shop started a sit-down strike, refusing to budge from their work stations until bosses negotiated with them, WLT actors entertained the strikers, carrying their props in and out through a store window. "The fantastic thing about our gang," Pro-Lab and WLT actor Will Lee later reminisced, "is that we weren't singers but we sang, we weren't dancers but we could move. Nothing fazed me—in pageants I used to slide down a fourteen-foot ladder. It had to be done."[6]

Prison scene from
They Shall Not Die
1934
Vandamm, gelatin
silver print

John Wexley's *They Shall Not Die* (1934) was one of several "socially conscious" New York plays that protested the racist mistreatment of African Americans in the South.

Confronting Fascism

Supporters greet the Abraham Lincoln Brigade 1938
Unknown photographer

New Yorkers gather at Manhattan's West Side piers to greet American volunteers returning from the unsuccessful fight to save the Spanish Republic.

"... [A]s a Jew and a progressive, I would be among the first to fall under the axe of the fascists," New Yorker Hyman Katz wrote to his mother in 1937 explaining his decision to join the Abraham Lincoln Battalion, the American volunteer force fighting for the Spanish Republic during the Spanish Civil War (1936-39). International events during the 1930s—the rise of Nazi Germany, Fascist Italy, and imperial Japan, and Francisco Franco's right-wing rebellion in Spain—alarmed leftist and liberal New Yorkers. The city's Communists, Socialists, and others, many of them heeding the Soviet Union's call for a global Popular Front against Fascism, sent thousands of tons of supplies, equipment, and medicine to the Republic, while conservative Catholic groups dispatched money and goods to Franco's victorious rebels. Some 3,000 Americans—between one-fifth and one-third of them New Yorkers—fought in Spain for the struggling Republic. A small number of black New Yorkers also went to Ethiopia to fight against Fascist Italian invaders in 1935.[7]

Anti-Fascisti
Demonstrate at
New York's Italian
Consulate 1933
Unknown photographer

Demonstrators organized by the United Front
Anti-Fascisti Action Committee protest
Mussolini's imprisonment of Italian Communist
leaders in a march to the Italian Consulate at 70th
Street and Lexington Avenue.

But New York itself also became a battleground. In the streets of the Bronx, Brooklyn, and Washington Heights, Jews fought members of the Christian Front, whose members were pro-Nazi followers of the Michigan-based "Radio Priest" Father Charles Coughlin. When the city's Nazis—the German American Bund—brought 20,000 attendees to a 1939 rally in Madison Square Garden,10,000 members of Jewish, African-American, leftist, and veterans' groups outside carried placards reading "KEEP THE NAZIS OUT OF NEW YORK," while fistfights broke out inside the hall. Italian anti-Fascists clashed violently with fellow Italians of the city's Duce Fascist Alliance, while marchers in Chinatown protested Japanese expansion in their homeland and labor unionists boycotted imported Japanese silk. Meanwhile, in the pages of *Partisan Review* and other New York periodicals, leftists who renounced the Soviet Union blasted Russian as well as German and Italian intervention in the Spanish conflict. Attuned to foreign events by the city's diverse ethnic communities and outspoken political groups, activist New Yorkers were mobilizing to fight World War II even before it erupted in 1939.[8]

**Untitled
[May Day parade, anti-Japanese Boy Scouts]** 1935–43
Lucy Ashjian, gelatin silver print

Boy Scouts march through Chinatown carrying banners denouncing Japan's protracted invasion of China, which began with the seizure of Manchuria (1931) and the siege of Shanghai (1932) and intensified in 1937.

Waiting for Lefty
1937
Vandamm, gelatin silver
print

Actor Elia Kazan (third
from left) stirs the
audience to support
a taxi drivers' strike in
Waiting for Lefty.

AGIT-PROP

Get yourself a trumpet, buddy, a big red trumpet.
And climb to the top of the Empire State Building
and blare out the news—Time to revolt! Black
man, white man, field man, shop man—Time
to revolt! Get yourself a trumpet, buddy, a big...
red... trumpet![9]

Such were some of the final words of *Newsboy*,
a short play presented by the WLT in their rehearsal
loft on East 12th Street in 1933. They would present it many more times, in New York's Fifth Avenue
Theatre, in Chicago, and elsewhere; workers' theaters, amateur groups, and college dramatic societies soon performed it nationwide, and it was staged
as far afield as London.

The forceful, repetitive simplicity of *Newsboy*'s
lines was deliberate. Left-wing theater troupes were
intent on finding the most effective means of arous-
ing and teaching their audiences. In New York, the
city where new ideas constantly crossed paths, they
had plenty to choose from. *Newsboy* and other New
York plays were most striking for their use of agit-
prop (Agitation-Propaganda), created during the
Soviet Union's early years to educate and convert
the Russian people to Communism. The Soviet government sponsored troupes of traveling actors who
used pantomime, song, chanting, repetition, dance,
and colorful posters to communicate with Russia's
millions of often illiterate peasants and laborers.
Members of New York's workers' theaters believed
that these tactics had helped forge the Russian
people into a revolutionary force; in America they
might do the same, or at least strengthen and unify
workers in their demands for a better life.

"You hear? Seventeen white men take a black
man for a ride, and string him up a tree, and fill his
body full of holes because a white woman said he
smiled at her." These lines, spoken by an African-
American actor in *Newsboy*, evoked another shared
aim of the agit-prop groups: their determination to
denounce racism as a twisted symptom of capitalist society. The crusade to prevent the execution of
eight of the "Scottsboro Boys"—nine young black
Alabamans convicted in 1931 of rape based on the
questionable testimony of two white women—became a focal point for leftist writers and performers
as well as for Communist and NAACP lawyers in
New York. Plays echoing the case hit New York stages, including the Prolet-Buhne's agit-prop *Scottsboro*,
John Wexley's *They Shall Not Die*, and the Theatre

Union's *Stevedore*, about a militant black worker falsely accused of rape. One viewer of *Stevedore*, an African-American woman from Philadelphia, proclaimed "I'd have walked to New York to see that play." The Scottsboro Boys were eventually exonerated, although they all served prison terms.[10]

In an era when racial segregation backstage was routine, and a Broadway charity, the Actors' Dinner Club, refused to serve black people, leftist artists also challenged the racism of their own profession. The black and white actors of *Stevedore* received equal pay and defiantly shared dressing rooms. Both the Theatre Union and the Group Theatre broke the illegal but common Broadway practice of seating black customers only in the balcony. Meanwhile, Harlem-based artists started their own "socially conscious" theaters. Rose McClendon's Players' Theatre Workshop, the Negro People's Theatre, and the Suitcase Theatre insisted on staging plays by, for, and about black Americans and their Depression-era struggles. Established and budding Harlem writers and artists—Langston Hughes, Gwendolyn Bennett, Romare Bearden, Ralph Ellison, and others—contributed to their productions.

"WELL, WHAT'S THE ANSWER?"

Not all audiences appreciated the agit-prop concoctions. "We'd drag ourselves out to Brooklyn or Queens, carrying our costumes in brown paper bags on a deserted subway train," the New Dance Group's Edna Ocko remembered, "...always [playing] starving workers, and the real starving workers wanted ballet dancers in tutus, or tap dancers." Reviewers for New York's leftist press, including *New Theatre* magazine and the Communist *Daily Worker*, sometimes criticized productions for not presenting the "correct" political interpretation, or for lack of originality. "In the first act we suffer, in the second we pass out leaflets, and in the third we go on strike," a *New Theatre* critic complained. More broadly, the plays tended only to reach that part of New York's population that already leaned leftward in its views, rather than winning large numbers of new converts to the cause of labor or revolution. "Agit-prop plays could convert nobody who wasn't already at least partly convinced," actor Jay Williams concluded.[11]

Despite criticism, by the mid-1930s the passion of such productions was spreading beyond the workers' theaters. On January 6, 1935, for example, the Civic Repertory Theatre on 14th Street became the showcase for an electrifying new drama staged

by the Group Theatre, a company founded in 1931 by New York directors Harold Clurman, Cheryl Crawford, and Lee Strasberg. Although not officially a "political" company, many Group members enthusiastically followed the progress of the workers' theaters, and some joined the Communist Party.

Now, one of their number—Clifford Odets—had written a play, *Waiting for Lefty*, which pulled audiences headlong into the action. Based on a 1934 strike by New York City taxi drivers, *Lefty* transformed the theater into an imagined union hall, where actors portraying cab drivers, some scattered in the audience, debated whether to strike for higher pay. The play climaxed in the shattering news that Lefty, the play's unseen hero, had been murdered by thugs working for taxi bosses and corrupt union leaders trying to prevent a strike.

On opening night, Clurman watched as the line separating cast and audience seemed to dissolve.

Program for *One Third of A Nation* 1938
Federal Theatre Project

The program for the Living Newspaper production of *One Third of a Nation* came in the form of a daily paper.

"[A] shock of delighted recognition struck the audience like a tidal wave," he wrote. "Deep laughter, hot assent... seemed to sweep the audience toward the stage." When the actors asked, "Well, what's the answer?" the audience roared back "Strike! Strike!" As Clurman saw it, "people went from the theater dazed and happy; a new awareness and confidence had entered their lives." Lefty ran for 144 performances at West 48th Street's Longacre Theatre; some 60 other productions opened in towns and cities across the country.[12]

A NEW DEAL FOR ARTISTS

"What we want is a free, adult, uncensored theater," Harry Hopkins declared in July 1935. Hopkins, a former New York City social worker, was head of the Works Progress Administration (WPA), President Roosevelt's new federal agency tasked with spending $4 billion to put 3.5 million Americans back to work. In August 1935 he inaugurated the Federal Theatre Project as part of the WPA's white-collar division, which aimed to provide work to 40,000 professionals, including painters, sculptors, writers, musicians, composers, and others. To run the FTP, Hopkins chose his college classmate Hallie Flanagan, director of the Experimental Theatre program at Vassar College in Poughkeepsie, New York. Although the FTP was a nationwide program, with funds flowing from Washington, Flanagan knew that the focal point of her efforts had to be in New York City, the country's theatrical heart. The FTP ultimately leased five Manhattan playhouses for its performances (as well as sponsoring troupes in the "outer boroughs"). Shows that began in New York often became the basis for productions by FTP theaters nationwide.[13]

In the program's first year, Flanagan established 200 theatrical groups across the country employing over 12,000 performers, directors, writers, stagehands, teachers, and technicians. To guarantee artistic quality, FTP rules allowed regional directors to hire 10 percent skilled professionals; the other 90 percent had to be men and women whose main qualification was being jobless. Soon the FTP was reaching nearly 400,000 Americans weekly with performances, most for free and the rest at an average of 15 cents a ticket.

In New York Flanagan viewed her job as helping to advance "the new frontier... against disease, dirt, poverty, illiteracy, unemployment and despair... special privilege and apathy." Eager for a regular paycheck, many veterans of New York's workers' theaters flocked into the FTP. Among its most provocative productions were the Living Newspapers, partly modeled on the Soviet agit-prop performances Flanagan and many FTP directors admired. Researched by a crew of newspapermen working under the direction of Morris Watson, head of the Newspaper Guild (the journalists' union), the Living Newspapers used pantomime, off-stage loudspeakers, stylized sets, film clips, and the latest headlines to educate audiences about the era's most timely social problems. Typical was *One Third of a Nation*, which addressed the ongoing crisis of urban slum housing, complete with a four-story tenement-house stage set, partly built out of pieces of demolished Manhattan buildings provided by the New York City Housing Authority.[14]

Yet, despite Flanagan's efforts to protect the creative freedom of her employees, Washington politics shaped the FTP's agenda well before *The Cradle Will Rock* was stripped of funds in 1937.

Rep. J. Parnell Thomas 1939
Harris & Ewing, glass negative

New Jersey Congressman J. Parnell Thomas was one of numerous conservative foes of the New Deal and the Federal Theatre Project. He would later be a key player in the House Un-American Activities Committee's interrogations of suspected Communists during the late 1940s.

Franklin D. Roosevelt with the cast of *Pins and Needles* 1938
Katherine Joseph, gelatin silver print

Some New York labor unions mounted their own politically pointed plays. Here, International Ladies' Garment Workers Union head David Dubinsky (left) and performers from the ILGWU's musical revue *Pins and Needles* visit President Roosevelt (holding program). Mutual support between FDR and unions aroused the anger of conservative opponents.

Conservatives saw the FTP as a prime example of the "subversive" tendencies of the entire New Deal. Especially targeted were New York City FTP productions such as the Negro Theatre Project's *Turpentine*, about the exploitation of black workers by southern white businessmen, and *Revolt of the Beavers*, which seemed to encourage its juvenile audience to side with the "masses" of ordinary beavers in a revolution against their king. New Jersey Republican Congressman J. Parnell Thomas described the FTP as "one more link in the vast and unparalleled New Deal propaganda machine… infested with radicals from top to bottom." Congressional opposition meant that it was only a matter of time before the FTP would be fully shut down, as it was in late June 1939.[15]

Two months later, World War II erupted when Hitler's troops invaded Poland. For many New York City Communists, the non-aggression pact between the Soviet Union and Nazi Germany that launched the war came as a bewildering betrayal of their belief that the Communist Party was committed to fighting Fascism. Some left the Party, and many who remained were deeply shaken. Only with the Nazi invasion of Russia in June 1941, and then America's entry into the war in December 1941, could American Communists wholeheartedly join their talents—artistic and otherwise—to what was now a shared military effort.

By then other conflicts and temptations had largely killed the workers' theater movement. Many went from the defunct FTP and workers' troupes to Hollywood or into the military. Wartime prosperity softened some leftists' anger and fervor. As Harold Clurman put it, "'poor guys' like ourselves, 'outsiders'—the opposition, in short—were able to swim into the main stream of money, security, respectability." For the moment, the war against Nazism—and opportunities in a reviving economy—brought a new chapter in their lives and careers. Few foresaw the price many would pay for their Depression-era radicalism in the postwar years to come.[16]

MARCANTONIO FIGHTS FOR YOU

RE-ELECT
MARCANTONIO
VOTE ROW C · AMERICAN LABOR PARTY

CHAPTER TWELVE

A Cold War: Activism and Anti-Communism in New York

Vito Marcantonio campaign poster
1948

This 1948 reelection poster for East Harlem congressman Vito Marcantonio (center) of the American Labor Party (ALP) identified him with other figures favored by liberal and leftist New Yorkers: (left to right) the late president Franklin D. Roosevelt, former mayor Fiorello La Guardia, and ALP presidential candidate Henry Wallace. Small parties like the ALP were able to gain seats in New York's city government beginning in 1937 through a system of proportional representation, instead of "winner take all." That system was repealed in 1949 as a political movement against leftists gained momentum.

In late 1947 hundreds of New York University students turned Washington Square Park into a rallying ground.

Their complaint: NYU had removed Professor Lyman Bradley as German Department chairman. Bradley and others had been convicted of contempt of Congress for refusing to hand over records of the Joint Anti-Fascist Refugee Committee (JAFRC). Although Bradley was awaiting an appeal, NYU had gone ahead and removed him.

Founded in New York in 1942, the JAFRC aided refugees from Spain's right-wing Franco regime. Bradley and other board members believed that handing over their papers would jeopardize the lives of activists within Spain, as well as subject thousands of American supporters to political persecution. To the House Un-American Activities Committee (HUAC), on the other hand, JAFRC was a dangerous organization, secretly controlled by Communists to advance their agenda of world revolution. In HUAC's view, obtaining the records was vital to the international fight against Communism.

By December 1947 pro-Bradley demonstrations had spread to City College, Columbia University, and Hunter College, as well as to Brooklyn College, where students were angered that novelist Howard Fast—also convicted over the JAFRC records—was barred from speaking on campus. The protests continued into the following year. On October 11, 1948, 200 students tried to crowd into a meeting between Bradley and NYU Dean Thomas Pollock. Students also started petitions and letter-writing campaigns; one letter praised Bradley for being "a *real* American, not un-American Committee brand... Shame on you!"[1]

But their own activism was becoming dangerous. NYU administrators warned that the protests were "strongly surcharged with Communist elements." Activists who continued to stand up against HUAC increasingly did so at the risk of their own livelihoods and privacy, as government agents and college officials tracked their activities. And, in the end, the students could do little for Lyman Bradley, even though he had never, in fact, joined the Communist Party. Along with his ten JAFRC colleagues, Bradley went to prison (in his case for three months) and he was dismissed from his professorship, despite his efforts to fight on in the courts. He never taught again.[2]

RED CITY, ANTI-RED CITY

New York was a special target for "red hunters" during the era of McCarthyism—a term describing Wisconsin Senator Joseph McCarthy's campaign against alleged Communists during the early 1950s. But McCarthyism was only one part of a broader array of government and private campaigns to purge leftists from American life between the late 1940s and early '60s. The city was the epicenter of the American left; its voters had repeatedly elected two Communists—Benjamin Davis and Peter Cacchione— to the City Council. From its headquarters near Union Square, the US Communist Party (CPUSA) was said to control the lives of some 74,000 card-carrying members nationwide, about half of whom lived in the New York area. The FBI's Soviet Espionage Division was based not in Washington but in Manhattan, where agents monitored the comings and goings at the Russian Consulate on East 61st Street.

To many conservatives, moreover, the city's liberalism was itself a form of subversion. They saw New York's left-leaning politics as a plot by Communists, aided by "fellow travelers" and well-meaning dupes. Among those dupes was anyone who had joined with the USSR in speaking out against Nazism in the 1930s. This included members of the American Labor Party (ALP), an organization founded in New York in 1936 to support President Roosevelt's New Deal, Fiorello La Guardia, and a pro-labor agenda in local politics. ALP spokesmen such as East Harlem congressman Vito Marcantonio worked comfortably with

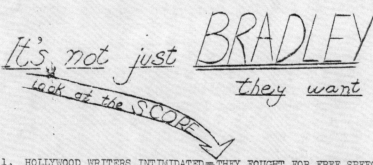

It's not just **BRADLEY**
look at the **SCORE**
they want

1. HOLLYWOOD WRITERS INTIMIDATED══THEY FOUGHT FOR <u>FREE SPEECH</u>

2. BOARD OF EDUCATION BANS BOOKS ══ <u>FREE THOUGHT</u> BECOMING "DANGEROUS"

3. "THE NATION" VERBOTEN ══<u>FREE PRESS</u> UNDER ATTACK

4. TRADE UNIONS SMEARED ══ <u>FREE UNIONS</u> UNDERMINED

<u>ADD IT UP FOR YOURSELF:</u>

<u>ONE</u> + <u>TWO</u> + <u>THREE</u> + <u>FOUR</u> ══AN ATTACK ON THE BILL OF RIGHTS FROM

EVERY SIDE —

THAT'S WHY PROFESSOR BRADLEY WAS CONVICTED! HE REFUSED TO
   GIVE UP HIS CIVIL RIGHTS TO THE THOMAS COMMITTEE!!

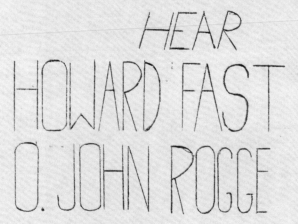

HEAR
HOWARD FAST
O. JOHN ROGGE

WEDNESDAY, AUG.4th at 2P.M. - EDUCATION AUDITORIUM

Sponsored by: Students for Wallace, American Veterans Committee,
              American Youth for Democracy.

"It's not just Bradley they want" protest flyer 1948

In 1948 New York University students handed out this flyer to rally others against "the Thomas Committee" (HUAC) and other "red hunters" who were accusing Professor Lyman Bradley, Hollywood screenwriters, *Nation* magazine, and labor unions of being Communists or Communist-influenced.

Communists, and "Marc" himself was rumored by some to be a secret CPUSA member. When 422,000 New York City voters—Communists and non-Communists alike—supported ALP candidate Henry Wallace for President in 1948, Wallace's vows to restore American-Soviet friendship and combat racial discrimination branded his supporters as radicals; many ended up on lists of "subversives."

In effect, many conservatives branded anyone who supported labor unions, or civil rights for African Americans and Puerto Ricans, as "Communist"; while some of those left-leaning New Yorkers were CPUSA members, many were not. And a current of anti-Semitic bigotry that blamed Communism on New York Jews ran just below (and sometimes above) the surface of anti-"subversive" campaigns in Congress and New York itself. (While Jews did make up the most noticeable ethnic group in the city's Communist Party and in other leftwing movements, the vast majority of New York's Jews were not Communists.) Communist-hunters also targeted gay men and women, largely out of homophobia and the belief that homosexuality was an insidious threat to America, but also because they

feared that "closeted" homosexuals with government jobs might be blackmailed by Communists who could then force them to spy for Russia.

Federal courthouses in lower Manhattan soon became settings for inquests including the 1949 trial of 11 CPUSA leaders who were convicted of conspiring to advocate the overthrow of the government by force and violence. And the city became an incubator of grassroots anti-Communist activism. Many of the city's two million-plus Roman Catholics agreed with Monsignor Fulton Sheen that Communism was "to the social body what leprosy is to the physical body." The Brooklyn Diocese's weekly *Tablet* charged that godless Communists had enslaved Catholics in Soviet-occupied Eastern Europe. Local chapters of the Catholic War Veterans, Knights of Columbus, Veterans of Foreign Wars, and others mobilized against Communist subversion. While fewer than 20,000 marched in the city's 1949 leftist May Day parade, 50,000 to 100,000 anti-Communists marched in the Manhattan Loyalty Day parade sponsored by publisher William Randolph Hearst and Catholic Cardinal Francis Spellman.[3]

Anti-Communist activism also came from the left

Demonstration against a Peace Conference in New York 1949
Keystone-France/
Gamma-Keystone,
photograph

Anti-Communists picket outside the Waldorf-Astoria Hotel in 1949. They were protesting the Waldorf World Peace Conference, a gathering of Soviet and leftist American writers and artists who blamed the United States for the Cold War between the two superpowers.

and center. Embittered by decades of rivalry with Communists, socialist and liberal union leaders did all they could to remove Communist influence. Other socialists, like the NYU philosophy professor Sidney Hook, outraged by Soviet dictator Joseph Stalin's oppression and violence, organized the American Committee for Cultural Freedom in 1949 (with funding from the CIA, the US government intelligence agency) to remove secret American Communists from positions of influence.

FEAR

New York Communists faced attacks from all sides— from government officials, conservatives, non-Communist leftists, and many liberals. But being in the party was a more complex matter than many of their foes understood. Members felt a passionate faith in the possibility of a better world. Even one of their harshest critics, Sidney Hook, admitted that American Communists had created "a network of social, emotional, and personal relationships that constituted a vibrant community." For most, by the late 1940s the party's attraction had little to do with fantasies of revolution, or even with hopes for converting the American working class in their lifetimes. Instead, the CPUSA's broad political agenda—anti-fascism, support for unions, and opposition to racism—lured supporters as much as did the supposed model of the Soviet Union as a classless society. On the other hand, the postwar CPUSA lost many members by expecting them to defend every twist and turn of Soviet policy and to ignore Stalin's massacres and repression of his own people.[4]

The death sentences meted out in 1951 to two New Yorkers convicted of being Russian spies, Julius and Ethel Rosenberg, sparked a global effort by Communists and other leftists to save their lives. Despite mass rallies and pleas for clemency, the US government executed the couple in 1953. Ironically, however, as the anti-Communist alarm heated up in the 1950s, other events—including disillusionment after the new Soviet premier Nikita Khrushchev publicly revealed Stalin's crimes—were already destroying American Communism. By one estimate, in 1955 when the CPUSA in New York had declined to around 10,000 members, 1,353 of them were actually undercover FBI agents. By mid-1957 only 3,500 men and women remained in the city's Communist Party.

Nevertheless, the campaign against Communist influence continued. During the 1950s, any New Yorker with a record of involvement in leftist

Demonstrators protesting Julius and Ethel Rosenberg's conviction and death sentence gather near Union Square hours before their execution
June 19, 1953
Lawrence Schiller, photograph

causes—black civil rights, union organizing, or early gay rights advocacy—ran the risk of being labeled a Communist or Communist sympathizer. Those who refused to testify, citing their constitutional right to their own political views or against self-incrimination, often faced contempt charges and jail time. This was especially true for those who refused to name others as party members. Meanwhile, many workers in schools and public offices had to sign loyalty oaths and disavow Communism in order to keep their jobs; even New York City high school students had to sign such an oath to receive their diplomas.

More shadowy was the blacklist, which cut "controversial" men and women out of work in the entertainment industry and other fields. Blacklisting became lucrative for a group of Manhattan anti-Communists, who went into the business of "talent clearance." In 1950 Counterattack, an agency run by three ex-FBI agents, published *Red Channels: The Report on Communist Influence in Radio and Television*, which named 151 actors, writers, directors, and producers, many of them New Yorkers, as members of Communist fronts. One of the report's co-authors went on to found AWARE, Inc., which sold television networks information on the politics of potential performers. Fearing boycotts, the

Hazel Scott defends herself before the House Un-American Activities Committee 1950
Unknown photographer

Singer Hazel Scott was listed in *Red Channels* in 1950. A dedicated civil rights activist and wife of Harlem's congressman Adam Clayton Powell Jr., Scott was the first African American to have her own television series. A week after her HUAC testimony, the Dumont Television Network canceled the series.

networks barred hundreds of men and women. Countless others were intimidated by the fear of being tainted as "red" (Communist) or "pink" (a Communist sympathizer). As novelist Howard Fast later recalled, one publisher "begged me not to submit my manuscript to him, and not put him in the terrible position of having to reject it out of fear. I abided by his wishes."[5]

LEFTIST ACTIVISM IN THE CROSSHAIRS

The purge diminished New York activism by taking aim at organizations dedicated to progressive causes. When JAFRC closed its doors in 1955 it joined a host of groups—including the Civil Rights Congress, the Jefferson School of Social Science, and the National Council of the Arts, Sciences and Professions—unable to survive government investigations. Anti-Communism also reshaped the city's

labor movement. Between 1946 and 1950 a generation of labor leaders abruptly found themselves fired, deprived of power in the unions they had helped to build, or barred from membership. Many foreign-born unionists left the country in the face of deportation laws aimed at Communists.

The anti-Communist crusade scored one of its biggest victories in the city's public school system through a multi-pronged campaign against the Teachers Union (TU). Since the mid-1930s the TU had been dominated by CPUSA members. They had campaigned vigorously for better pay and working conditions for the membership. Following party policy the union also fought against unequal conditions for black and Puerto Rican children, who crowded into decaying public schools while the Board of Education concentrated resources in largely white middle-class neighborhoods.

The union denounced inferior schooling as part of a larger pattern of "Jim Crow practices" of discrimination in New York. Teachers active in the TU, including Alice Citron (a secret Communist Party member, who was Jewish) and her African-American colleagues Lucille Spence and Mildred Flacks, worked to combat the problem by mobilizing parents, clergy, and other community members to pressure the Board of Education. They also fought to eliminate racial stereotypes and introduce black history into the public school curriculum. In 1941—almost 30 years before Afro-American Studies became a rallying cry for young black activists—Citron and other TU members called for a new curriculum to make students "aware of the great part Negro people have played in the building and progress of our country." Reflecting the Communist Party's campaign against "male chauvinism," the TU also denounced texts in which "women and girls were portrayed in inferior roles." These campaigns helped plant the seeds of changes that the civil rights, student, and women's liberation movements would successfully bring to American education in the 1960s and beyond.[6]

CRACKDOWN

In 1950 the Board of Education cracked down, calling the Teachers Union "an instrument of the Communist Party" and banning it from negotiations. Board member George A. Timone, a Bronx lawyer with ties to ultraconservative Catholic groups, led the charge. One conservative leader asserted that "even a teacher who is not a Communist can be led to

Blacklisting the Weavers

In the summer of 1950 the recording of the song "Goodnight, Irene" by the Weavers, a New York-based folk-singing quartet, became a runaway hit, selling two million copies. "[N]o American could escape that song unless you plugged up your ears and went out into the wilderness," Pete Seeger, the group's split-tenor and banjo player, later recalled. Over the next two years, however, the Weavers found themselves shunned by the same radio stations and nightclubs that had so recently welcomed them. The reason for the turn-around was the publication on June 22, 1950 of *Red Channels*, a listing of 151 individuals accused of spreading "Communist influence in radio and television." Seeger, identified as a performer at various left-wing events over the previous four years, was among those listed.[7]

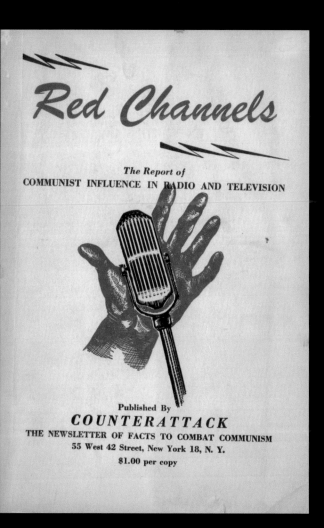

Red Channels 1950

In addition to Pete Seeger and Hazel Scott, *Red Channels* named as "subversive" such New Yorkers as composers Aaron Copland and Leonard Bernstein, writers Dorothy Parker and Langston Hughes, and playwrights Arthur Miller and Lillian Hellman.

Unknown photographer

In this federal courtroom in Manhattan in 1961, Pete Seeger (right) was sentenced to one year in prison for refusing to answer HUAC questions about his Communist affiliations. An appeals court overturned the conviction in 1962.

The Weavers were already being investigated by the FBI for their association with leftist causes and the "subversive" nature of their songs, some of which commemorated the anti-Fascist fighters of the Spanish Civil War. Since the 1930s, many folk musicians in New York had, indeed, been strongly tied to Communist or Communist-inspired movements for labor unions, African-American civil rights, and against fascism and Nazism in Europe. Seeger was, in fact, a member of the Communist Party, and his good friend Woody Guthrie wrote for the Communist newspaper *Daily Worker*.

In 1952 an ex-Communist testified before HUAC that Seeger and two of his Weavers colleagues were party members. The group's work quickly dried up. "Then we went lower and lower as the blacklist crowded us in," Seeger later observed. But Seeger and other New York folk singers continued their political activism despite being squeezed out of performing venues. Seeger reemerged as one of the nation's leading artists and activists in the civil rights, disarmament, anti-nuclear, anti-Vietnam War, and environmental movements until his death in 2014. His songs would be part of the soundtrack of protest in America for over half a century.[8]

Pete Seeger performing at a free concert sponsored by his environmental organization, the Hudson River Sloop Clearwater, in the Bronx 1981
Paul Mozell, photograph

indoctrinate children with pro-Communist propaganda stemming from the Teachers' Union."[9]

Between 1948 and the late 1950s over 1,100 TU members were interrogated by Board of Education officials, aided by the New York Police Department "red squad," the FBI, HUAC, and informers inside the union. Often the suspects were given no notice before hearings and many were not allowed any legal counsel. Hundreds, including Alice Citron, lost their jobs. The crackdown effectively ended the TU as a functioning labor union, setting the stage for the rise of a politically more moderate and anti-Communist United Federation of Teachers (UFT) to dominate the labor movement for educators in New York City.

TU leaders and members fought back vigorously but futilely, participating in picket lines, angry public hearings, and legal challenges. After losing its status as a bargaining agent, the union reinvented itself as a lobbying organization, pursuing the same goals it had advocated during the 1930s and '40s. Among its causes were training programs for black teachers, support for civil rights, and a plan for integrating New York City schools published three weeks before the landmark 1954 *Brown v. Board of Education* case.

THAW

Other allies also fought back against the "witch hunt" in the schools. At one contentious public hearing at the Board of Education's headquarters in 1950, Communist-affiliated officials from the United Public Workers Union, the Harlem Trade Union, and the International Jewelry Workers Union joined the TU to vigorously oppose the resolution barring the TU. They argued that it "would deny teachers... the right to freely join any organization of their own choosing" and end "every vestige of independence." Some New York anti-Communists also opposed the teacher firings, especially when the Communist ties of the accused were unproven or only fleeting. Meanwhile, anti-communist New York intellectuals writing for magazines like *Dissent, The New Leader,* and *Partisan Review* blasted McCarthy's "excesses and demagogic exaggerations," even as they also decried the Soviet Union and criticized one another.[10]

By the mid-1950s opponents of the purges were beginning to score some successes. Echoing other liberal journalists, broadcaster Edward R. Murrow exposed Senator McCarthy's smear tactics before millions of viewers in 1954, the same year that national events opened the door for broader challenges to the purge. These included the end of the Korean War, Joseph McCarthy's fall from senatorial power, and the appointment of the moderate Earl Warren as the Supreme Court's chief justice. In addition to its *Brown v. Board of Education* ruling, the Warren court soon began declaring some key components of the anti-Communist crusade to be unconstitutional. Here and there in the city, dissenters also challenged the climate of fear. In Queens in 1960 several Flushing High School students were denied their diplomas when they refused to sign loyalty oaths. The following year, students struck for the right to hear the Communist Benjamin Davis and the black Muslim Malcolm X when Queens College refused to let the two men speak on campus.

In 1962 a Foley Square courtroom became the setting for another pivotal legal victory when John Henry Faulk, a liberal radio humorist who had been fired by WCBS, won his lawsuit against the blacklist organization AWARE, Inc. Faulk's "offense" had been to organize union members to challenge the blacklist. His victory effectively ended blacklisting in the broadcast industry.

By then, however, the Cold War "witch hunts" had had their impact, chilling the climate for social activism. The expulsion of Communists from unions and professional organizations narrowed the terms of debate on issues ranging from health insurance and racial equality to the arms race. By the mid-1950s older leftists also lamented a "missing generation" of activists. As a Queens College professor observed in 1954, his students were "not given to controversy. They don't even argue in the lounge about music and art the way we did. This is a generation that grew up in the cold war."[11]

LEGACIES FOR A NEW GENERATION

By the dawn of the 1960s, as the "baby boom" generation entered high school and a new wave of student activism began to gain momentum, the legacies of the Red Scare remained complex. The growing civil rights movement distanced itself from any taint of Communism, emphasizing instead the "Americanism" of the cause. The "Old Left" was largely absent from new protests against the US-Soviet nuclear arms race. When hundreds of New York activists protested in City Hall Park and on college campuses against a Cold War civil defense drill in May 1961 they cited the pacifism of Gandhi, not the revolutionary ideas of Marx or Lenin.

But, in more subtle ways, the legacies of the Old Left continued to echo through New York's activism. Ex-Communists reemerged in the city's unions, drives for community control of schools, the antiwar movement, and women's liberation. And a new generation of so-called "red-diaper babies"—children of Communists and ex-Communists—played their own roles, such as sustaining the city's progressive private schools as bastions of educational innovation. Together they would carry into the 1960s and beyond the commitments they had absorbed from the city's Communist-influenced political culture.

New Leftists and surviving Old Leftists disagreed, often furiously, over an array of issues. Yet even the soundtrack of the new activism—protest songs strummed by Bob Dylan in MacDougal Street coffeehouses and by amateurs in Washington Square—echoed the folk music of Woody Guthrie, Pete Seeger, and other New Yorkers who had sought a better world through the Communist Party in the years before the Cold War.

UE Fights for Women Workers booklet cover 1952
United Electrical, Radio and Machine Workers of America

The Communist-affiliated United Electrical (UE) union promoted gender equality while defying the anti-Communist "witch hunt." Betty Friedan, the author of this 1952 pamphlet, went on to become a "Founding Mother" of the women's liberation movement during the 1960s.

1 **Joseph Papp**
Keystone Pictures USA,
photograph

2 **Jesús Colón (at right)** 1943
Alexander Alland, acetate
negative

3 **Lena Horne** c. 1943
Unknown photographer

4 **Annie Stein** 1979
Unknown photographer

5 **Betty Friedan** 1960
Fred Palumbo, photograph

6 **Jack Bigel** 1982
Unknown photographer

7 **Jane Jacobs** 1962
Phil Stanziola, photograph

8 **Ewart Guinier** 1949
Unknown photographer

9 **Stanley Levison**
Blackstone Shelburne, photograph

Some New Yorkers who lived through the anti-Communist "purge" went on to play major roles in the city. Interrogated by HUAC and fired by CBS, Joe Papp later founded the Public Theater and Shakespeare in the Park. Puerto Rican-born poet and journalist Jesús Colón fathered the Nuyorican literary movement. Singer-actress Lena Horne, blacklisted for supporting Communist city councilman Ben Davis and other political activities, resumed her career when she renounced the party. Communist Party member Annie Stein survived to be a major figure in campaigns for racial integration and community control of schools in Brooklyn. Betty Friedan, a journalist for the United Electrical (UE) union, became a leader of the women's liberation movement. Labor consultant Jack Bigel helped to forge the agreement saving the city from bankruptcy during its 1975 fiscal crisis. Although an anti-Communist, future urban activist and theorist Jane Jacobs questioned the federal government's "fear of radical ideas" in 1952. Ewart Guinier of the United Public Workers Union would be the first chairman of Harvard University's Afro-American Studies Department. Stanley Levison became a major adviser to Martin Luther King Jr.

Refusing to Hide: Anti-Civil Defense Protests

"I will not raise my children to go underground," Janice Smith, a 21-year-old mother of two, told policemen and reporters in New York's City Hall Park on April 15, 1959. Smith was demonstrating against Operation Alert, an annual drill that required pedestrians to seek shelter in subway stations and basements as if a Soviet nuclear attack was taking place. The protest was the fifth since 1955 when Dorothy Day of the Catholic Worker movement and 26 other New York pacifists, including A. J. Muste of the Fellowship of Reconciliation and Bayard Rustin of the War Resisters League, were arrested in City Hall Park for refusing to take shelter during Operation Alert. "We will not obey this order to pretend, to evacuate, to hide," Day declared in a pamphlet. "We know this drill to be a military act in a cold war to instill fear, to pre-pare the collective mind for war."[12]

Dorothy Day picketing civil defense drill in New York City 1959
Vivian Cherry, photograph

Dorothy Day (center), seen here protesting at City Hall Park in 1959, continued her activism against war, nuclear weapons, and poverty until her death in 1980.

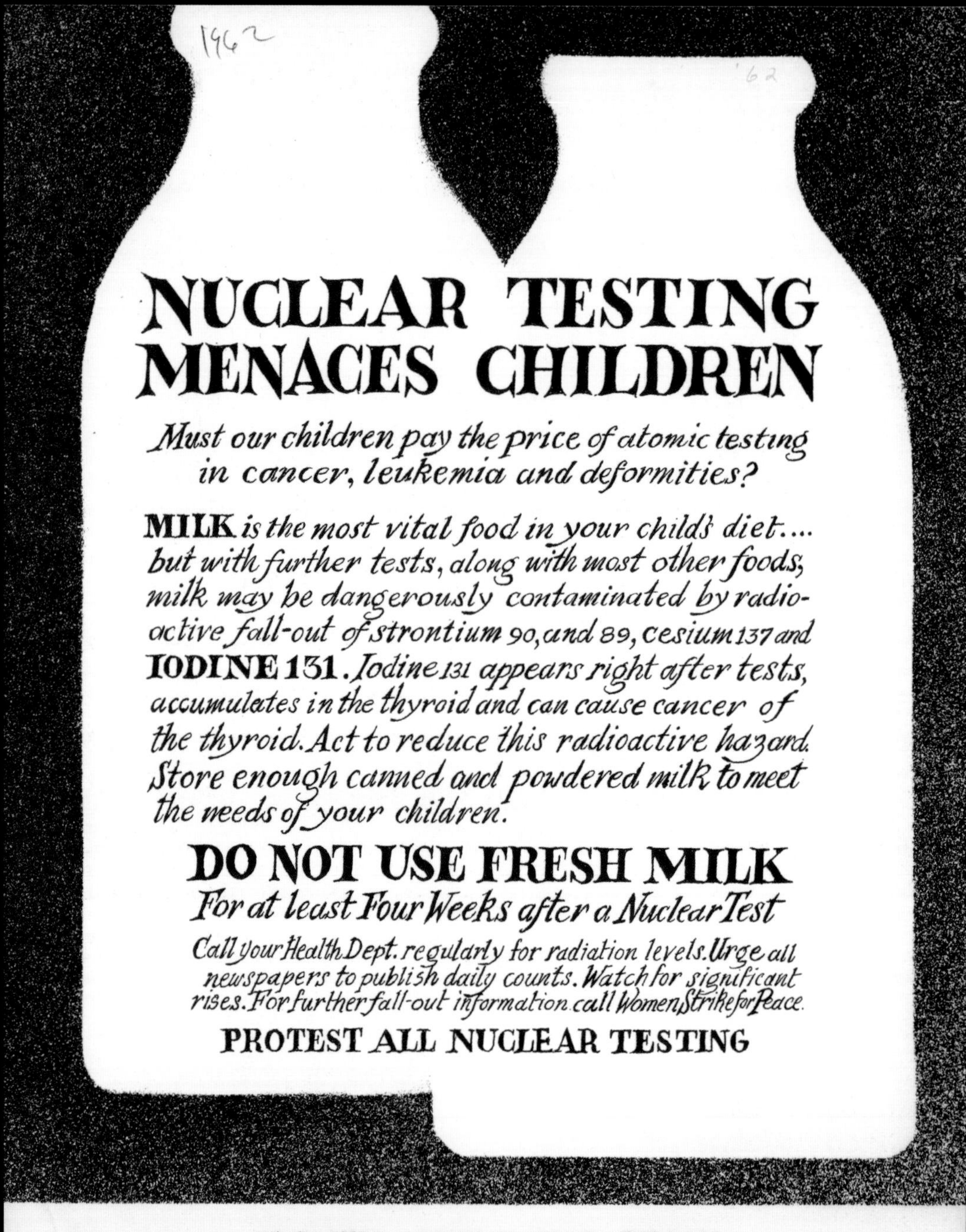

1962

'62

NUCLEAR TESTING MENACES CHILDREN

Must our children pay the price of atomic testing in cancer, leukemia and deformities?

MILK *is the most vital food in your child's diet.... but with further tests, along with most other foods, milk may be dangerously contaminated by radioactive fall-out of strontium 90, and 89, cesium 137 and* **IODINE 131.** *Iodine 131 appears right after tests, accumulates in the thyroid and can cause cancer of the thyroid. Act to reduce this radioactive hazard. Store enough canned and powdered milk to meet the needs of your children.*

DO NOT USE FRESH MILK
For at least Four Weeks after a Nuclear Test

Call your Health Dept. regularly for radiation levels. Urge all newspapers to publish daily counts. Watch for significant rises. For further fall-out information call Women Strike for Peace.

PROTEST ALL NUCLEAR TESTING

WOMEN STRIKE FOR PEACE
750 THIRD AVENUE · NEW YORK CITY · OX 7-0527

"Nuclear Testing Menaces Children" flyer 1962
Women Strike for Peace

In a 1962 campaign, Women Strike for Peace focused on the environmental and dietary dangers of nuclear weapons testing. The threat of nuclear war and the health risks of atomic radiation would give environmentally-minded and pacifist New Yorkers common ground for activism in the years to come.

Driven by her adopted Catholic faith to preach and practice non-violence, Day had been an outspoken pacifist since cofounding the Catholic Worker movement in Manhattan in 1933. With the Cold War between the United States and Soviet Union threatening to become an atomic holocaust, civil disobedience struck a chord among growing numbers of New Yorkers. By the seventh protest in 1961, 2,500 New Yorkers crowded into City Hall Park and similar demonstrations spread to other cities. Facing popular pressure and increasingly negative editorials, John F. Kennedy's White House quietly ended Operation Alert.

Janice Smith and other young middle-class parents continued their activism in new organizations such as the Civil Defense Protest Committee (1959) and SANE (1957). Women Strike for Peace, founded in New York by lawyer Bella Abzug and artist Dagmar Wilson in 1961, proved so effective at organizing and lobbying that the group helped persuade President Kennedy to sign a limited nuclear test ban treaty in 1963. Some of these fledgling activists would soon shape new insurgencies—against the Vietnam War, for women's rights, and for protection of the environment—as the 1960s unfolded.

Protest against nuclear weapons
1963
Neil Haworth, photograph

A.J. Muste (center), a pacifist leader since World War I, was joined by Judith Malina of New York's Living Theatre (right), Miriam Levine (left) and about 75 others in a three-day vigil against atomic weapons outside the Atomic Energy Commission's New York office in 1963.

The Sixti in New Y

"By general consent, Manhattan is the U.S.'s cultural capital, the greatest concentration of taste and wealth in the nation," *Time* magazine reported in 1962.

As the 1960s began New York City was not only America's "glamour" metropolis, it also remained the nation's largest city and its most important center of corporate and financial business, shipping, and trade. Yet, beneath the surface, broad changes were transforming the city's economy and population. Escaping the city's strong labor unions, high wages, taxes, and regulations, many industries started leaving for suburbs or distant states during the 1950s; others automated production and laid off workers. Meanwhile, between 1940 and 1970 some two million New Yorkers—most of them white and middle-class—followed an expanding highway system to nearby suburbs, taking their money with them. As they left, their places were taken by African Americans from the South and Puerto Rican migrants seeking better lives in the urban North.

But black and Puerto Rican newcomers arrived at the same time the city was losing the industrial jobs that had provided work and an economic foothold for earlier immigrants. They also faced racial discrimination in the workplace, deteriorating conditions in overcrowded tenements, public housing that was segregated by income levels, government and bank lending policies that blocked them from moving out of poor neighborhoods, tensions with police, and

1960– 1973

a public school system increasingly divided between poorer "minority" schools and richer "white" schools. By 1965 alarmed observers in New York—and in many other American cities— were discussing an "urban crisis" that was unfolding in the form of racial friction, destructive riots (notably in Harlem and Brooklyn in July 1964), crime, deepening poverty, drug addiction, and anger.

In the same years the city once again became a major incubator of social and political activism, much of it driven by a new generation born during the post-World War II "baby boom." The civil rights movement against racial segregation and discrimination both North and South engaged young black, white, Puerto Rican, and Asian New Yorkers, who infused their activism with a variety of political and religious views. When President Lyndon Johnson's "War on Poverty" (1964–68) brought federal dollars earmarked for community planning, housing, healthcare, and education, some

Tenants from Greenwich Village arriving at City Hall in a "sightseeing train" 1960
Phil Stanziola, photograph

"Urban Renewal"—a city policy of demolishing aging neighborhoods to build new highways and housing with federal money— provoked opposition in communities across the city. Here, Greenwich Village residents resisting plans for new development arrive at a "Save the Village" rally at City Hall.

young men and women also became grassroots organizers in poor neighborhoods. Meanwhile, in Manhattan's East Village, on college campuses, and in high schools, a new counterculture energized young people with its promises of physical, sexual, and mental liberation from outdated values.

But many young activists also found themselves growing impatient with the traditional liberal politics represented by Johnson and local politicians. With schools and neighborhoods still segregated, liberalism seemed to promise more than it delivered in bringing racial equality and ending poverty. And as draftees headed for battlefields in Southeast Asia, where 58,000 Americans (1,741 of them from New York City) would lose their lives between 1964 and 1973, New York became a hub of the national movement to end the Vietnam War.

By the late 1960s an angrier, more militant mood was evident among many young activists. Bent on launching revolutions to transform power relationships, the distribution of property, and sex roles, some worked to overturn rather than reform the American political and economic system. A student takeover of Columbia University in April 1968—in protest against racial segregation and the war—ended with clashes between students and police that left over 100 injured. Conservative New Yorkers launched their own movements, resisting school desegregation plans, supporting "law and order" political candidates, and marching in support of the Vietnam War.

Yet it was the militancy, defiance, and influence of "New Left" activists—advocates of Black

Fulton St. and Nostrand Ave., Bedford-Stuyvesant, Brooklyn
July 21, 1964
Stanley Wolfson, photograph

The Harlem and Bedford-Stuyvesant riots of 1964, triggered when a white policeman shot and killed a black teenager, left one person dead and over 100 injured. The first of several riots in minority neighborhoods over the next four years, it fueled a mood of increasing racial polarization.

Protestor at Weinstein Hall demonstration for the rights of gay people on campus
1970
Diana Davies, photograph

A student demonstrator marching for gay rights at New York University in 1970 holds a placard summarizing several of the late 1960s' "New Left" causes.

"Bike-In" flyer, with illustration by Red Grooms 1973
Transportation Alternatives

On April 7, 1973, 400 cyclists chanting "Bikes don't pollute" rode through midtown Manhattan in a "Bike-In" organized by a new group, Transportation Alternatives, whose members called for separate bike lanes on city streets. The artist Red Grooms illustrated this flyer for the event. The growing environmental movement fueled the call for a more bike-friendly city.

The masked "Operation Breathe Free" motorcade prior to departure from South Beach, Staten Island 1967
Matthew Black, photograph

Pollution from traffic and industry sparked an emerging environmental movement in New York and across the country during the 1960s. Staten Islander William O'Connell, chairman of "Operation Breathe Free," pressured nearby New Jersey towns to control their "air-fouling smoke and polluted wastes" under the federal Clean Air Act of 1963.

Power, Puerto Rican Power, Gay Liberation, Women's Liberation, welfare rights, housing rights, community rights, student rights, and an end to the war—that made the city a flashpoint for demonstrators and insurgents across the country and the world. In many ways the 1960s—a decade that transformed the way Americans think about race, war, sex, gender, and personal freedom—remain a benchmark and inspiration for New York activists half a century later.

CHAPTER THIRTEEN

"Gay Is Good": The Rise of Gay Power

Stonewall Inn nightclub raid
June 28, 1969
Unknown photographer

A crowd tries to stop police from arresting patrons of the Stonewall Inn on the first morning of the riots.

At 1:20 a.m. on June 28, 1969, a squad of police officers raided the Stonewall Inn, a gay club and barroom on Christopher Street in Greenwich Village.

By selling alcohol without a liquor license, Stonewall was in violation of state law. But, as the club's patrons knew, the real reason for the raid was that the club was a known gay gathering place. For years Stonewall and the city's other scattered gay and lesbian bars had been the target of raids by the police and New York State Liquor Authority agents. Now, in the early morning hours, the police divided the people they found inside the Stonewall into two groups: those carrying personal identification, who were allowed to leave, and those—transvestites, club employees, and customers without I.D.s—who were marched into a police truck waiting at the curb.

As a curious crowd gathered outside, some reflected on the double penalty they paid for being gay in New York City. To "protect" the Stonewall's customers from police and liquor authority harassment, members of the Genovese crime family had gained ownership of the club, where they sold overpriced, watered-down liquor to a clientele that had few other places to go. But the regular payoffs the Mafia made to policemen and agents still did not prevent unpredictable raids like this night's. For decades gay men and lesbians in New York had resented—but usually accepted—their double exploitation by criminals and the forces of law and order, a humiliation they endured in order to have places where they could meet, drink, socialize, dance, and relax.

Now, as some patrons milled around while the police marched others into the truck, anger erupted. Sylvia Rivera, a male transvestite detained inside the club, came close to hitting an officer. "It had got to the point where I didn't want to be bothered anymore," Rivera later recalled. Tammy Novak, another male transvestite, began to fight back. Some present also remembered a lesbian in men's clothing (violating a law against public crossdressing) tussling with police. The officers soon found themselves dodging coins, bottles, and bricks (carried from a nearby construction site). From the front stoop of a nearby brownstone, bookstore owner Craig Rodwell began shouting a novel slogan: "Gay Power!"[1]

The confrontation became a riot as the crowd, using a broken parking meter as a battering ram and setting fire to the front of the Stonewall Inn, forced the police back into the club. A detachment of the Tactical Police Force, sent in to free their colleagues, found that when they dispersed the crowd on Christopher Street, its members simply raced around the block and regrouped to jeer and taunt them.

The tactical unit freed those inside the bar, and arrestees were driven to the Sixth Precinct station house a few blocks away. But the next morning the *Daily News* made the event a headline story. That

Marty Robinson speaks before first Gay Pride March
July 27, 1969
Fred W. McDarrah, photograph

A month after the riots the Stonewall Uprising was becoming a mass movement. Marty Robinson, shown here addressing Gay Pride marchers near the Stonewall Inn, later helped found the Gay Activists Alliance, and eventually the AIDS activist group ACT UP.

This Mattachine Society of New York flyer sums up the group's efforts to win gay rights through persuasion, appeals for acceptance, and reminders of the nation's tradition of civil liberties.

night—and again, four nights later—a crowd gathered outside the club. To Rodwell, the second night was "a public assertion of real anger by gay people that was just electric." Once again police and angry gay New Yorkers (along with some straight sympathizers) played a cat-and-mouse game of insults and hurled objects on the street in front of the Stonewall Inn.[2]

"Stonewall," as the event came to be known, immediately electrified New York's gay and lesbian communities, as well as LGBT people across the country and the world. Never in historical memory had homosexuals fought back so aggressively, publicly, and in such numbers against discrimination. Stonewall was not, in fact, the starting moment of a gay rights movement in America; that movement had already been alive for two decades. Yet those nights marked a crucial turning point, a moment when defiance and self-empowerment ignited a gay movement of unprecedented vitality, visibility, and diversity. For gay men and women, it was a revolution in their self-understanding, their willingness to be public about their identities, and their commitment to fight for their rights. "Something lifted off my shoulders," Sylvia Rivera said of the riots.[3]

GAY NEW YORK

Gay people were already a significant minority in New York City, but largely invisible to other New Yorkers. By the late 19th and early 20th centuries, when medical authorities first defined homosexuality as a full-fledged personal identity, gay men and women were making their own communities in the city. In the 1920s they even enjoyed a relatively open environment for expressing their sexuality on the city's stages and in its nightclubs. At the same time, they faced the larger society's conviction that homosexuality was criminal, sick, immoral, and shameful. In New York, as throughout the nation, government employees ran the risk of being fired if they were revealed as being gay, while "outed" gay soldiers and sailors were dishonorably discharged from military service. At every turn, gay people faced harassment, arrest, blackmail, job loss, and violence. As a result, most LGBT New Yorkers lived "in the closet"—terrified that others might discover their hidden orientation.[4]

Fourth Reminder Day picket, Independence Hall, Philadelphia July 4, 1968
Randy Wicker, photograph

Members of the Daughters of Bilitis and the Mattachine Society, including New Yorkers, marched in the July 4th Annual Reminder every year between 1965 and 1969.

A MOVEMENT TAKES SHAPE

The founding of the Mattachine Society in Los Angeles in 1950 marked the beginnings of a sustained gay rights movement. Founder Harry Hay named his organization after a medieval secret society. Hay, who had been schooled in Marxism by New York actor Will Geer, created a network of affiliated "cells"—smaller sub-groups—to promote the idea that homosexuals were a distinct minority group with their own legitimate culture and a need to liberate themselves from persecution. In 1955 New Yorkers Tony Segura and Sam Morford founded The Mattachine Society of New York (MSNY) to bring the cause to the nation's largest and most

influential city. In the same year San Francisco lesbians formed their own activist organization: the Daughters of Bilitis (DOB), named for a fictional gay woman poet who had supposedly lived in ancient Greece. "What we were looking for was a safe place, where we could meet other women and dance," co-founder Phyllis Lyon recalled. Barbara Gittings started New York City's DOB chapter in 1958.[5]

By the early 1960s the New York City MSNY and DOB chapters were at the forefront of what their leaders called the "homophile" movement. But some younger members grew impatient with what they saw as a lack of concrete achievements. In 1960 Mattachine nationally claimed only 230 full members, and DOB only 110, even though both groups had chapters across the country. Many participants used aliases to conceal their identities. Both organizations were dominated by conservatives who, rather than demand that gay men and women be recognized as citizens with equal rights, turned meetings into forums where "experts" explained that same-sex attraction was a form of perversion that should be cured.

A GAY CIVIL RIGHTS MOVEMENT

The African-American civil rights movement became the force that reshaped gay activism. In Washington, DC, Frank Kameny, a Brooklyn-born astronomer fired from his government job after employers learned of his arrest for "lewd and indecent acts," energized that city's Mattachine chapter. Inspired by Martin Luther King Jr.'s civil rights crusade, Kameny launched a public campaign against government firings and the idea that homosexuality was a sickness. "This is a movement... of down-to-earth, grass-roots, sometimes tooth-and-nail politics," Kameny told the New York Mattachine chapter in a 1964 speech.[6]

New Yorkers heeded Kameny's call for a more assertive and public gay civil rights movement. A public rally he organized in Washington, DC, in 1965 generated a new tactic called the Annual Reminder. For the next four years several gay men and women converged on the sidewalk in front of Philadelphia's Independence Hall every Fourth of July to demand, as Craig Rodwell put it, "their basic rights to life, liberty and the pursuit of happiness."[7]

Meanwhile, other young activists joined the movement in New York. Randy Wicker, a New Jersey native, focused on making the cause as visible as possible. Like generations of other activists, he

Craig Rodwell in the Oscar Wilde Memorial Bookshop, New York 1971
Kay Tobin, photograph

Craig Rodwell's Greenwich Village bookstore, named to honor the 19th-century British writer imprisoned for his homosexuality, became a center for gay activism.

Mattachine Society "Sip-In" April 21, 1966
Fred W. McDarrah, photograph

John Timmons (with coat over his shoulder) and (left to right) Dick Leitsch, Craig Rodwell, and Randy Wicker during the "Sip-In" at Julius's bar.

relied on New York's role as a national media center to attract publicity, ultimately managing to gain the attention of WBAI radio, *Newsweek*, and *The New York Times*. Greenwich Villager Craig Rodwell opened the nation's first gay bookstore, the Oscar Wilde Memorial Bookshop, on Mercer Street in 1967. Despite the threatening graffiti scrawled by unknown homophobes on the front of the store, the shop survived as a vital center of news, political conversation, and community-building for gay New Yorkers.

In 1966 civil rights and antiwar "sit-ins" inspired MSNY president Dick Leitsch, his lover John Timmons, Wicker, and Rodwell to adapt the tactic

to their cause. They reasoned that New York State's law revoking the licenses of bars serving drinks to homosexuals could be challenged in court as a civil rights violation. To do so, however, they needed to prove that bars were, indeed, discriminating against gay customers. On April 21, 1966, they launched the "Sip-In": the four men, trailed by invited reporters, sought to be turned away from a bar after identifying themselves as homosexuals. At Julius's, a well-known West Village gay bar, the bartender agreed not to serve them, allowing Mattachine to take legal action. In 1967 they scored a victory: the New York Appellate Division ruled that the State Liquor Authority could not prevent bars from serving gay clients without evidence of "indecent behavior." But, in practice, police and liquor authority harassment of the city's gay bars continued.[8]

By then events nationwide were heating up the temperature of militancy. Movements for Black Power, Women's Liberation, and Mexican-American, American Indian, Puerto Rican, and Asian-American rights were emerging across the country. A youthful "counterculture" espoused the public celebration of a liberated sexuality. And the anti-Vietnam War movement took on a harder edge as some student activists came to believe that only violent revolution might end the war. For the homophile movement too, ongoing discrimination sparked moments of militancy. In 1966 several transgender patrons of San Francisco's Compton's Cafeteria fought back when police tried to arrest them. This was the simmering world in which the Stonewall Uprising exploded in June 1969.

AFTER STONEWALL

On July 4, 1969, seven days after the Stonewall riots began, a meeting at St. John's Church in Greenwich Village turned into a collision between two generations of gay activists. MSNY's Dick Leitsch, Randy Wicker, and other older activists condemned the violent resistance at Stonewall as counterproductive. Emulating Martin Luther King Jr.'s goal of ending segregation peacefully, they aimed to integrate gay men and women into the mainstream of American society as healthy and normal citizens. The road forward, they believed, was to persuade officeholders to pass anti-discriminatory laws; active resistance would only alienate potential allies. But at the church meeting, Jim Fouratt, a 24-year-old actor, defiantly celebrated Stonewall as an act of revolution, rejecting pleas to mainstream

Gay Liberation Front strategy meeting at Washington Square Methodist Church, New York 1970
Diana Davies, photograph

The GLF's Jim Fouratt later said of his challenge to the Mattachine Society, "They were committed to being nice, acceptable, status quo Americans... we had no interest at all in being acceptable."

GAY LIBERATION

The outpouring of youthful enthusiasm and New Left ideas was transforming the "homophile" movement. But the new militant Gay Liberation movement quickly generated its own internal divisions. In December 1969, 19 people gathered in journalist Arthur Bell's Greenwich Village apartment to found the Gay Activists Alliance (GAA), which separated from GLF in order to pursue its own agenda. GAA members focused closely on advocating for gay rights, rejecting GLF's argument that Gay Liberation required gay activists to join a coalition to fight for the rights of racial minorities, straight women, and workers.

GAA members were as militant as GLF activists, but their narrower focus led them to adopt tactics

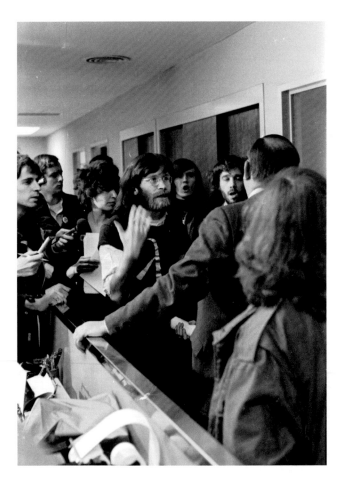

Gay Activists Alliance Household Finance Corporation "zap" 1971
Rich Wandel, photograph

Arthur Evans, Jim Owles, and Pete Fisher (center, left to right) of the Gay Activists Alliance confront managers of the Household Finance Corporation about the company's policy of denying loans to gay applicants. The action was one of several surprise "zaps" aimed at homophobic discrimination.

society: "We don't want acceptance, goddamn it! We want respect!" Fouratt, a co-founder of the Youth International Party (Yippies), was a man of the New Left. "We have got to radicalize," Fouratt shouted in the church. "Be proud of what you are... And if it takes riots or even guns... well, that's the only language that the pigs [police] understand!"[9]

Leaving the church, Fouratt led a group of like-minded young men and women to Alternate U., a space for radical activities in a building at Sixth Avenue and 14th Street. That night they founded Gay Liberation Front (GLF), dedicated to connecting an unfolding Gay Power movement to a whole range of revolutionary New Left "fronts." GLF began issuing its own periodical, *Come Out!*, urging gay men and women to "come out of the closet" and proclaim their gay identities with pride. They also staged a sit-in to protest New York University's policy of prohibiting gay student dances because homosexuality was a "mental disorder."[10]

Stonewall unleashed other new ideas as well. The riots confirmed Craig Rodwell's sense that the Annual Reminder in Philadelphia was too concerned with presenting gay people as respectable and "acceptable" to straight America. Rodwell now began planning something different: an annual Christopher Street Liberation Day to mark the anniversary of Stonewall and allow gay New Yorkers to express themselves in public however they wanted.

Resisting the Vietnam War

On August 8, 1964, some 60 young men and women gathered in mid-town Manhattan's Duffy Square with placards reading "U.S. Troops Out of Vietnam." Many were college students, members of small Marxist groups that had emerged as McCarthyism waned in the late 1950s. They were protesting the Gulf of Tonkin Resolution, passed by Congress to allow President Lyndon Johnson to commit American forces to fight against Communist North Vietnam. When the demonstrators resisted a police order to disperse, 17 were arrested. It was the nation's first anti-Vietnam War protest. Many more would follow in New York City and across the nation before direct American military involvement in Vietnam ended in 1973.[11]

Burning of Draft Cards 1965
Benedict J. Fernandez, gelatin silver print

Pacifists (left to right) Tom Cornell, Marc Edelman, Roy Lisker, Jim Wilson, and David McReynolds burn their draft cards in Union Square in protest against the Vietnam War. A counter-demonstrator sprayed the cards with a fire extinguisher, but failed to keep them from being burned.

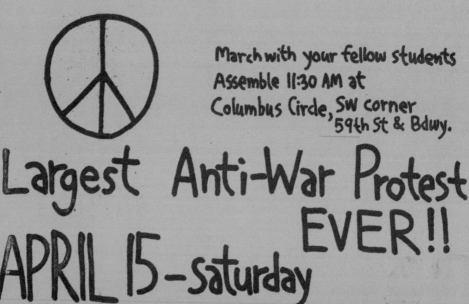

NO DRAFT for VIETNAM
END the WAR in VIETNaM

It is two years since the U.S. government began bombing North Vietnam. For two years the U.S. government has continued to escalate the war and has spent ever-increasing sums of money. In Vietnam, the war is being paid for by the increased shedding of the blood of American and Vietnamese soldiers, and the mounting deaths of Vietnamese civilians. At home, the war is beung paid for by higher food prices, higher tuition, and the disruption of the lives of American youth. Recent proposals have increased the likelihood of Stuyvesant students being drafted to fight in Vietnam even if they go on to college.
We are ashamed of what our government is doing in Vietnam. Our government is conducting an immoral war against the people of Vietnam in violation of the Geneva agreements, our Constitution, the United Nations Charter, Lyndon Johnson's 1964 campaign promises, and all standards of humanity.

March with your fellow students
Assemble 11:30 AM at
Columbus Circle, SW corner
59th St & Bdwy.

Largest Anti-War Protest EVER!!
APRIL 15 - saturday
Stuyvesant Students Against the War in Vietnam

"No Draft for Vietnam, End the War in Vietnam" 1967
Stuyvesant Students Against the War in Vietnam, printed leaflet

Thousands of high school students, including this group at Stuyvesant High School, were part of the city's antiwar movement. The circular emblem on the leaflet was a popular symbol of peace during the 1960s.

As US intervention in the war between North and South Vietnam
escalated during the mid-1960s, New York became an organizational
base for antiwar activists. Veterans of the city's earlier pacifist and
civil rights organizations mobilized to help the growing numbers of
students drawn to the movement against the war and its draft. Five
Beekman Street in lower Manhattan—home to A. J. Muste's Fellowship
of Reconciliation, Norma Becker's Fifth Avenue Peace Parade
Committee, the offices of Bayard Rustin and David Dellinger of the
War Resisters League, and other pacifists—became a nerve center for
nationwide agitation. Becker, Dellinger, and Cora Weiss of Women
Strike for Peace worked tirelessly for the "Mobe" (the National
Mobilization Committee to End the War in Vietnam, founded in 1967)
and for other, later umbrella organizations that worked to unify the
diverse national movement.

But such unity was hard to maintain. Groups frequently splintered
along political fault lines: pacifists versus Marxists, supporters of
civil disobedience versus those who believed breaking laws would
only alienate potential allies and, by the early 1970s, advocates of
nonviolence versus a small minority (such as the Weathermen) bent
on acts of terrorist bombing to end the war and start a revolution. At
the same time, New York political and labor leaders—including Mayor
John Lindsay; representatives Bella Abzug, Adam Clayton Powell Jr.,
Shirley Chisholm, Herman Badillo, and Ed Koch; civil rights champion A. Philip Randolph; and Victor Gotbaum of DC 37, the city's largest

municipal union—became nationally recognized figures pressuring Presidents Lyndon Johnson and Richard Nixon to bring the troops home from a bloody, seemingly endless war.

New York City provided dramatic settings for displaying rising public discontent with the war. When several young Christian pacifists burned their draft cards in front of the US Army's Whitehall Street induction center in July 1965, photographs of the event in *Life* magazine reached millions of readers across the country. On April 15, 1967, Martin Luther King Jr. and the pediatrician Benjamin Spock led between 100,000 and 400,000 marchers—the country's largest antiwar demonstration to that date—from Central Park to the United Nations. Nationwide "Moratorium" demonstrations on October 15, 1969, supported by tens of thousands of New Yorkers, and a march by half a million Americans on Washington a month later, largely organized by Norma Becker, played a role in persuading Nixon to call off a planned escalation of the war.

Pro-Vietnam-War Demonstration, New York 1970
Benedict J. Fernandez, gelatin silver print

After attacking antiwar students, flag-waving construction workers tussle with police during the "Hardhat Riot" on Wall Street, May 8, 1970.

Yet the city also became a setting for a different type of demonstration: Loyalty Day Parades (1967 and 1968) attended by tens of thousands of conservative marchers calling for America to persevere in the anti-Communist war. In "the Hardhat Riot" (May 8, 1970), conservative construction workers attacked antiwar students rallying in lower Manhattan. Indeed, along with struggles over civil rights, Black Power, and Women's and Gay Liberation, conflict over the war played a role in unraveling the coalition of leftists, Jews, African Americans, unionized workers, and working-class white Catholics that had sustained the city's liberal politics ever since the Great Depression. Still, the 50,000 antiwar activists and ordinary New Yorkers who flocked to Central Park's Sheep Meadow on May 11, 1975, after North Vietnamese forces defeated South Vietnam, felt exhilaration and relief as they raised a banner and balloons proclaiming, "THE WAR IS OVER!"[12]

Three members of Lavender Menace at the Second Congress to Unite Women, New York 1970
Diana Davies, photograph

GLF women, including Martha Shelley (far right), during the Lavender Menace "zap" at Intermediate School 70.

designed to force changes in the political mainstream, rather than launch a revolution to overturn the "Establishment." GAA's most dramatic tactic was the "zap"—a carefully planned confrontation meant to maximize media coverage and pressure officials into advancing gay rights. GAA members, for example, infiltrated the studio audience of Mayor John Lindsay's taped television program, then shouted questions and demands at him: "We want free speech! Lindsay, you need our votes." GAA leaders also lobbied liberal City Council members to support gay rights legislation. Although Intro 475, a law that would have made discrimination on the basis of sexual orientation illegal in the city, failed to pass the Council in 1971, Mayor Lindsay did sign an executive order outlawing discrimination against gay city employees and job applicants—one of the nation's first such measures.[13]

THE LAVENDER MENACE

Meanwhile, lesbians were launching their own independent movement. In the months following Stonewall, Lois Hart, Martha Shelley, Rita Mae Brown, Karla Jay, and others who identified both as feminists and as lesbian activists felt themselves caught between two forms of discrimination within New York activism: an emerging Women's Liberation movement whose straight members were often uncomfortable with lesbianism, and a Gay Liberation movement dominated by men who ignored lesbian voices. By April 1970 the GLF's Women's Caucus had forced GLF to provide funds for an all-woman dance, an event that proved deeply empowering for many of the hundreds of lesbians who attended. "In New York State it was illegal for two people of the same sex to dance together," Karla Jay later recalled. "Just by dancing, we were challenging a system that refused to let us be ourselves."[14]

At the same time, a group of GLF women planned their own "zap" to dramatize homophobia in the women's movement. They knew that leading feminist Betty Friedan had denounced lesbians as "the lavender menace," "man-haters" who scared away potential supporters of women's rights. In response, on May 1, 1970, Rita Mae Brown, Karla Jay, and 15 other GLF lesbians wearing "Lavender Menace" T-shirts confronted 300 women attending a feminist conference in a school auditorium on West 17th Street. The insurgents turned Friedan's argument upside down: gay women, they asserted, were the true feminists. "A lesbian is the rage of all women condensed to the point of explosion," declared *The Woman Identified Woman*, the printed manifesto that Jay and her friends handed down the rows of seats.[15]

Out of the "Lavender Menace" zap and other activities came a separate lesbian rights movement,

1 **Barbara Gittings printing Daughters of Bilitis newsletter** 1962
Kay Tobin, photograph

2 **(left to right) Frank Kameny, Randy Wicker, and Jim Owles** 1971
Kay Tobin, photograph

3 **Sylvia Ray Rivera (front) and Arthur Bell at a gay liberation demonstration, New York University** 1970
Diana Davies, photograph

4 **Marsha P. Johnson at a Gay Liberation Front meeting** c. 1970
Diana Davies, photograph

5 **Gay Liberation Front picketing Time, Inc.** 1971
Diana Davies, photograph

6 **Harvey Milk in front of his Castro Street camera store** 1977–78
Daniel Nicoletta, photograph

Veteran gay rights activists and new-comers both collaborated and clashed during the 1960s. Barbara Gittings founded New York's Daughters of Bilitis chapter; she went on to march in the Annual Reminders and worked to get the American Psychiatric Association to stop listing homosexuality as a mental illness. Mattachine Society activist Frank Kameny and GAA's Randy Wicker and Jim Owles developed different forms of public protest for gay rights. Stonewall Uprising participant Sylvia Rivera and GAA founder Arthur Bell marched together against NYU's prohibition of gay dances. Marsha P. Johnson cofounded Street Transvestite Action Revolutionaries with Rivera. GLF's Linda Rhodes, Lois Hart, Ellen Broidy, and Jim Fouratt picketed against a homophobic *Time* magazine article in 1971. New Yorker Harvey Milk, a former lover of Craig Rodwell, became California's first openly gay elected official as a member of San Francisco's Board of Supervisors in 1977.

Christopher Street Liberation Day
June 20, 1971
Diana Davies, photograph

Starting in 1970 marchers from across the nation and the world came to the annual Christopher Street Liberation Day parade, marking the anniversary of the Stonewall Uprising. Today it continues as the New York City LGBT Pride March. In 2016 it drew an estimated 30,000 participants and two million spectators.

based in new organizations such as Radicalesbians, in which Brown and Jay played leadership roles. But even as lesbian activists forced straight feminists and male gay activists to face lesbian concerns, Gay Liberation generated new splinter groups. "Both the women's and gay movements were much more white and middle class than we would like to admit," Jay reflected later. Gay New Yorkers who felt like outsiders in their own movement—African Americans, Latinas, and transvestites—soon formed their own groups, including the Black Lesbian Counseling Collective, *Las Buenas Amigas*, and STAR (Street Transvestite Action Revolutionaries).[16]

A NEW ERA

The Stonewall Uprising had changed everything. A movement with two decades of history had abruptly broadened as the Christopher Street riots reached vast audiences through broadcasts, publications, word of mouth, and organizing efforts. A new generation of young gay men and women quickly embraced the anger and public visibility of Stonewall to press for their own liberation across the country and the world. In a resounding victory, activists in the New York-based National Gay Task Force and other groups persuaded the American Psychiatric Association to remove homosexuality from its list of mental disorders in 1973.

On June 27, 1970—the first anniversary of the Stonewall Uprising—Craig Rodwell's Christopher Street Liberation Day Committee kicked off the world's first gay rights parade on Sixth Avenue from Greenwich Village to Central Park. Other commemorative marches began in Chicago, Los Angeles, and San Francisco; by the next anniversary in 1971, London and Paris would have their own parades. At least 2,000 people marched up Sixth Avenue that day. Surveying the marchers stretching along fifteen city blocks, Jim Fouratt thought about the year that had transformed the movement and his own activism. "I saw what we had done," he later remembered. "It was remarkable. There we were in all our diversity." A decade later, Fouratt and other gay rights pioneers would find themselves building on their Stonewall-era achievements to rally new activists, this time to "zap" those they accused of standing in the way of solving an unfolding AIDS crisis (see page 261).[17]

Women's Liberation in New York

In 1963 a Rockland County housewife helped plant the seeds of a revolution by writing about something she called "the problem that has no name": the unhappiness of well-educated, middle-class American women like herself. Betty Friedan's *The Feminine Mystique* became a bestseller as three million readers confronted her unsettling demand: "I want something more than my husband and my children and my home." Friedan's words echoed her work as a writer for New York's leftist United Electrical, Radio and Machine Workers union during the early 1950s, when American Communists were among the few groups seriously discussing "the Woman Question."[18]

Cover of the first issue of *Ms.* magazine Spring 1972
Miriam Wask

Published in Manhattan, *Ms.* magazine was the first periodical created, owned, and operated entirely by women. The first cover image modernized the multi-armed Hindu goddess Kali, showing her juggling work and household tasks.

African-American women attending the International Women's Day rally
March 12, 1977
Freda Leinwand, gelatin silver print

Some New York feminists, both black and white, argued that the housework they performed should earn wages, just like labor performed in the workplace.

Bella Abzug and Gloria Steinem at "Solidarity Day" demonstration in Washington, DC 1981
Hal Reiff, gelatin silver print

New Yorkers Gloria Steinem (left, holding sign) and Bella Abzug (center right, in hat) helped reinvent feminism in the 1960s and '70s. Here they demonstrate for the Equal Rights Amendment.

By 1966, when Friedan, Pauli Murray, Shirley Chisholm, and others founded the National Organization for Women (NOW), this criticism of the limits placed on American women resonated with a younger generation. Across the country, women active in the civil rights, student, and antiwar movements were voicing their own frustration with the sexism they encountered from male associates. By 1967-68 some, including New Yorkers Shulamith Firestone and Kathie Sarachild, called for "women's liberation." Robin Morgan and other members of a new group, New York Radical Women, protested the 1968 Miss America pageant in Atlantic City, New Jersey, by symbolically throwing girdles, bras, false eyelashes, cosmetics, and other "instruments of torture" into a "Freedom Trash Can," attracting nationwide news coverage.[19]

New York became a major base of operations for these New Feminists. A spectrum of organizations ranging from NOW and New York Radical Women to Redstockings, The Feminists, and WITCH (Women's International Terrorist Conspiracy from Hell) proposed sweeping changes to American society. Feminists demanded equal access, pay, and advancement in the male-dominated workplace; government-funded daycare to help working mothers; equal participation by men in housework and parenting; abortion rights; affirmation of women's sexuality; and the elimination of sexist stereotypes, domestic and sexual violence, and male treatment of women as "sex objects." Many focused on winning passage of the Equal Rights Amendment (ERA) to the Constitution, first proposed by Alice Paul in 1923.

As the nation's center of media and business, New York offered ample opportunity for protest and organizing. Angered by workplace discrimination and sexist portrayals of women, feminists picketed *The New York Times* and National Airlines; sat in at *Newsweek* and *Ladies' Home Journal*; and sued the *Times* and *Fortune*, *Time*, and *Life*

Demonstration protesting anti-abortion candidate Ellen McCormack at the Democratic National Convention, New York City
July 14, 1976
Warren K. Leffler, photographic negative

Feminists' support for abortion rights, and for the 1973 *Roe v. Wade* Supreme Court ruling legalizing abortions, triggered a decades-long struggle between "pro-choice" and "pro-life" activists that continues to shape American politics and law today.

On August 26, 1970, the fiftieth anniversary of the adoption of the 19th Amendment giving American women the vote, feminists draped a huge banner over the Statue of Liberty reading "Women of the World Unite." The statue was a fitting symbol for the empowerment New York feminists were claiming for all women.

WOMEN'S LIBERATION

magazines. Women also forcibly integrated all-male spaces including bars at the Hotel Biltmore, Plaza Hotel, and McSorley's Alehouse. In 1972 journalist Gloria Steinem, Dorothy Pitman Hughes, and several others founded *Ms.* magazine in Manhattan; it quickly became the nation's leading feminist publication. Meanwhile, political changes—the election of Chisholm and Bella Abzug to Congress, Mayor John Lindsay's executive order banning sex discrimination in city employment, and the Supreme Court's *Roe v. Wade* decision legalizing abortion (1973)—ushered in a new era.

At the same time, Women's Liberation was not a uniform movement; like other activists, feminists divided over important issues. Some worked with men in hopes of bringing gender equality; others rejected collaboration and created separate women's institutions. The primarily white, middle-class focus of NOW and other mainstream groups alienated radical leftists, poor women, and women of color, and they launched their own organizations, such as Flo Kennedy's and Margaret Sloan-Hunter's National Black Feminist Organization, and Brooklyn's National Congress of Neighborhood Women. And the rise of militant Gay Liberation in 1969 fueled tensions between heterosexual and lesbian feminists that led to angry confrontations and the rise of an independent gay feminist movement.

Failure to pass the ERA (1982) and the rise of a conservative anti-feminist movement across the country signaled that continued victories would not be attained easily. Still, a generation of New York women had played a crucial role in launching a national and global revolution—one aiming at nothing less than transforming the rights and ambitions of half the world's population—whose struggles continue to unfold half a century later.

CHAPTER FOURTEEN

"¡Basta Ya!": The Young Lords and Puerto Rican Activism

Garbage Offensive—
Summer/Fall 1969
Hiram Maristany.
photograph

With help from neighbors, the Young Lords
blocked East Harlem traffic during their 1969
"garbage offensive."

Smoke rose from the burning trash into the air over 110th Street in East Harlem.

Similar piles of garbage, some stacked five feet high, backed up traffic along Second and Third Avenues between 106th and 118th Streets. It was August 17, 1969, the fourth Sunday of the "garbage offensive," a protest launched by the Young Lords Organization (YLO), a new group of youthful Puerto Rican activists. Three weeks earlier the New York Young Lords had officially announced their existence at a rally in Tompkins Square Park on the Lower East Side, like East Harlem, a neighborhood with a large population of poor Puerto Rican residents. Canvassing their East Harlem neighbors about the problems they faced, the young activists heard repeated complaints about the lack of garbage collection. Now the Young Lords were insisting that the city's Sanitation Department clean East Harlem's neglected streets and haul away its garbage as regularly as in the city's white middle-class and wealthy neighborhoods.

When a group of about a dozen Young Lords tried to borrow brooms from the Sanitation Department to help clean up the neighborhood themselves, sanitation workers had refused. The Lords took the brooms anyway. The traffic-stopping garbage offensive was their next step. "The only choice we had was confrontational politics," Mickey Melendez, one of the participants, later recalled. "... It was a collective cry of '¡Basta ya!'—'Enough!'" In addition to its political impact, the offensive filled the activists with a feeling of pride. "We all felt the spirit of winning," Melendez recalled, "the triumph of good over evil, where justice, in this moment, prevailed."[1]

CREATING THE YOUNG LORDS

The Young Lords Organization had gelled when young Puerto Rican New Yorkers came together during the summer of 1969. Some were recent graduates or students at Columbia University, the State University of New York at Old Westbury, and other colleges. Juan González, for example, was a member of Students for a Democratic Society (SDS) and had joined in the takeover of Columbia by student protesters in April 1968. Others came from neighborhood organizations. Luis Garden Acosta had already been an activist for welfare recipients' rights and against the Vietnam War, while Denise Oliver had worked with the Student Nonviolent Coordinating Committee (SNCC) and the Congress of Racial Equality (CORE) to empower poor African Americans. The Real Great Society/Urban Planning Studio, an anti-poverty organization pledging to attain "self control and self determination" for El Barrio ("the neighborhood," as East Harlem was called), provided members. So did the Sociedad de Albizu Campos, a reading and discussion group dedicated to Puerto Rican nationhood. Other activists joined the Lords through José Martínez, a Lower East Side activist, and through a photography workshop led by Hiram Maristany, a young East Harlem resident.[2]

Formal Introduction of the Young Lords Organization— Tompkins Square Park July 26, 1969
Hiram Maristany, photograph

The Young Lords publicly announced their existence at this rally in the East Village (a neighborhood known to many Puerto Ricans as Loisaida).

Puerto Ricans demonstrate for civil rights at City Hall, New York City 1967
Al Ravenna, photograph

A Puerto Rican civil rights movement was already underway in New York before the Young Lords appeared in 1969. Here, members of the Council of Puerto Rican & Hispanic Organizations of the Lower East Side rally at City Hall for better public schools in their neighborhood and better access to jobs and housing.

Inspired by the Chicago Young Lords, a Puerto Rican street gang that had evolved into a community activist group, the New Yorkers adopted the Chicagoans' name and commitment to change. By 1970 the New York Young Lords Party (as it renamed itself) had several hundred core members and thousands of sympathizers, a storefront headquarters on Madison Avenue between 111th and 112th Streets, and a Central Committee: deputy chairman Felipe Luciano, deputy minister of defense David Pérez, deputy minister of information Pablo "Yoruba" Guzmán, deputy minister of education Juan González, and deputy minister of finance Juan "Fi" Ortiz.

The idealism and anger that drove "the Youth Revolution" of the mid and late 1960s inspired many of these young Latinos to create their own variety of activism. They were disillusioned with President Lyndon Johnson's War on Poverty, which spent millions of federal dollars to fund anti-poverty programs across the nation but had not fundamentally changed the conditions of decrepit housing, joblessness, segregation, and police brutality that plagued the nation's black and Puerto Rican "inner cities." By 1968 the civil rights movement, long dedicated to racial integration by peaceful means, was evolving toward a more militant assertion of "Black Power." In New York, a movement for control of neighborhood public schools by black, Puerto Rican, and Asian American parents and community members in 1968 pitted minority activists against the city's largely white teachers' union.

Meanwhile, the Vietnam War mobilized students of all races against what seemed like an endless bloodbath. "My neighbor, Pedro, came back in a body bag...," Melendez recalled. "Was there any reason for him to die? The news on the TV, the radio, or the papers did not provide a good answer to that question." Radical history inspired them as well. Young New York Puerto Ricans read the writings of radical thinkers Mao Zedong, Malcolm X, Frantz Fanon, Régis Debray, and the Black Panther leader Huey P. Newton. They were moved by the example of Fidel Castro's and Che Guevara's Marxist revolution in Cuba and the history of Puerto Rico's own radical leaders, especially Pedro Albizu Campos. At the same time, young Latina women like Iris Morales, Nydia Mercado, Lulu Carreras, and others were energized by the emergence of the Women's Liberation movement, even as they distrusted the white middle-class focus of the National Organization for Women (NOW) and other new feminist groups. Young Lords, both male and female, were willing to envision socialist revolution rather than peaceful reform as the answer to the ills of poverty, war, racism, and inequality.[3]

KEY DEMANDS

As Puerto Rican New Yorkers, the Young Lords evolved their own distinct agenda, one that combined two key demands: the elimination of the poverty, racism, and sickness that limited the lives of New York's Latinos and political independence for the island of Puerto Rico. By the late 1960s about 800,000 New Yorkers—over ten percent of the city—were natives of Puerto Rico or their descendants. Seeking jobs and economic opportunity during and after World War II, thousands of poor Puerto Rican families had migrated to the city they knew as "Nueva York." But, rather than finding an abundance

of well-paying jobs, most encountered a factory economy in decline as industries left the city, low pay, overcrowded housing and schools, and racist discrimination. "It seemed that all the institutions—from the local school to the Social Security office to the hospital emergency room—were willing to experiment with and throw away our lives," future Young Lord Iris Morales felt.[4]

Their communities in East (or Spanish) Harlem, the Lower East Side, and the South Bronx, though beset with poverty, became a launch pad for the young men and women who created the Young Lords. "We want control of our communities... to guarantee that all institutions serve the needs of our people," their 13 Point Program and Platform, issued in October 1969, asserted. "People's control of police, health services, churches, schools, housing, transportation and welfare are needed." The same manifesto targeted a trend that was making Puerto Rican community-building harder in 1960s New York: "urban removal" (also called Urban Renewal), which pushed poor people out of certain neighbor-hoods to make way for new highways, apartment buildings, campuses, and corporate offices serving middle-class and wealthy New Yorkers.[5]

At the same time, the Young Lords insisted that Puerto Rico be freed from American control, even though many of them had never visited their parents' home island, and spoke Spanish only as their second language after English. Acquired by the United States in the Spanish-American War of 1898, the island was now officially a commonwealth territory, and Puerto Ricans had been US citizens since 1917. But island residents could not vote for US president, had no voting representation in Congress, and labored in an economy largely controlled by American corporations. While some Puerto Ricans on the island and in New York supported the mod-erate goal of US statehood, others embraced the more radical aim of complete independence as a nation. The Young Lords embraced the latter posi-tion. In doing so, they also embraced the tradition of Pedro Albizu Campos's Puerto Rican Nationalist Party, whose members had launched an assassi-nation attempt against President Harry Truman in 1950 and an attack that injured five congressmen in the US House of Representatives in 1954, all for the cause of island independence. "WE WANT SELF-DETERMINATION FOR PUERTO RICANS—LIBERATION ON THE ISLAND AND INSIDE THE UNITED STATES," the 13 Point Program and Platform insisted.[6]

First People's Church
1970
Hiram Maristany,
photograph

Felipe Luciano
(holding microphone)
and other Young Lords
and supporters rally
outside "the People's
Church."

TAKING ACTION

While the Young Lords advocated the liberation of their ancestral homeland, most of their day-to-day activism focused on drawing attention to and fighting the poverty and harsh living conditions facing Puerto Rican New Yorkers. When, in December 1969, the conservative pastor of East Harlem's First Spanish Methodist Church refused to let the Lords use the church to distribute free breakfasts, clothing, and medical services to neighborhood children and families, 30 Young Lords took over the building and renamed it "the People's Church." The New York police, bent on evicting them, cordoned off the church. Committed to the idea of revolutionary confrontation when necessary, the occupiers hoped for a peaceful resolution of the standoff. Negotiators sent by John Lindsay, the city's liberal mayor, managed to resolve the crisis by convincing 105 Young Lords and supporters to submit peacefully to arrest after eleven days. The YLO largely got what it wanted out of the sit-in: free media attention that dramatized the problems of hunger and poverty in El Barrio and an opportunity to attract new members and supporters.

The high rates of lead poisoning and tuberculosis afflicting Puerto Rican families living in unhealthy tenement apartments and the shoddy medical care available to the city's poor people of color sparked other Young Lord actions. In late 1969 about 30 Young Lords launched a sit-in at the city's Department of Health demanding the release of 200 lead-testing kits. Its members then went door to door with students from New York Medical College collecting blood samples proving that many children in run-down tenement apartments were swallowing loose paint chips that were full of toxic lead. (Landlords often neglected to repaint tenement walls and ceilings with new lead-free paints because of the cost.) Their campaign, along with pressure from newspapers, health advocates, some officeholders, and other activists, helped drive the city into enacting and enforcing measures that cracked down on landlords who were slow to remove lead paint. The city also created the Bureau of Lead Poisoning Control to oversee lead removal.

Most dramatic of all was the Young Lords' one-day takeover of the city-run Lincoln Hospital in the South Bronx. Long notorious for the poor care it provided Puerto Rican and African-American residents of the South Bronx, the hospital infuriated the Young Lords and others. Aided by sympathetic hospital workers (organized as the Health Revolutionary

Unity Movement) and doctors, a group of 150 Young Lords occupied the facility on July 14, 1970. The negotiations that followed resulted in reforms that improved care at the hospital including innovative preventive treatment. After a second sit-in in November, organized by the Young Lords, the Black Panthers, and others, Lincoln Hospital started a heroin detoxification program, one of the first to use acupuncture to treat the secondary effects of addiction.

FIGHTING AGAINST "MACHISMO"

As the YLO worked to improve the conditions of daily life for Puerto Ricans, members found themselves in conflict over the organization's internal workings and philosophy. A pressing issue, for example, was the "male chauvinism" of many of the group's male leaders and members. About one-third of all Young Lords were women, yet the all-male Central Committee and many male members continued to embrace "machismo," the Latino version of male chauvinism that expected women—even in a revolutionary movement—to cook, clean, follow male orders, and be sexually available. "The men selected each other to be the leaders," Iris Morales recalled. "Although several women were already working with them, none was chosen for a leadership position." In response, about 12 members formed

Young Lords Party women at International Women's Day demonstration 1970
Katherine Ursillo, photograph

Iris Morales (at lectern), Denise Oliver (behind her to right), and other Women's Caucus members insisted on equality for women in the Young Lords. In this photograph they wear the Young Lords' signature purple berets, part of the group's paramilitary garb.

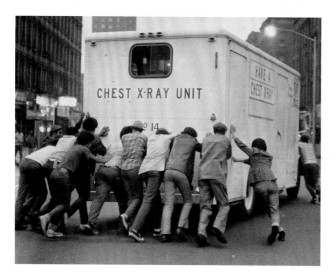

The Take-Over of T.B. Testing Truck 1970
Hiram Maristany, photograph

In addition to occupying Lincoln Hospital, the Young Lords temporarily hijacked a city-owned medical truck to offer chest X-rays to El Barrio residents suffering from tuberculosis; over 770 were tested. The city's Health Department later agreed to test regularly in Puerto Rican neighborhoods.

the Women's Caucus in 1970 to overcome their organization's ingrained sexism. In June Denise Oliver was appointed as the new Minister of Finance on the Central Committee, and Morales, Martha Duarte, and other Women's Caucus members also moved into positions of decision-making power alongside male Young Lords. The Women's Caucus also achieved the revision in November 1970 of the 13 Point Program and Platform. Originally, the document had declared "WE WANT EQUALITY FOR WOMEN. MACHISMO MUST BE REVOLUTIONARY... NOT OPPRESSIVE." The new version stated, "WE WANT EQUALITY FOR WOMEN. DOWN WITH MACHISMO AND MALE CHAUVINISM." As Oliver later wrote, "[We] made it very clear that we were not going to be just secretaries, that we were warriors too, and that we had a right to be in every area."[7]

Similarly, as the gay liberation movement emerged following the 1969 Stonewall Riots and a

From Civil Rights to Black Power

In 1963 thousands of New Yorkers demonstrated at Brooklyn's Downstate Medical Center construction site to protest the refusal of white labor unions to train or hire African Americans for skilled, high-paying construction jobs. Black and white members of CORE (the Congress of Racial Equality, founded in 1942), the Urban League, the NAACP, and members of black church congregations blocked construction trucks; hundreds were arrested. They based their tactics on the peaceful civil disobedience advocated by Martin Luther King Jr. and his colleagues in the ongoing campaign to end racial segregation and discrimination in the South. But, as the Downstate demonstrations dragged on, some protesters, frustrated at their failure to gain concessions from unions or city officials, began scuffling violently with police. Some also voiced impatience at the involvement of white activists in demonstrations for black rights; as one African-American activist told another, "We have to take care of business ourselves!" In the wake of the protest's failure a more militant movement for black empowerment began to unfold in New York.[8]

Since 1960 young CORE members had spearheaded an interracial movement to combat discrimination in the city's workplaces and housing market, and to end segregation in public schools. Activists

African American woman carried to a police patrol wagon during a demonstration in Brooklyn, New York 1963
Dick DeMarsico, photograph

Inspired by the southern civil rights movement, protesters like this one at Downstate Medical Center blocked entrances and courted arrest. CORE members also picketed other job sites that did not employ black workers, including Harlem Hospital's annex construction site in 1963.

like Brooklyn's Oliver and Marjorie Leeds and Jerome and Elaine
Bibuld (both interracial couples) drew inspiration from the southern
civil rights movement and earlier efforts by New Yorkers to combat
local "Jim Crow" conditions during the 1950s. They collaborated with
a wide spectrum of other New York activists, including Bayard Rustin,
organizer of the 1963 March on Washington for Jobs and Freedom, and
the Reverend Milton Galamison of the Parents' Workshop for Equality
in New York City Schools.

Civil rights activists sustained the distinctive feature of New York's
long history of advocacy for racial justice: a tradition of cooperation
between diverse players—black nationalists and mainstream black
politicians, Communists and Socialists, Christians, Jews, and Muslims,
whites and blacks, men and women. Among the supporters of the
Downstate Medical Center protest was Malcolm X, the Nation of Islam's
militant young Harlem minister.

But, by 1963, many civil rights activists—in New York and across
the country— were also growing frustrated with the slow progress
of using peaceful civil disobedience in pursuit of racial integration.
White bureaucrats, union leaders, realtors, parents, and officials
dragged their feet or actively resisted change; meanwhile, decent
housing, jobs, and schools remained elusive for hundreds of thousands
of African Americans. When Harlem exploded in a riot in July 1964,
Jesse Gray—leader of successful rent strikes against slumlords and a
victim of police beating—called for "100 skilled black revolutionaries
who are ready to die" to fight "the police brutality situation in Harlem."[9]

Gray's plea for a more aggressive, even violent, defense of black
rights—one that echoed Malcolm X's views—soon rippled through
the city's activist organizations. By 1966 a phrase coined by New Yorker
Stokely Carmichael—Black Power—was being embraced by young

African Americans across the country. For many the term meant a newly defiant approach to activism: self-empowerment for black communities rather than integration with white society. For some it also meant working to bring a radical revolution to overturn capitalism and racism.

While a small number of black New Yorkers joined the Black Panther Party and advocated using arms to defend black lives against white aggression, it was in schools that Black Power took its most volatile form. Weary of failed efforts at integration, a group of educators and activists obtained funding from the Ford Foundation to experiment with "community control"—a program in which blacks and Puerto Ricans would run their own neighborhood public schools.

In 1968 Rhody McCoy, the black administrator of the new community-controlled school district in Brooklyn's Ocean Hill-Brownsville neighborhood, transferred out several white teachers for being uncooperative. The United Federation of Teachers (UFT), the powerful teachers' union, responded with a wave of strikes. An uproar followed as most students in the nation's largest school system were left without teachers.

While many white liberals and leftists supported McCoy and the call for neighborhood control of schools, the largely white teachers' union used scattered statements by black Ocean Hill-Brownsville activists to paint the community control movement as anti-white and anti-Semitic. City and state officials ultimately reorganized the school system, but in ways that empowered few community control reformers and fostered little racial integration. The conflict also strained the traditional alliance between African Americans and Jews that had helped sustain the city's liberal politics.

In the end New York activists would carry forward both civil rights and Black Power approaches, working within the system to integrate institutions while insisting on community self-determination. With social and economic discrimination, poverty, and racially motivated brutality still harsh realities, the legacies of the 1960s continued to inspire activists of color and their allies in the decades to follow.

African-American children on way to PS 204 pass mothers protesting the busing of children to achieve integration
1965
Dick DeMarsico, photograph

When white parents resisted the racial integration of local public schools—as here, in Bensonhurst, Brooklyn, in 1965— Black Power activists turned to the idea of controlling their own schools in minority neighborhoods to improve the education of black students.

"All Power to the People" c. 1970
Black Panther Party, celluloid and metal button

Founded in Oakland, California, in 1966, the Black Panther Party vowed to defend African Americans against white oppression. New York's Black Panthers, described by *The New York Times* as "an anti-integration group of articulate young militants," emerged in the same year and pushed for black control of Harlem schools.

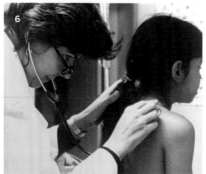

1 **Maria Lorenzi and Petra Santiago during voter registration campaign** c. 1963
Unknown photographer

2 **Manny Díaz and unidentified woman talking** 1960-79
Unknown photographer

3 **Antonia Pantoja** undated
Unknown photographer

4 **Gilberto Gerena Valentín picketing in front of a Canadian Bank on Wall Street** 1975
Unknown photographer

5 **Evelina López Antonetty at a Bronx school board meeting** 1970s
Unknown photographer

6 **Dr. Helen Rodríguez-Trías examining a young patient** undated
Unknown photographer

Puerto Rican New Yorkers engaged in a variety of activist movements during the 1960s and '70s. Petra Santiago and Maria Lorenzi (in dark coats) founded Mobilization of Mothers (MOM) on the Lower East Side to pressure local public schools to provide better services for Puerto Rican children. Manuel "Manny" Díaz worked with African-American activists to mobilize Puerto Ricans for the March on Washington for Jobs and Freedom (1963) and school integration. Antonia Pantoja founded ASPIRA (1961) to help Puerto Rican students get to college and prepare them for community leadership. Labor organizer, civil rights activist, and politician Gilberto Gerena Valentín founded the Puerto Rican Day Parade (1958) to instill pride and display the community's political clout. Evelina López Antonetty created United Bronx Parents to fight for better schools in the South Bronx. Pediatrician Helen Rodríguez-Trías campaigned for better medical care for Latinos, women, and the poor.

gay and lesbian caucus emerged inside the Young Lords, the group's straight males tried to let go of their "macho" homophobia. "From the time you were a kid your folks told you the worst thing you could be was gay," Pablo "Yoruba" Guzmán wrote in 1971. He added, "Now, I'm not gay, but maybe I should be. It would probably give me a better outlook on a whole lot of things... Gender is a false idea, because gender is merely traits that have been attributed through the years to a man or a woman." The YLO thus became one of the groups confronting anti-gay bias within the so-called New Left itself. In 1970 the Young Lords welcomed Sylvia Rivera, the Stonewall Riots veteran and Latino transgender activist, into their fold, although Rivera's main work continued in her own group, Street Transvestite Action Revolutionaries. Young Lords attributed their own inner growth to the belief that colonialism and capitalism created unjust ways of thinking, mental "chains" that had to be defeated just as surely as poverty and illness.[10]

DECLINE, FALL, AND LEGACIES

By 1971 the Young Lords were riding high. In New York about 1,000 women and men identified themselves as Young Lords, and the group had earned national recognition. Modeled on the New York office, other branches had been, or were being, founded in Philadelphia, Newark, Boston, and Bridgeport. Their biweekly, bilingual newspaper *Palante* (Forward), published in Manhattan, reached as many as 10,000 or more readers; a weekly radio program on the progressive station WBAI, also called *Palante*, was broadcast to thousands of listeners. Their campaigns to call attention to unequal sanitation collection, hunger, poverty-related disease, slum conditions, police brutality, abuse of prison inmates, and other social ills had succeeded in pushing some changes in city policies and services. Collaborating with the Black Panthers, Third World Women's Alliance, I Wor Kuen, Gay Liberation Front, and other leftist groups, the Young Lords helped lead 10,000 protesters in a march to the United Nations in October 1970 demanding self-determination for Puerto Rico.

Internally, however, the organization faced a series of simmering conflicts during 1971 and 1972. The group's paramilitary regimen, which required round-the-clock availability, political education classes, and arms and martial arts training, turned off some, especially those with full-time jobs and

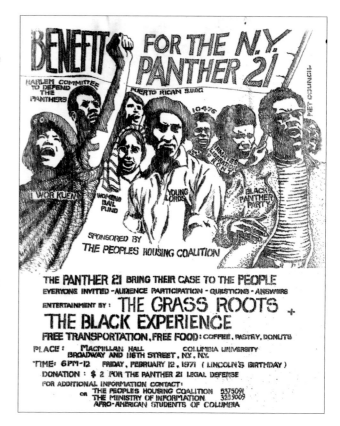

"Benefit for the N.Y. Panther 21" flyer
1971
Unknown artist

The Young Lords collaborated with other activists in New York, including the Black Panthers, the Asian American group I Wor Kuen, and the Metropolitan Council on Housing, as this poster shows. The "Panther 21," a group of Black Panthers tried for allegedly planning terrorist bombings in New York City, were acquitted of all charges in May 1971.

families to raise. Additionally, the Young Lords' attempt in 1971 to establish branches in Puerto Rico and to assume command of pro-independence forces merely spread the group's resources to the breaking point. Many members also resented the growing power on the Central Committee of a faction led by Gloria Fontanez, who espoused a rigidly revolutionary ideology and "banished" dissenters to the Philadelphia branch. "[M]embers spent most of their days in endless debates about Marxist-Leninist-Maoist philosophy," charged Iris Morales. "Isolated from the reality of [the] Puerto Rican/Latino community, the organization became irrelevant."[11]

Meanwhile, internal tensions were being manipulated by undercover agents and informers working for the New York Police Department and the Counterintelligence Program (COINTELRPO), a top-secret FBI campaign that infiltrated and

The Nuyorican Poets Café, East Village, New York City
undated
Philip Scalia, photograph

New York Puerto Rican activism and art became intertwined in the late 1960s, as the Young Lords and others helped to shape an emerging Nuyorican literary movement. The Nuyorican Poets Café (1973) on the Lower East Side remains a vital cultural presence today.

helped undermine New Left radical groups by turning members and leaders against each other. By 1972 when the Young Lords Party transformed itself into the Puerto Rican Revolutionary Workers Organization (PRRWO), it was unraveling as a meaningful player in New York's "street politics" or in the Puerto Rican independence movement. The PRRWO disbanded in 1976.

The demise of the Young Lords resembled that of many New Left organizations during the early and mid-1970s. It was the result of internal divisions, COINTELPRO, the decline of radical momentum with the end of US involvement in the Vietnam War, and the desire of many young activists to move on to another phase of their lives. Yet the impact of the Young Lords continued to be felt in New York and across the country. Individual members like Iris Morales, Denise Oliver, Juan González, Pablo Guzmán, Felipe Luciano, Minerva Solla, and others went on to influential careers as journalists, writers, educators, and labor organizers. Young Lords

played pivotal roles in the lasting revival of Lincoln Hospital, the movement for prison inmates' rights, the creation of Puerto Rican and Hispanic Studies departments in the city's colleges, the movement for bilingual English-Spanish education in New York's schools, and the Nuyorican literary movement.

More than anything else, they fostered a confident pride in Puerto Rican identity that stimulated new generations of Puerto Rican New Yorkers to attain important roles in the city's politics and institutions. As Pablo Guzmán put it, the Young Lords inspired a "sea change in perception" that helped open unprecedented opportunities for at least some Latino New Yorkers, despite the persistence of poverty and unequal access to resources and power. "While some may describe us as dreamers… we aspired to create a new society," former Young Lord Martha Duarte Arguello reminisced in 2015. "How else do you change a community, a society, without dreaming about another and daring to act and work toward bringing that about?"[12]

Asian American Activism

On May 12, 1975, over 2,500 Chinatown residents marched to City Hall protesting the police beating of Peter Yew, a young Chinese American engineer who had intervened in a traffic dispute. Other marches against alleged police racism followed. A broad coalition of community groups, including a New Left organization, Asian Americans for Equal Employment (AAFEE), mobilized the protests. "I'm joining the demonstration because I'm Chinese," noted Mak Nui, an 80-year-old woman. The actions succeeded in getting the local police commander transferred and helped fuel the city's growing Asian American rights movement.

Between 1960 and 1970 Chinatown's population had grown from 20,000 to 45,000 as a 1965 law opened the nation to increased immigration. The influx diversified the city's Asian immigrant population, but it also brought overcrowding, poverty, illness, and, especially for college-age Asian Americans, anger over racist stereotypes and political powerlessness. As a "Yellow Power" insurgency emerged on West Coast campuses in the late 1960s, New Yorkers in the anti-Vietnam War movement like Kazu Iijima and Minn Matsuda started their own Asian American movement to fight racism and gain economic and political power.

Protesters from Chinatown demonstrate at City Hall against alleged police brutality 1975
Neil Boenzi, photograph

Chinatown activists took to the streets when engineer Peter Yew was beaten by police in 1975.

Protest against the detention of Chinese illegal immigrants
1994
Osamu Honda,
photograph

As New York's Asian American population grew, immigrant rights became a focal point for activism. Here, New Yorkers picket the Immigration and Naturalization Service's Manhattan Detention Center, protesting the imprisonment of 286 asylum-seeking illegal immigrants from the ship *Golden Venture*, which ran aground off Queens in 1993.

New groups included I Wor Kuen (1969), a revolutionary Maoist organization that opened a Chinatown health clinic to combat widespread tuberculosis, and Concerned Asian Students (1971) who demanded and got an Asian American Studies program at City College. AAFEE (1974) gained construction jobs for Chinatown workers by picketing at a local building site. As part of the drive for cultural self-empowerment, the Basement Workshop's New York Chinatown History Project (1980) evolved into the Museum of Chinese in America.

The legacy of these early movements can still be felt in the city today. The Chinese chapter of the Coalition of Labor Union Women has pressed for services for Asian immigrant women in the city's garment industry, and the Committee Against Anti-Asian Violence (1986) has supported women's and LGBT rights and the fight against residential gentrification in neighborhoods across the five boroughs. In the 21st century diverse activists—drawn from the city's Chinese, Japanese, Korean, South Asian, Southeast Asian, and other Asian American communities—continue working to forge what one writer has called a "bold culture, unashamed and true to itself."[13]

Triangle Fire 100th Anniversary Rally and March, Union Square
2011
Steven H. Jaffe, photograph

Asian Americans and other members of the International Ladies' Garment Workers Union march to mark the 100th anniversary of the Triangle Fire in 2011.

Urban Cr and Revi

In the late 20th century New York City rode a roller coaster that plunged downward in the 1970s before heading upward again in the 1980s and '90s.

In 1975 the city government ran out of money to pay its bills. Without enough support from taxes or funds from Albany and Washington, officials had spent years borrowing money to pay the rising costs of city services. Emergency action by a combination of politicians, municipal unions, and major banks saved the city from defaulting on its loans, but at a frightful cost. City Hall balanced its books by slashing services and laying off thousands of teachers, police officers, fire fighters, and other civil servants. The city's decaying infrastructure and high crime rates worsened, fostering a negative public image of New York around the world. When the urban economy finally bounced back in the 1980s, New York was no longer the manufacturing and shipping powerhouse it had been since the mid-19th century. Instead, its economic growth revolved around banks and investment houses, real estate development, and professional and clerical services.

New Yorkers, however, did not give up during the years when their home city became a symbol of "urban blight." Many organized against budget cuts, staging protest marches, sit-ins at city offices, and occupations of closed firehouses. Meanwhile, movements rooted in the fervor of the 1960s spread and developed. Gay New Yorkers entered mainstream politics, becoming

isis
val 1973– 2011

an important voting bloc behind liberal Democratic candidates. They fought to expand their legal rights, and they created a spectrum of gay organizations, periodicals, and community centers. New York also remained an intellectual and political headquarters for feminists, and it became the launch point for new campaigns for abortion rights, equal pay, and daycare programs, as well as debates over whether crusades against pornography were the best use of feminist energies.

Other causes drew New York activists. A growing environmental movement gave rise to annual Earth Day celebrations, recycling drives, laws limiting pollution, and bicycle advocacy. On the Lower East Side, a group called the Green Guerillas (1973) helped launch the community garden movement by throwing "bombs" containing flower and vegetable seeds over fences into abandoned lots. In the late 1970s many New Yorkers joined the "No Nukes" movement against the perceived dangers of nuclear

People's Firehouse, Northside, Brooklyn
1976
Janie Eisenberg, photograph

When the city's fiscal crisis led to the shutdown of their local firehouse in 1975, angry Williamsburg residents occupied the building, renamed it People's Firehouse No. 1, and held its fire engine "hostage" while demanding restored services. The Fire Department agreed in 1977; ex-occupiers went on to advocate for affordable housing and other community needs.

Protest against Christadora House conversion 1988
Clayton Patterson, photograph

The conversion of a former settlement house called Christadora House into expensive condominiums for the wealthy became a symbol of East Village "gentrification" and displacement of the poor. Anger over the conversion helped fuel the Tompkins Square riot in 1988. The building remained a flashpoint for neighborhood protest.

power as an energy source. In the largest political rally in American history to that date, peace activists drew 700,000 people to a Manhattan march for a global nuclear arms freeze on July 12, 1982. Protesters also organized against US involvement in the Persian Gulf War (1990–91). And as a new federal immigration law (1965) once again brought waves of newcomers—this time from Asia, Latin America, the Caribbean, and Africa, as well as Europe—new communities founded their own labor, legal aid, and advocacy groups.

Conflicts over class and race intertwined in new ways during the 1980s and '90s. The city's "new economy" greatly enriched some entrepreneurs and professionals, but it left many middle-class New Yorkers feeling left behind, and it did not ease

the plight of the poor: in 1990 one-quarter of all New York City residents lived below the federal poverty line. A socially conservative and pro-business political shift—under President Ronald Reagan (1981–89) and Mayors Ed Koch (1978–89) and Rudolph Giuliani (1994–2001)—alarmed leftists, activists of color, feminists, and gay rights advocates. This was especially true as the AIDS epidemic, crack cocaine addiction, and homelessness made life far more difficult for hundreds of thousands of New Yorkers. Gay Men's Health Crisis (1982), ACT UP (1987), and other groups fought for the rights and the very survival of the city's HIV-positive population. In the East Village, where high-priced real estate development threatened to displace poor tenants, squatters, and the homeless, activists and

their allies clashed violently with the police who tried to impose an overnight curfew in Tompkins Square Park in 1988, leaving dozens wounded. Self-proclaimed anarchists and others challenged politicians, police, and developers over the city's dwindling supply of affordable housing and unregulated public spaces.

Racial tensions mirrored financial ones, as black and Latino New Yorkers remained overrepresented on the lower rungs of the city's economic ladder. And a series of tragedies—including the deaths of Michael Griffith in Howard Beach, Queens, (1986), Yusef Hawkins in Bensonhurst, Brooklyn, (1989), and Amadou Diallo in Soundview, the Bronx, (1999)—showed that African Americans were vulnerable to white violence (sometimes, as in the case of Diallo and others,

Demonstration in the Jay Street Borough Hall subway station, Brooklyn
1987
Ricky Flores, photograph

On a "Day of Outrage" demonstrators protested the failure of a jury to find defendants guilty of murder rather than manslaughter in the death of Michael Griffith, a young African American who was chased by a white mob and then hit by a car. Hundreds blocked mass transit routes, stopping or slowing more than 700,000 New York City commuters.

by New York police). Meanwhile, tensions between African Americans and new immigrants sparked boycotts and picket lines in front of the shops of allegedly abusive Korean grocers in Brooklyn in 1990-91.

The tragedy of the World Trade Center attack of September 11, 2001, which took over 2,700 lives, drew diverse responses from activists. Some protested the hate crimes directed at Muslim Americans in the attack's wake. Others focused on health advocacy for the first responders who toiled in "Ground Zero's" toxic environment. Many became participants in debates over the proper balance between an "open society" and national security needs and, in 2010, in a heated conflict over a planned Islamic Cultural Center near the Twin Towers site. Two American wars—in

Afghanistan (2001–present) and Iraq (2003–11)—made New York a stage for new peace protests, though never reaching the scale of those of the Vietnam era.

Despite polarization over wealth and poverty, race, and "turf," working for a better city was the common goal of activist New Yorkers, who pursued it in diverse and sometimes conflicting ways. They rebuilt abandoned housing, planted community gardens, started block associations, advocated for community input in city planning decisions, fought for environmental regulations, argued over the proper direction of the women's and gay rights movements, and competed for funds and media attention. In 2011 a diverse coalition came together to launch Occupy Wall Street in response to the financial crisis triggered by big banks and

investors in 2008. Despite their different causes and approaches New York activists of the late 20th and early 21st centuries all could agree with 20-year-old college student Edwin Hernandez, a participant in the 1982 nuclear freeze march: "I have a future to take care of. That's the most basic issue there is."

CHAPTER FIFTEEN

"Don't Move! Improve!": The New Housing Activists

Members of East Brooklyn Congregations (EBC) prepare to break ground for the first Nehemiah homes in Brownsville 1982
Unknown photographer

The Brownsville, Brooklyn, Nehemiah homes were the first of several affordable housing projects across the city organized or inspired by EBC.

"If you believe the city is worth saving… say amen."
"Amen!"
"If you believe the city can be saved, say amen."
"Amen!"
"If you believe we are the saviors of the city, say amen."
"Amen!"[1]

In a church gymnasium on a fall day in 1990, Reverend Johnny Ray Youngblood stirred up the action team of East Brooklyn Congregations (EBC), the organization he had co-founded a decade earlier. EBC, a coalition of 52 churches and one synagogue, had spent that decade fighting to improve daily life for the residents of some of Brooklyn's most stressed neighborhoods, places like Brownsville, Ocean Hill, Bedford-Stuyvesant, and East New York. EBC's crowning achievement was the Nehemiah homes, a complex of 2,400 two-story row houses owned by their occupants, families whose average yearly income was about $25,000. The name was inspired by Old Testament verses in which the prophet Nehemiah, beholding the ruined city of Jerusalem, urged its people to rebuild: "let us build up the wall of Jerusalem, that we be no more a reproach."[2]

EBC was just one of dozens of community organizations that had emerged in New York City since the late 1960s and '70s when the so-called "urban crisis" had led some to doubt whether parts of the city could survive. In a process of decay that had been building for years, joblessness, crime, drug addiction, and housing abandonment overtook entire neighborhoods. Many of the African-American and Puerto Rican newcomers who had flocked to New York in the decades following World War II

found themselves caught between two programs sanctioned by federal and city officials. One was "redlining," in which federal agencies and local banks, viewing minorities as poor financial risks and threats to residential "stability," kept them from borrowing money to buy or upgrade homes in their

New York City Firemen fighting fire in South Bronx abandoned tenement building 1977
Alain Le Garsmeur, photograph

Fires in abandoned buildings in the South Bronx and other poor neighborhoods were a daily occurrence during the 1970s.

Among the last residents, [an] African-American boy standing in rubble, his "neighborhood," with abandoned buildings in the background 1976-82
Mel Rosenthal,
gelatin silver print

Photographer Mel Rosenthal, who had grown up in the South Bronx, used his camera to record—and protest—the area's decline and neglect during the 1970s.

block after block; 12,300 fires hit the South Bronx in 1974 alone. To the remaining residents of these areas the unmistakable message was that New York City had given up on them.

By then several well-intentioned efforts to save the South Bronx and other poor, predominantly minority neighborhoods had failed to stop their continuing decline. Starting in 1964 President Lyndon Johnson's War on Poverty had brought millions of dollars in federal funds to New York and other cities where new nonprofit "community corporations" spent the money on drug treatment, job training, and other social programs. In 1967 another federal program, Model Cities, injected yet more government money into efforts to tear down slums and replace them with new affordable housing. But community residents and activists complained that the money did not go far enough. Meanwhile, housing abandonment increased, and residents of surrounding neighborhoods feared that "blight" would soon overwhelm their own homes.

Yet many people held on, and they invented their own resources, strategies, and tactics for rebuilding. In the process they learned that activism was not only about replacing broken locks, renovating deserted buildings, or constructing new ones. It also meant finding ways to attract attention and money, to pressure officials and bankers, and to find new allies—in short, to empower themselves. This was Reverend Youngblood's message to his fellow EBC leaders and activists on that fall day in 1990 as he reminded them of their past accomplishments while encouraging them to continue fighting: "Remember... This land is our land. This city is our city. Of the people. For the people. By the people."[3]

NOT GIVING UP

Across New York City during the late 1960s and '70s, groups of people began organizing to save their neighborhoods. As Father Louis Gigante recalled of the Hunt's Point section of the South Bronx, where he was parish priest at Saint Athanasius Roman Catholic Church, "Drugs really took a toll. Crime really took a toll...Then there was the heat and hot water problem. People froze terribly." In 1968 Gigante, Sister Miriam Thomas, and neighborhood residents founded the South East Bronx Community Organization (SEBCO). By December 1969 Gigante mobilized 300 people living on East 163rd Street to stage a bonfire of trash collected from nearby buildings to protest the area's abandonment. The idea of

own communities or move to middle-class areas. The other was Urban Renewal, in which powerful figures like the city's "master builder" Robert Moses used federal funds to construct apartment complexes, arts centers, and highways (like the Cross-Bronx Expressway) that tore apart existing neighborhoods without providing adequate housing for displaced poor people, who then had to crowd into slums or low-income public projects elsewhere. By the mid-1960s embittered African-American New Yorkers had a nickname for Urban Renewal: Negro Removal.

When the city government ran out of money during its fiscal crisis in 1975, budget cutbacks hit poor neighborhoods hardest. Across the city, but especially in the South Bronx and central Brooklyn, landlords began to abandon thousands of apartment buildings. Fires, some intentionally set, consumed

Tenant leaders of Northwest Bronx Community and Clergy Coalition 1983
Jim Mendell, photograph

NBCCC leaders (left to right) Anne Devenney, Junior Soto, Joyce Ketter, Elizabeth Roman, America Garcia, Essie Reese, and Lisa Lindsay hold a planning session in their campaign to preserve the northwest Bronx from deterioration.

Squatter sign on the fire escape of an abandoned tenement in Alphabet City 1987
Stacy Walsh Rosenstock, photograph

On Manhattan's Lower East Side, housing activism took the form of "squatting" by people who occupied and renovated abandoned tenements without paying rent. In 2002, the city signed agreements with a nonprofit organization and residents of 11 surviving "squats," turning their buildings into limited equity co-ops and preserving them as affordable housing.

organizing residents to rescue their own neighborhoods spread to nearby areas.[4]

"We needed everything, including decent housing," Genevieve Brooks, an African-American accountant living in Crotona Park East, recalled, describing her work with several other women and Father William Smith in founding the Mid-Bronx Desperadoes Housing Corporation (MBD) in 1974. MBD vowed to revive the neighborhood "building by building, person by person, block by block," by renovating and managing apartment buildings for low and moderate-income Bronxites. In the same year Ramon Rueda, a young Puerto Rican New Yorker inspired by Chinese Communist leader Mao Zedong, created the People's Development Corporation (PDC). The group practiced "homesteading"—using their own unpaid labor to renovate and claim an abandoned city-owned apartment building, Venice Hall. PDC resorted to assertive tactics: in 1975, for instance, Rueda and his colleagues, dressed in their homesteading hardhats and work boots, staged a sit-in at the city's Housing Development agency. The resulting publicity helped PDC obtain over $300,000 in loans from a combination of city agencies and foundations. Although Venice Hall ultimately failed after its renovators fell out with each other, PDC's work helped inspire other homesteaders across the South Bronx.[5]

Seeking to maintain their own neighborhoods as stable and livable communities, members of the Northwest Bronx Community and Clergy Coalition (NBCCC), founded in 1974 by a group of 16 Catholic parishes and tenant organizations, fought to expose hidden decisions they blamed for their borough's deterioration. They used the federal Home Mortgage Disclosure Act of 1975 to obtain bank records that showed how several important Bronx and Manhattan savings banks had created an "investment desert." NBCCC accused the banks of secretly discriminating against Bronx borrowers, worsening the social decay that bankers used as justification for abandoning the borough. "We wanted to make them live up to their responsibility," the coalition's Richard Gallagher, a postman from Moshulu-Woodlawn, explained. Gallagher and his neighbors were part of a larger movement, led by the non-profit New York Public Interest Research Group (NYPIRG), to challenge discriminatory lending practices. During the late 1970s neighborhood committees formed by ordinary citizens successfully pressured eight Brooklyn banks to give up their "redlining" policies.[6]

On April 1, 1977, 150 NBCCC members and friends formed a picket line outside a branch of the Eastern Savings Bank, one of their prime targets. When a furious bank employee accused an Irish-American picketer named Anne Devenney of being a communist, Devenney responded by rolling her eyes and simply sighing, "Oh, mister." As she put it later, "It was fun to take on a bank and let them know—hey, the old days are over. It was like David and Goliath." Their campaign, along with threats of boycotts, succeeded in persuading several banks

"Don't Move Improve," Westchester Avenue at Third Avenue in The Hub 1980

Lisa Kahane, photograph

A banner bearing the NBCCC motto hangs over a busy intersection in 1980, expressing the determination of grassroots activists to save and rebuild their Bronx neighborhoods.

Charlotte Street cleanup 1980

Allan Tannenbaum, photograph

President Jimmy Carter had visited this site in Crotona Park East, one of the Bronx's most stressed neighborhoods, in 1977, and pronounced it a "disaster area." This photograph shows a cleanup during the People's Convention, an alternative to the Democratic National Convention held in New York in 1980. The flag at left proclaims the determination of the area's Puerto Rican community activists to rebuild.

to reinvest in at-risk neighborhoods. A slogan devised by Anne Devenney—"Don't move! Improve!"—became a rallying cry in the north Bronx and was soon taken up by activists in neighborhoods to the south.[7]

NOT ENOUGH

During the 1970s, however, many New Yorkers were learning that picket lines, sit-ins, bonfires, and homesteading were not enough. To bring meaningful change activists needed access to money and power, which meant pressuring and persuading city officials as well as learning how to navigate the world of foundations, philanthropies, and government agencies. Members of nonprofit community development corporations (CDCs) like SEBCO, MBD, and the Banana Kelly Community Improvement Association (named for the curved shape of the South Bronx's Kelly Street, where residents defied city demolition crews and refused to leave their

homes) learned how to court politicians and apply
for funds. Gigante's SEBCO, for instance, figured
out how to obtain housing funds from the city, state,
and federal governments, and to attract redevelop-
ers with legal tax shelters they could offer to other
investors. (The fact that Father Gigante's neighbors
elected him to a seat on the City Council in 1973
certainly allowed him new leverage for obtaining
money.) By 1976 the money enabled SEBCO to renovate 360 apartments in nine Hunt's Point buildings,
the first of 1,070 units the CDC would create over
the next five years. A few blocks away, Banana Kelly
developed some 1,500 units.

Across the city, much of this learning process
was aided by outside organizations. The Industrial

Areas Foundation (IAF), for example, came to play
a leading role. Founded in 1940 by radical Chicago
sociologist Saul Alinsky, IAF had become a national
force for community activism, dedicated to helping neighbors empower themselves through organizing, developing their own leaders, and seizing
control of their own futures. They often worked with
concerned Catholic and Protestant pastors and
their congregations, whom IAF saw as ready-made
blocks for building neighborhood democracy. IAF's
"graduates" included Mexican-American labor leaders Cesar Chavez and Dolores Huerta. (And a young
community organizer in Chicago, Barack Obama,
would be influenced by IAF during the 1980s.)
The IAF also became a force for racial integration,

1   **EBC leaders Rev. Youngblood and Bishop Mugavero with Mayor Koch at the Groundbreaking of Nehemiah homes** undated
Unknown photographer

2   **Father Gigante** undated
Harry J. Fields, gelatin silver print

3   **Sister Miriam Thomas Collins (at right)** undated
Unknown photographer

4   **Genevieve Brooks Brown** undated
Unknown photographer

5   **Edward Chambers** 1966
George Tames, photograph

6   **Yolanda Garcia, Founder of Nos Quedamos** undated
Unknown photographer

7   **Mayor Ed Koch** undated
Unknown photographer

New Yorkers mobilized their communities to rebuild. Bishop Francis Mugavero (at lectern), Reverend Johnny Ray Youngblood, Mike Gecan, and Mayor Ed Koch (all to the right of Mugavero) brought Nehemiah homes to challenged neighborhoods. Father Louis Gigante and Sister Miriam Thomas founded SEBCO to improve conditions in Hunt's Point in 1968. Genevieve Brooks was instrumental in the rise of Mid-Bronx Desperadoes (1974) in Crotona Park East; she later became the first woman Deputy Borough President of the Bronx. Ed Chambers of the Industrial Areas Foundation helped East Brooklyn Congregations and other groups launch grassroots movements for change. Yolanda Garcia founded Nos Quedamos (We Stay) to bring new housing and social services to her Bronx neighborhood, Melrose, in 1992. Though activists across the city fought Mayor Ed Koch on a range of issues, he collaborated on a ten-year program of affordable housing.

Neighborhood leader Ralph Porter (right) takes President Bill Clinton on a tour of Charlotte Gardens, built by Mid-Bronx Desperadoes as a set of suburban-style, single-family ranch houses on the site of abandoned apartment blocks. The complex opened in 1985.

working with white and black city dwellers to foster and maintain interracial neighborhoods.

By the late 1970s IAF was making New York City a major target. Alinsky had long relied on New York philanthropists for funding and on New York journalists and writers—including the urban activist Jane Jacobs—for publicity. In 1979 Ed Chambers, the new IAF director, moved IAF's main offices to Franklin Square, Long Island, in part, as one observer noted, to bring IAF near Manhattan, "the media capital of the world."[8]

EAST BROOKLYN CONGREGATIONS

In 1980 several Brooklyn clergymen approached Chambers and the IAF for help. The result was a new organization, East Brooklyn Churches (later renamed East Brooklyn Congregations), guided by professional IAF organizer Michael Gecan. EBC became one of the nation's most important groups in rebuilding urban neighborhoods.

EBC started small: its first campaign was to improve local food shopping. Over several weekends in the spring of 1981, dozens of members of EBC-affiliated church congregations—armed with clipboards, survey forms, and badges labeled "EBC Shopper Inspector"—swarmed ten grocery stores in East Brooklyn known for high prices, spoiled food, and rudeness to customers. The EBC "inspectors" made note of health violations and jotted down customers' complaints. When one shop owner threatened to call the police, the inspector shot back, "Don't worry... We already did." Seven of the store owners quickly signed an agreement promising to upgrade conditions. The three holdouts agreed to attend an EBC meeting at Reverend Youngblood's Saint Paul Community Baptist Church, not realizing that 400 EBC members would also be there to hold an informal "trial." Those three signed as well and store conditions improved.[9]

From this victory EBC went on to others: pressuring the city government to install 3,000 missing street signs, to finish renovating a local park and swimming pool, and to tear down 300 abandoned buildings. By June 1982, when EBC was ready to take on the task of building affordable housing, the members pulled another strategy—personal persuasion and negotiation—out of their activist toolbox. When EBC leaders met with Mayor Ed Koch to ask for city-owned land, tax deferments, and loans, Koch was initially uninterested and hostile, still seething over a confrontation with another IAF group four years earlier. But the leaders had also brought along an ally, Brooklyn's Roman Catholic Bishop Francis Mugavero, a personal friend of the mayor's. Mugavero's charm and his ability to connect with Koch helped to smooth the way for a city agreement to aid in building the Nehemiah homes.

Although EBC followed up with public rallies and press conferences to keep pressure on the city, their strategy showed an understanding that personal relationships between powerful "players" like Mugavero and Koch were critical ingredients in rebuilding their communities. By 1984, with city support and loan money from Catholic, Episcopalian, and Lutheran church sources, the first Nehemiah one-family row houses in Brownsville were occupied by local working people and their families.

SOUTH BRONX CHURCHES AND THE TEN-YEAR PLAN

In 1985 Bronx clergymen and activists inspired by the Brooklyn example founded South Bronx Churches (SBC) to build Nehemiah homes in their borough. But IAF's mix of pressure and persuasion played out differently under different local conditions.

SBC set its sights on a vacant three-block plot of land—"Site 404"—in the Melrose neighborhood. But SBC found itself competing with another nonprofit organization, the New York City Housing Partnership (NYCHP), which had city backing and its own vision for affordable housing on the site. SBC argued that NYCHP's planned complex would prove too expensive to house many working poor people who needed it. The group also made the mistake of criticizing and offending Bronx Borough President Fernando Ferrer, a powerful potential ally. In the end SBC did not gain access to Site 404. But it did succeed, with the help of city officials and nonprofit housing groups, in building Nehemiah houses on nearby blocks, which ultimately housed nearly 2,000 South Bronx families.

By the late 1980s a new ambitious ten-year housing plan, set in motion by Mayor Koch, was investing in rebuilding vast stretches of the city. Between 1986 and 1996 the project created over 250,000 new units of low and moderate-income housing, erasing most evidence that large swaths of Brooklyn and the Bronx had once been burned-out ruins. EBC, SBC, and community development corporations,

including new ones like Melrose's Nos Quedamos/We Stay, now worked to bring schools, community centers, clinics, and businesses back to neighborhoods once written off as dead or dying and involved themselves in the complicated process of planning for the urban future. As Koch's successor at City Hall, David Dinkins, noted at the groundbreaking for the South Bronx Nehemiah homes in 1991, "nurses' aides and paralegals, transit workers, young teachers, secretaries and postal workers will finally have the opportunity to become homeowners."[10]

INTO THE FUTURE

Even with their successes in building housing, activists sometimes found themselves at the center of controversies. Critics of Nehemiah homes, for example, complained that these new residences for New York's working poor had, in some cases, displaced "the poorest of the poor"—jobless people who could not afford homeownership even at low Nehemiah rates. Across the city, housing activists found themselves competing with advocates for community gardens and public greenspaces who had their own plans for abandoned lots.

Community Garden, South Bronx c. 1980
Unknown photographer

Young South Bronx residents work in one of the gardens planted by neighbors in deserted lots to improve the streetscape and provide a focal point for community action. The blackened front of the abandoned building behind them shows that a fire had taken place there.

South Bronx Rebirth
1995
Ralph Fasanella,
oil on canvas

Ralph Fasanella—
machinist, labor
organizer, Spanish
Civil War veteran, and
artist—celebrated
the South Bronx's
revival in this painting,
which documents
the presence of com-
munity development
corporations (CDCs)
in the neighborhood.
Fasanella painted
himself in the scene
(at left), helping a
family move into a
new apartment on
Fox Street.

Individual leaders came under criticism as well: In the 2000s New York's press scrutinized Father Gigante for his lavish personal lifestyle and his family links to the Mafia, while some SEBCO tenants complained of deteriorating conditions. And in 2002, after incurring large debts and being accused of mismanagement, the Board of Directors of another South Bronx CDC, Banana Kelly, was replaced by a new board that included Fernando Ferrer. More broadly, even as a measure of stability returned to parts of eastern Brooklyn and the South Bronx, these areas remained burdened by widespread poverty. In 2010 the 16th congressional district, comprising the central and South Bronx, was the nation's poorest. At the same time, as some "reborn" Bronx and Brooklyn blocks became desirable places to live, the arrival of wealthier newcomers drove up rents and prices, threatening the future of poorer, mostly black and Latino residents in their own revitalized neighborhoods. Would a new cycle of real estate development, ironically due to improvements fought for by longtime residents, price out those very residents?

Whatever the answer and whatever the criticisms, Bronx and Brooklyn residents—with the help of outside organizers, government officials, and non-profit organizations—had turned their home boroughs around. They had used all means within their reach—the collective energy of church congregations, appeals to potential funders, boycott threats, personal ties to powerful politicians—to improve their own lives and gain greater control over their own neighborhoods. In doing so, they had reinvented the meaning of community and civic participation for themselves and others. As one observer of SBC noted in 1995, the group "is not just building housing; it wants to create a community." "My grandparents, parents, and I saw the Bronx burn down, but we didn't want to leave…," Mary Martinez, a young legal secretary living in an SBC Nehemiah home, explained that same year. "[My daughter] Theresa was only five—I wanted something more for her… [We] are beginning to work with the tenants who still live in the apartment buildings on the street to make it better for all of us."[11]

"Silence = Death": AIDS Activism

"If what you're hearing doesn't rouse you to anger, fury, rage, and action, gay men will have no future here on earth," activist Larry Kramer warned a Greenwich Village audience in 1987. AIDS, initially detected in gay men, was affecting not only the gay community, but also recipients of infected blood transfusions, intravenous drug users and their partners, Haitian immigrants made vulnerable by malnutrition and other diseases, and babies of infected mothers. Since 1981 it had become an epidemic sickening and killing tens of thousands.[12]

Backed by a gay community that had become increasingly assertive since the Stonewall Uprising in 1969 (see Chapter 13), New York activists publicized and fought the disease. Kramer had cofounded Gay Men's Health Crisis (GMHC) in 1982 to provide the city's AIDS patients, who made up between one third and one half of the nation's affected population, with support and counseling. Now, in 1987,

"Talk to Us" button advertising the AIDS Hotline c. 1989
Keith Haring, metal and celluloid button

Activist Rodger McFarlane began an AIDS crisis counseling hotline on his home telephone; it evolved into the Gay Men's Health Crisis AIDS Hotline. Artist Keith Haring, who would himself succumb to AIDS in 1990, designed this button for the Hotline.

Kramer and his allies founded the AIDS Coalition to Unleash Power (ACT UP). Their goal was to publicize the epidemic, educate people about "safe sex," and force government, the media, and drug companies to take action. For ACT UP the struggle was political, since the Reagan administration was at best indifferent and even openly hostile to the cause. Activists also charged that city and state officials ignored AIDS because so many victims were gay, drug users, homeless people, and/or poor people of color.

ACT UP devised confrontations that echoed the 1960s "street theater" of New Left groups and the "zaps" of early gay militants. In 1989 ACT UP members chained themselves to a New York Stock Exchange balcony to protest the high price of the AIDS drug AZT; two weeks later the drug's manufacturer lowered the price. More controversial was the "Stop the Church" rally that same year, when ACT UP members disrupted mass at St. Patrick's Cathedral to protest the anti-gay and anti-"safe sex" positions of Roman Catholic Archbishop John O'Connor. By the mid-1990s acts of civil disobedience and public pressure by ACT UP and allied groups had pressured the government to speed up testing and approval of new drugs, expand benefits for patients, and allow the distribution of clean needles to IV drug users. The rage and action that Kramer had called for had fostered meaningful, life-prolonging results, and emboldened new generations of LGBT and public health activists. Looking back on those years, ACT UP activist Jay Blotcher asked in 2007, "How do you explain to [a newcomer] that hopelessness is sometimes the only thing that engenders hope?"[13]

ACT UP Protest, Grand Central Terminal 1991
Ron Frehm, photograph

In 1991 ACT UP protesters climbed to the train schedule board in Grand Central Terminal with a banner telling commuters that a person was dying from AIDS every eight minutes.

ACT UP Protest, City Hall 1994
Betsy Herzog, photograph

ACT UP members rally in City Hall Park on Rudolph Giuliani's first day as mayor. The "Silence=Death" emblem, designed by a New York activist-artist collective in 1987, was based on an upside-down version of the pink triangle that Nazi Germany forced homosexuals to wear. It became a symbol on ACT UP posters, T-shirts, and buttons across the city and then the world.

CHAPTER SIXTEEN

"We are the 99 Percent!": Occupying Wall Street

A General Assembly Meeting, Occupy Wall Street 2011
Natan Dvir, photograph

Crowds of protesters filled Zuccotti Park during the 60 days of Occupy Wall Street.

"Mic check!"
"MIC CHECK!"
"We have a problem here—"
"WE HAVE A PROBLEM HERE—"
"Look around."
"LOOK AROUND."
"We're a circle of palefaces."
"WE'RE A CIRCLE OF PALEFACES."
"We need outreach into the neighborhoods!"
"WE NEED OUTREACH INTO THE NEIGHBORHOODS!"[1]

This was the sound of the "people's mic" (short for microphone) in Lower Manhattan's Zuccotti Park during the fall of 2011. Barred from using an electronic sound system, the activists collectively known as Occupy Wall Street (OWS) used their unaided voices to communicate with fellow protesters crowded into the block-long park. "To take the floor," participant Hena Ashraf explained, "a person would shout, 'Mic check!' And others would repeat this back until they had the attention of the whole general assembly. Then the speaker would speak their mind in phrases of a few words at a time, which were repeated by the entire crowd until the message was complete."[2]

Some in OWS saw the people's mic not merely as a tool for communication and debate, but something deeper: part of a revolutionary change in American society they hoped to ignite. As activist Sarah van Gelder put it, the mic "encourages deeper listening because audience members must actively repeat the language of the speaker. It encourages consensus because hearing oneself repeat a point of view one doesn't agree with has a way of opening one's mind."[3]

The people who gathered in Zuccotti Park between September 17 and November 15, 2011 came for various reasons, but all were deeply distressed by the direction of the US economy. For most the trigger for their discontent was the financial meltdown of 2008, which some of the world's richest banks and firms had set off by selling hundreds of billions of dollars in risky investments. Among those investments were hundreds of thousands of home mortgages that these same banks and firms had sold to Americans. Many borrowers could not afford to pay back the loans and when they defaulted the impact rippled through the world economy. The result was the collapse or near-collapse of America's most powerful financial companies, a panicked freezing of credit, and economic crises throughout the world. Action by the Bush and

The Occupied Wall Street Journal 2011

Newspaper

Protesters published *The Occupied Wall Street Journal* (its title a satire on the pro-business newspaper *The Wall Street Journal*), which printed news and opinions on global movements for change.

Obama administrations and the Federal Reserve eventually stabilized conditions, but at the cost of trillions of dollars spent to "bail out" banks considered "too big to fail." Meanwhile, as unemployment soared and hundreds of thousands lost their homes, the banks' executives continued to earn salaries, bonuses, and exit packages worth tens or hundreds of millions of dollars.

Ever since the 1830s Wall Street in downtown Manhattan had been the nerve center of American capitalism: the place where bankers, brokers, and investors made and lost fortunes and accumulated power in ways that baffled and alarmed other Americans. Now, in 2011, with joblessness and foreclosures still at high levels, New York City—home to JPMorgan Chase, Citigroup, Goldman Sachs, and other firms central to the meltdown—became a natural target for those demanding change. As one OWS participant, Patrick Bruner, explained, he was taking his anger to the "place where most of the

OWS participants gathered across the city to protest bank foreclosure proceedings that had forced out homeowners who could not afford to pay their mortgages. They also advocated for the rights of the homeless. In some cases they reclaimed and moved into vacated apartments.

On December 6, 2011 Occupy Wall Street, O4O and the NYC housing justice movement, along with homeowners, tenants and homeless people came together to reclaim foreclosed homes and declare that housing is a human right.

FORECLOSE ON BANKS NOT PEOPLE

OCCUPIED REAL ESTATE

world's problems originated—Wall Street."[4]

The thousands of mostly young people who "became" OWS in Zuccotti Park also brought a range of other grievances with them. Many worried that their college loans might financially burden them forever. They were outraged by the role of corporate money in politics, especially in the wake of the Supreme Court's *Citizens United v. FEC* decision (2010), which enabled corporations and interest groups to spend massive amounts in political advertising and publicity. Some focused on wealthy companies that were exporting American jobs to low-wage countries where workers had few protections. Others emphasized the global impacts of climate change, fracking (hydraulic fracturing), and other environmental problems that they blamed on corporations and irresponsible governments. Many, like one young man, worried about multiple problems: "Look, I'm twenty-five years old. I'm never going to have a real job. And the ice caps are melting."[5]

Unifying them was one shared perception: Life was getting harder for middle-class and working Americans, while the very rich continued to acquire wealth and power. Statistics supported them: the Congressional Budget Office found that the income of the nation's richest one percent grew by 275 percent between 1979 and 2007, while that of the bottom 20 percent increased by only 18 percent. By 2011 the wealthiest one percent controlled about 40 percent of the nation's wealth. Summarizing their anger, OWS activists embraced a memorable and lasting slogan: "We are the 99 percent!" Within weeks people in 1,500 cities around the world would be repeating that slogan as they "occupied" their own plazas and parks.

ORIGINS

OWS emerged in a period of worldwide activism. In Spain, *Indignados*—"indignant" young people—flooded into urban centers to protest joblessness and government budget cuts. In Madison, Wisconsin, workers and others rallied at the statehouse to oppose a Republican tax and budget plan that would erode the power of public sector labor unions. And the "Arab Spring" of early 2011, which swept across North Africa and the Middle East, was symbolized for many by the 250,000 protesters who occupied Cairo's Tahrir Square and helped to depose Egypt's President Hosni Mubarak.

On July 13, *Adbusters*, a Canadian magazine opposed to consumerism and corporations, ran an invitation: "Are you ready for a Tahrir moment? On Sept 17, flood into lower Manhattan, set up tents,

"Don't Let the One Percent Take Another Cent" flyer
2011

Occupy Wall Street encouraged New Yorkers to form "flash mobs" at local bank branches to protest bank policies and persuade customers to withdraw their money.

kitchens, peaceful barricades and occupy Wall Street." By the time this call to action went viral on social media, New Yorkers were already organizing. In June about 100 members of New Yorkers Against Budget Cuts (NYABC) camped out near City Hall to protest Mayor Michael Bloomberg's proposed budget cuts, insisting "There is no revenue crisis; there is an inequality crisis." In August, at a protest rally at Bowling Green, anthropologist David Graeber and artist Georgia Sagri, both anarchists, argued that future activism must be "horizontal"—that is, leaderless and participatory. NYABC, Graeber, Sagri, and others began mobilizing people and resources to answer the *Adbusters* call.[6]

On the appointed day, September 17, police and guards blocked marchers from occupying Chase Manhattan Plaza, home to JPMorgan Chase, the world's wealthiest bank. About 1,000 protesters moved two blocks away to Zuccotti Park instead. Although it was a privately owned space, the park was, by law, open to the public 24 hours a day. Several hundred Occupiers, many with sleeping bags, filled the park and renamed it "Liberty Square." They set to work creating a "micro-city" as one participant put it, constructing "flimsy assemblages of tent poles, tarpaulin, cardboard, plywood, and polystyrene." They also organized protest marches across the Brooklyn Bridge, to Union Square, and to Wall Street itself just two blocks away. Although the press paid little attention at first, OWS got the word out through websites, tweets, Tumblr, Facebook, live streaming, and other forms of digital media. When a New York Police deputy inspector

pepper-sprayed several detained protesters in the face during a march on September 24, phone videos of the spraying went viral, and new supporters flocked to Liberty Square.[7]

TAKING IT TO THE STREETS

Without formal leaders, OWS depended on its participants. They came from many places, with many concerns. Shen Tong, for example, had been a leader in the movement by Chinese students for greater freedom in Beijing's Tiananmen Square in 1989; now an American software entrepreneur, he threw himself into OWS. Priscilla Grim, a 37-year-old single mother and former fanzine publisher from Tennessee, "who has lived near the financial margin for much of her life," came to Liberty Square and helped edit an OWS Tumblr website. Yotam Marom, a New Jersey-born son of Israeli immigrants, had gone to the West Bank to resist Israeli policy there. So had Palestinian-American Amin Husain, who worked as a financier in a Manhattan law firm before becoming a performance and video artist in Brooklyn. Others, mostly in their 20s and 30s, had been active in movements against police brutality, against the Iraq War, or for LGBT rights.[8]

The activists mixed old and new tactics. Like earlier generations, they recognized that New York's parks and avenues were useful settings for "'spectacles' that can turn spectators into participants." Working with labor unions, OWS organized rallies that drew large numbers of chanting, banner-waving marchers, such as the 10,000 or more who appeared for a Day of Action for Students and Unions in Lower Manhattan on October 5. OWS chants echoed moments in the nation's activist past. "The Whole World Is Watching" was first popularized by anti-Vietnam War demonstrators when they were attacked by Chicago police in 1968. "This Is What Democracy Looks Like!" came from the 1999 "Battle in Seattle," when some 75,000 anti-corporate activists managed to shut down the World Trade Organization meeting in that city. Guitar-strumming musicians played Woody Guthrie's 1940 classic "This Land is Your Land" and "We Shall Not Be Moved," an old labor and civil rights anthem.[9]

Other tactics reflected the Occupiers' own inventiveness. To protest the bank foreclosures that were taking the homes of tens of thousands of New Yorkers, members of "the People's Bailout" entered Brooklyn and Queens housing courts and disrupted the proceedings with songs. A sleepover for 50 families with children was held in Zuccotti Park to deflate the "assumption that the only people supporting the movement are solely homeless or unemployed…" Marchers chanted "You're sexy, you're cute, take off your riot suit!" at policemen in full riot gear who blocked their paths, while others challenged officers to engage in verbal "Rap Battles." Artists created a mock Police Brutality Coloring Book, and they used a projector to beam a huge "We Are the 99%" slide onto the side of lower Manhattan's Verizon Building.[10]

But OWS strategies were not merely amusing. For "Bank Transfer Day" (November 5), OWS used the internet to help persuade hundreds of thousands of depositors to move an estimated $4.5 billion of their money out of large corporate banks and into non-profit credit unions or community-based banks. In fact, social media made OWS possible, just as it had sparked a people's revolution in Tunisia and drawn thousands to Cairo's Tahrir Square. Digital technology supported Liberty Square in countless ways, large and small. Seeking to feed the crowd, Occupier Justin Wedes tweeted the contact information for Liberato's, a nearby pizzeria; soon Liberato's was "inundated with calls from around the world" as sympathizers donated food orders on their credit cards.[11]

OWS's leaderless and formless nature baffled outside observers. But for many in the movement its "horizontal" orientation was its most important quality. Many participants identified as anarchists. Whether or not they realized they were echoing the ideas of Emma Goldman and other New Yorkers from an earlier century, many expressed the same disdain for government as a tool of greedy business interests. In pursuit of maximum equality and participation, they embraced the General Assembly (GA) as OWS's governing body. Inspired by protesters in Spain and Greece, the GA was a daily gathering, open to all, held at the park's east end. Using the people's mic and hand signals, facilitators guided discussions and votes on an ever-shifting variety of issues. Decision-making was by consensus, defined as approval by at least 90 percent of those present. The GA reflected the views of many (but not all) Occupiers who rejected traditional voting to invent their own form of direct small-scale democracy as a model for the future.

Meanwhile, some 35 self-organized Working Groups (WGs) kept the occupation running. The Kitchen WG served at least 3,000 free meals a day, while the Security WG patrolled the grounds. The Sanitation WG removed 200 pounds of trash daily,

NYC GENERAL ASSEMBLY | HAND GESTURES

There are four basic hand gestures used during the General Assembly to express an opinion. These are used to ensure everyone's voice is heard and every opinion is respected.

a. Yes/Agreement

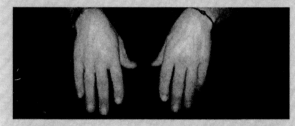

b. No/Disagree

c. Point of Process – a valued interruption

d. Block –This action will stop a proposal from being accepted unless retracted after further dialogue.

"NYC General Assembly: Hand Gestures" brochure 2011

This brochure explains the meaning of hand signals used to aid communication at Occupy Wall Street's General Assembly meetings.

Policemen restrain a protester on the "International Day of Action"
November 17, 2011
Natan Dvir, photograph

Nearly 2,000 protesters were arrested during Occupy Wall Street marches and acts of civil disobedience.

and the Medics WG—staffed by volunteer doctors and nurses working on shifts—met health needs. The Direct Action Working Group (DAWG) helped plan new protests. Occupiers peddling stationary bikes, provided by the environmentalist group Time's Up!, generated electricity.

VICTORIES, QUESTIONS, AND DISAGREEMENTS

The Occupiers experienced several small but exciting successes. On October 12, despite rules prohibiting tents in the park, members of Occupy Judaism NYC built a *sukkah*—a tent-like booth used to celebrate the Jewish holiday Sukkot. The police planned to tear it down, but backed off when First Amendment religious rights were raised. When a medical tent was threatened, a ring of protesters, including former presidential candidate Jesse Jackson, prevented the police from demolishing it. When Brookfield Properties, the park's owner, insisted that the protesters leave so it could be cleaned, 3,000 men and women cleaned it themselves. On the wider political scene, Occupiers took credit for pressuring New York Governor Andrew Cuomo to maintain high tax rates on the wealthy. They also gained the attention of President Barack Obama, who publicly acknowledged their frustration. And the Zuccotti Park protesters inspired a widening movement. From Philadelphia, Atlanta, and Oakland to Vancouver, Santiago, Dublin, Tel Aviv, and Melbourne, people took action to occupy their own public spaces in protest.

But along with such victories came challenges. Sociologist Todd Gitlin, a sympathetic observer, noted that "the people's mic didn't always work… Some meetings broke down in chaos." Tensions flared up between groups. GA facilitators set up procedures to ensure that women, people of color, and LGBT participants had speaking opportunities equal to those of the straight white males who made up the OWS majority. But some, including members of subgroups such as Occupy the Hood and the Women's Caucus, still felt disempowered, and they charged that the movement was not reaching out to all communities. When the Town Planning WG helped designate the park's west end as a site for drummers (and the homeless people they attracted), some complained that OWS was "gentrifying" the park, blaming the better-educated "Ivy Leaguers" and "Brooklyn Hipsters" they saw as monopolizing the park's east end. [12]

Yet the most pressing questions were about the movement's goals. Occupiers easily listed the things they were against. But what was OWS *for?* Many ideas were voiced: breaking up large banks, work programs for the jobless, healthcare for all, getting "big money" out of politics. But many of the park's anarchists resisted the idea of issuing "demands" because it would mean accepting compromises with the very politicians whose authority they rejected. As an activist named Lisa put it, "we need to create alternative economies… that enable people to disengage. And disobey unjust governments and unjust laws." But others felt that getting involved in the nation's politics was the only way to build the movement. "I try to be pragmatic," another participant named Curt noted. "Change within the system is possible… I am not an anarchist. I don't believe that people can do it themselves." Matt Smucker, a veteran of the Catholic Worker, peace, and environmental movements, went further, arguing that forcing politicians to act would be empowering: "The fact that establishment Dem[ocrat]s are clamoring to figure out how to co-opt this energy is a serious victory for genuine progressives and Left radicals. This is what *political leverage* looks like." In the end OWS had trouble unifying around a coherent set of goals that translated directly into political change.[13]

A SPACE OF POSSIBILITY

On November 15, 2011, OWS's 60th day, Mayor Bloomberg, citing the need to clean the park, sent in police to evict the Occupiers. Dispersed across the city, OWS mobilized 32,000 people two days later for a protest march across the Brooklyn Bridge. Occupiers regrouped in various spots in Lower Manhattan to plan their next moves. But by January 2012 many were discussing OWS in the past tense. Though other events followed, including a May Day rally that attracted between 15,000 and 30,000 marchers and a May 17 Woman's Caucus rally in Washington Square, the overall visibility and vitality of OWS seemed to dissolve. The movement was briefly reincarnated the following fall as Occupy Sandy, when a massive hurricane disproportionately impacted some of the most marginalized neighborhoods and citizens of New York. Occupiers who believed in electoral politics threw themselves into the 2016 presidential campaign of Democrat Bernie Sanders. But Occupy's presence as a living force was largely gone.

The lasting impact of OWS is still hard to assess. The movement's short-term achievements were few. Yet specific tactics drawing on OWS have endured: Artists from the Chinatown Art Brigade projected images onto buildings to resist gentrification

in 2016, and the "people's mic" was used in the January 2017 Women's March on Washington. Most enduring is the idea of the "99 percent," which continues to move progressive activists and ordinary Americans seeking a way forward in a world of economic imbalances, divisive politics, and environmental challenges.

In retrospect OWS was part of a larger story: the ways in which the city's diversity, its energy, and its dense concentration of people and resources have made it an incubator for change, and a seedbed for visions of a better world. "Occupy has had to learn from the longer history of organizing and activism in New York," CUNY graduate student and Occupier Manissa McCleave Maharawal reflected. "It has had to learn what it means to listen to groups and people from diverse places and with diverse experiences and to work with them." She noted, "I felt something pulling me back to that space. It felt like a space of possibility, a space of radical imagination. And it was energizing to feel that such a space existed."[14]

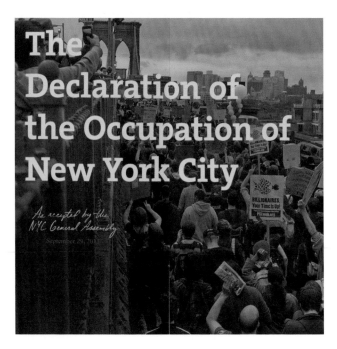

The Declaration of the Occupation of New York City booklet 2011

The printed version of the General Assembly's *Declaration of the Occupation of New York City* included this photograph of some 1,500 OWS marchers trying to cross the Brooklyn Bridge, one of the city's most iconic symbols, on October 1, 2011. Over 700 of them were arrested for using the bridge's roadway rather than its walkway.

A New Era of Activism

In the years since Occupy Wall Street (2011) New Yorkers have organized themselves for activism in both familiar and novel ways. Many of the most urgent issues centered around race, as accusations of discrimination continued to arouse and divide New Yorkers. The police department's "stop and frisk" policy, largely aimed at young African-American and Latino men, sparked popular pressure that led new Mayor Bill De Blasio to greatly reduce the number of such police stops in 2014. But the choking and restraining of Staten Islander Eric Garner in July 2014 and the shooting of Brooklyn resident Akai Gurley four months later—two in a series of deaths of African-American men at the hands of police across the country—moved New Yorkers to join others in a nationwide Black Lives Matter movement. In addition, an outcry against the racist histories of some of the people honored by New York's statues prompted the city to start an ongoing and controversial review of the political and racial meanings of public art.

Other campaigns against discrimination took varied forms reflecting the city's diverse communities and issues: ongoing AIDS advocacy and the successful drive for same-sex marriage in New York State (2011) and nationwide (2015); defense of undocumented immigrants and those from Muslim countries; action to remove legal and physical barriers for the city's people with disabilities; and the mass protest against the election of President Donald Trump that brought over 400,000 people to New York's Women's March on January 21, 2017. (Four New Yorkers—Bob Bland, Tamika Mallory, Carmen Perez, and Linda Sarsour—organized the concurrent march that drew nearly half a million protesters to Washington, DC.)

The rezoning of large areas of the city under Mayor Michael Bloomberg (2002–13) led activists to denounce much of the resulting redevelopment, which they claimed was pushing lower-income New

New York City Silent March protesting racial profiling and "stop and frisk" June 17, 2012
Sandra Baker, photograph

Environmental activists protest the Carbon Trading Summit in Lower Manhattan
January 13, 2010
Richard B. Levine, photograph

Yorkers out of their own neighborhoods to make way for upper middle-class and rich newcomers. The gentrifying trend sparked ongoing acts of resistance including lawsuits, fights against evictions, calls for an expanded community voice in local planning, and campaigns for affordable housing by the Brooklyn Anti-Gentrification Network, Queens Neighborhoods United, Take Back the Bronx, the Chinatown Tenants Union, Make the Road New York, and other groups.

Hurricane Sandy (October 29–30, 2012) killed 43 residents and flooded neighborhoods even as the city continued to recover from the 2008 Wall Street financial meltdown. The storm raised new questions about the future of urban space and unequal access to resources.

Bengali-speaking parent Munni Akter and the New York Immigration Coalition Education Collaborative June 16, 2015
Bryan Smith, photograph

In a diverse city, diverse activists sustained ongoing campaigns while also launching new movements to shape the future. Their tactics included everything from rallies, marches, and humorous street theater to e-blasts, lawsuits, lobbying, and "flash mobs." Their causes spanned concerns over economic and racial justice, gender equality, transgender rights, civil liberties, affordable housing, public health, equal access to education, prison and drug law reform, the uses of public space, fighting climate change, and many other issues.

Activists, allies, and performers participate in the Heritage of Pride March during NYC LGBT Pride June 25, 2017
Sean Drakes, photograph

Brooklyn Anti-Gentrification Network protest at the New York City Department of City Planning Urban Design Division January 4, 2017
Erik McGregor, photograph

#NeoSlaves activist protesting the statue of George Washington in Union Square August 28, 2017
G. Ronald Lopez, photograph

Meanwhile, the wireless communications revolution—and the eagerness of young people to use social media to effect change—has generated excitement, while also raising questions about the fragility of
digitally-driven activism. From campaigns combating climate change
to the successful drive to gain a $15.00 hourly minimum wage for the
city's workers (2012–15), from street comedy promoting advocacy of
public bike lanes to the #MeToo movement against sexual abuse and
harassment (2017–18), New York City has been—and will remain—one
of the world's great settings, incubators, battlegrounds, provocations,
and inspirations for activists across the country and the world.

**Demonstrator at a "Fight for $15" rally op-
posing the nomination of Andy Puzder as US
Labor Secretary, lower Manhattan**
February 13, 2017
Erik McGregor, photograph

**Times Up! Bike Lane Liberation Clowns
whipped cream pie fight**
March 14, 2009
Richard B. Levine, photograph

**International Women's Day March for Gender Equality and Women's
Rights, New York** March 8, 2015
Ethel Wolvovitz, photograph

Introduction: A City of Activists

[1] "The extraordinary thing ...": Pete Seeger speaking in the documentary film *Woody Guthrie: This Machine Kills Fascists* directed by Stephen Gammond (London: Snapper Music, 2005).

[2] "Inhabiting a hothouse...": Richard Kostelanetz, "The Center of the Fringe World," in *Resistance: A Radical Social and Political History of the Lower East Side*, ed. Clayton Patterson (New York: Seven Stories Press, 2007), xxxvii.

Chapter One

Let us Stay: The Struggle for Religious Freedom in Dutch New Netherland

[1] "If any of...": Haynes Trebor, *The Flushing Remonstrance (The Origin of Religious Freedom in America)* (Flushing, NY: Bowne House, n.d.), 4.

[2] "mutinous and detestable...": Edwin Burrows and Mike Wallace, *Gotham: A History of New York City to 1898* (New York: Oxford University Press, 1999), 61.

[3] "began to quake...": Jaap Jacobs, *New Netherland: A Dutch Colony in Seventeenth–Century America* (Leiden: Brill, 2005), 306; "continued to cry out...": Henri and Barbara Van der Zee, *A Sweet and Alien Land: The Story of Dutch New York* (New York: Viking Press, 1978), 294.

[4] "heretics, deceivers, [and] seducers": George Leslie Smith, *Religion and Trade in New Netherland: Dutch Origins and American Development* (Ithaca, NY: Cornell University Press, 1973), 228; "abominable Heresy": Burrows and Wallace, *Gotham*, 61.

[5] "erring spirits": Jacobs, *New Netherland*, 311.

[6] "some homeless Polish...": Van der Zee, *A Sweet and Alien Land*, 314.

[7] "long since been...": E. B. O'Callaghan, *Laws and Ordinances of New Netherland, 1638–1674* (Albany, NY: Weed, Parsons and Company, 1868), 36.

[8] "according to the...," "enjoy liberty of...," "the law of...," "be glad to...": Trebor, *Flushing Remonstrance*, 4, 12.

[9] "offend no more": Ibid., 20.

[10] "We are known...," "to consider whether...": Herbert F. Ricard, ed., *Journal of John Bowne, 1650–1694* (New York: Friends of the Queensborough Community College Library/New Orleans: Polyanthos, 1975), 33.

[11] "allow every one...": Michael Kammen, *Colonial New York: A History* (New York: Scribner, 1975), 62.

[12] "and other sectarians...," "proceed against them...": Van der Zee, *A Sweet and Alien Land*, 296; "heretics and fanatics": Burrows and Wallace, *Gotham*, 59.

Chapter Two

The Zenger Case: Fighting for Freedom of the Press

[1] "How must a...": James Alexander, *A Brief Narrative of the Case and Trial of John Peter Zenger, Printer of the New York Weekly Journal*, ed. Stanley Nider Katz (Cambridge, MA: Harvard University Press, 1963), 95; "many things tending...": Livingston Rutherfurd, *John Peter Zenger, His Press, His Trial, and a Bibliography of Zenger Imprints* (New York: Dodd, Mead & Co., 1904), 182.

[2] "A governor [who] turns...": Bernard Bailyn, *The Origins of American Politics* (New York: Random House, 1968), 137; "SLAVERY," "an overgrown criminal...," "Who is it...": Alexander, *A Brief Narrative*, 11, 16–17.

[3] "a deluded and...": Alexander, *A Brief Narrative*, 6.

[4] "middling," "industrious poor," "courtiers": Ibid., 225; "Dregs of the...," "unthinking... of no Credit...": Burrows and Wallace, *Gotham*, 153.

[5] "secret arrows that...," "the exposing...of...": Alexander, *A Brief Narrative*, 11, 15; "Freedom of speech...": Ian C. Friedman, *Freedom of Speech and the Press* (New York: Facts On File, Inc., 2005), 107.

[6] "truth makes a...": Rutherfurd, *John Peter Zenger*, 83.

[7] "the words themselves...," "the just complaints...," "to be upon...," "a free people," "were not obliged...": Alexander, *A Brief Narrative*, 62, 65, 80–81, 98–99.

[8] "leaving it to...," "jurymen are to...," "The question... is...": Rutherfurd, *John Peter Zenger*, 93, 114, 123.

[9] "a Catechising School...": Jill Lepore, "The Tightening Vise: Slavery and Freedom in British New York," in *Slavery in New York*, eds. Ira Berlin and Leslie M. Harris (New York: The New Press and New–York Historical Society, 2005), 83.

[10] "be Born again...": Jon Butler, *The Huguenots: A Refugee People in New World Society* (Cambridge, MA: Harvard University Press, 1983), 162.

[11] "Is there no...": C. C. Burlingham, "Denial of Visa Protested," in *The New York Times*, September 10, 1948, 10.

[12] "All the high...": Rutherfurd, *John Peter Zenger*, 94.

Chapter Three

Leather Aprons and Silk Stockings: The Coming of the American Revolution in New York

[1] "You now hear...," "The first act...": Isaac Newton Phelps Stokes, *The Iconography of Manhattan Island*, vol. 4 (New York: R.H. Dodd, 1915–1928), 866.

[2] "to wear the...": Richard M. Ketchum, *Divided Loyalties: How the American Revolution Came to New York* (New York: Henry Holt, 2002), 240–241.

[3] "leather aprons" : Gary B. Nash, *The Unknown American Revolution: The Unruly Birth of Democracy and the Struggle to Create America* (New York: Viking Penguin, 2005), 96, 178, 280.

[4] "the Love of…": Burrows and Wallace, *Gotham*, 216.

[5] "an effigy of…": *New York City during the American Revolution. Being a Collection of Original Papers (Now First Published) from the Manuscripts in the Possession of the Mercantile Library Association of New York City* (New York: Privately printed, 1861), 45.

[6] "with the end…": Burrows and Wallace, *Gotham*, 199; "windows and doors…," "the mob went…": *New York City during the American Revolution*, 48, 49.

[7] "men of sense…": Thomas Jefferson Wertenbaker, *Father Knickerbocker Rebels: New York City During the Revolution* (New York: Scribner, 1948), 37.

[8] "those who own…": Burrows and Wallace, *Gotham*, 222.

[9] "some individuals…," "Liberty, Liberty," "when great numbers…": Ibid., 193–194, 202.

[10] "The mob begin…": Nash, *The Unknown American Revolution*, 100; "a mob of…": Joseph S. Tiedemann, *Reluctant Revolutionaries: New York City and the Road to Independence, 1763–1776* (Ithaca, NY: Cornell University Press, 1997), 221.

[11] "taken from his…": Wertenbaker, *Father Knickerbocker Rebels*, 81.

[12] "melted majesty": Stokes, *The Iconography of Manhattan Island*, vol. 5, 992.

Chapter Four

Workingmen & Aristocrats: New York's Labor Movement Takes Shape

[1] "The Rich against…": Sean Wilentz, *Chants Democratic: New York City & the Rise of the American Working Class, 1788–1850* (New York: Oxford University Press, 1984), 291.

[2] "riot and conspiracy…": "Reported for the Journal of Commerce. Court of Oyer and Terminer," in *New York Evening Post*, June 1, 1836, 2.

[3] "illegal combinations": Burrows and Wallace, *Gotham*, 606.

[4] "a ringleader": "Journeymen Tailors," in *Ulster Republican*, June 15, 1836, 2; "assembled in front…": "New York Police—Sunday—Fighting Under False Colours," in Boston *Columbian Centinel*, March 16, 1836, 4 (reprint of *New-York Enquirer* article).

[5] "a spirit of…," "vile foreigners": Philip Hone, *The Diary of Philip Hone, 1828–1851*, vol. 1, ed. Bayard Tuckerman (New York: Dodd, Mead and Company, 1889), 210; "lawless combination," "evil consequences": "Police Office—January 28," in New York

Commercial Advertiser, January 30, 1836, 2.

[6] "We have nothing…," "equal food, clothing…," "General Division": Wilentz, *Chants Democratic*, 183, 194, 195.

[7] "destroy the dearest…": Edward Pessen, *Most Uncommon Jacksonians: Radical Leaders of the Early Labor Movement* (Albany, NY: State University of New York Press, 1967), 161; "plain, practical mechanics": Walter E. Hugins, *Jacksonian Democracy and the Working Class: A Study of the New York Workingmen's Movement, 1829–1837* (Stanford, CA: Stanford University Press, 1960), 18.

[8] "Workies," "Loco Foco" : Wilentz, *Chants Democratic*, 173, 235.

[9] "organized bodies of…," "the right to…": Ibid., 241, 383.

[10] "the natural weakness…": Christine Stansell, *City of Women: Sex and Class in New York, 1789–1860* (New York: Alfred A. Knopf, 1986), 137.

[11] "If it is…": Burrows and Wallace, *Gotham*, 604; "tyrant employers," "the women instantly…": Wilentz, *Chants Democratic*, 350, 351.

[12] "Here is a…," "the number of…": Samuel F. B. Morse, *Foreign Conspiracy Against the Liberties of the United States: The Numbers of Brutus, Originally Published in the New-York Observer. Revised and Corrected with Notes, by the Author* (New York: Leavitt, Lord & Co., 1835), 62.

[13] "I know nothing": Tyler Anbinder, *City of Dreams: The 400-Year Epic History of Immigrant New York* (Boston: Houghton Mifflin, 2016), 197.

[14] "subversive of the…": Wilentz, *Chants Democratic*, 284, 284.

Chapter Five

Practical Abolitionists: David Ruggles and the New York Committee of Vigilance

[1] "I was walking…": Frederick Douglass, *My Bondage and My Freedom* (New York and Auburn: Miller, Orton & Company, 1857), 336.

[2] "the city was…," "there were hired…," "an easy prey…": Ibid., 338.

[3] "Mr. Ruggles was…": Ibid., 341.

[4] "the deep and…": Leon F. Litwack, "The Abolitionist Dilemma: The Antislavery Movement and the Northern Negro," *The New England Quarterly* 34 (March 1961), 63; "the pro-slavery…": Ezra Greenspan, ed., *William Wells Brown: A Reader* (Athens, GA: University of Georgia Press, 2008), 170.

[5] "practical abolition," "whatever necessity requires…": Graham Russell Gao Hodges, *David Ruggles: A Radical Black Abolitionist and the Underground Railroad in New York City* (Chapel Hill, NC:

University of North Carolina Press, 2010), 88, 93.

[6] "protect unoffending, defenseless…": *The First Annual Report of the New York Committee of Vigilance, for the Year 1837, Together with Important Facts Relative to their Proceedings* (New York: Piercy & Reed, 1837), 4; "one of the…": Hodges, *David Ruggles*, 97.

[7] "kidnapping clubs": Hodges, *David Ruggles*, 88.

[8] "was a respectable…," "equal right to…": John H. Hewitt, "The Search for Elizabeth Jennings, Heroine of a Sunday Afternoon in New York City," *New York History* 71, no. 4 (October 1990), 391, 393.

[9] "go by foot…": Ibid., 398.

[10] "slave-catchers": Douglass, *My Bondage and My Freedom*, 338.

[11] "Was woman formed…": Hodges, *David Ruggles*, 121.

[12] "that you will…": "The Presidency. Speech of Hon. Wm. L. Yancey at the Cooper Institute," *The New York Times*, October 11, 1860, 8.

[13] "I have tried…": Hodges, *David Ruggles*, 162.

Chapter Six

"Propaganda by Deed": New York City Anarchists

[1] "Men and women…": Emma Goldman, *Living My Life*, vol. 1 (New York: Alfred Knopf, Inc., 1931), 122–123.

[2] "the social revolution": Ibid., 187.

[3] "direct action": Ibid., 122.

[4] "literally submerged in…": "The Health of New York," in *Harper's Weekly*, April 1, 1865, 194.

[5] "strike terror in…": Goldman, *Living My Life*, vol.1, 87, 105 ; "It was but…": Tom Goyens, *Beer and Revolution: The German Anarchist Movement in New York City, 1880–1914* (Urbana, IL: University of Illinois Press, 2007), 89.

[6] "I did not…": Goldman, *Living My Life*, vol. 1, 229.

[7] "the neighbors threw…": Goyens, *Beer and Revolution*, 102.

[8] "we wished to…": Ibid., 27; "in the mediaeval…": Robert M. Fogelson, *America's Armories: Architecture, Society, and Public Order* (Cambridge, MA: Harvard University Press, 1989), 163.

[9] "that cold monster…": Goldman, *Living My Life*, vol. 2, 896.

[10] "we resemble voices…": Goyens, *Beer and Revolution*, 213; "the people are…": Goldman, *Living My Life*, vol. 1, 304.

[11] "Montessori Method," "authoritarian": Paul Avrich, *The Modern School Movement: Anarchism and Education in the United States* (Princeton, NJ: Princeton University Press, 1980), 110, 173.

[12] "have made us…," "In a short…": Jennifer Guglielmo, *Living the Revolution: Italian Women's Resistance and Radicalism in New York City, 1880–1945* (Chapel Hill, NC: University of North Carolina Press, 2010), 166, 167.

[13] "We know now…": Jacob A. Riis, *How the Other Half Lives: Studies Among the Tenements of New York* (New York: Charles Scribner's Sons, 1890), 2.

[14] "a clean and…": Ibid., 4.

[15] "Philanthropy and five…": Ibid., 5, 266.

Chapter Seven

"Inside the Monster": Latino Activism in 19th-Century New York

[1] "Cuba and Puerto Rico…": Cordelia Chávez Candelaria, "Lola Rodríguez de Tió," in *Encyclopedia of Latino Popular Culture*, vol. 2, ed. Cordelia Chávez Candelaria (Westport, CT: Greenwood Press, 2004), 703.

[2] "I lived inside…:" Alfred J. López, *José Martí: A Revolutionary Life* (Austin, TX: University of Texas Press, 2014), 316.

[3] "it appears as…": Lisandro Pérez, "Cubans in Nineteenth Century New York: A Story of Sugar, War and Revolution," in *Nueva York: 1613–1945*, ed. Edward J. Sullivan (New York: New-York Historical Society with Scala Publishers, 2010), 97.

[4] "frail": Bernardo Vega, *Memoirs of Bernardo Vega: A Contribution to the History of the Puerto Rican Community in New York*, ed. César Andreu Iglesias (New York: Monthly Review Press, 1984), 74; "nearly 300 people…": López, *José Martí*, 221–222.

[5] "disturbed only by…," "These people speak…": José Martí, *Selected Writings*, ed. and trans. Esther Allen (New York: Penguin Books, 2002), 92, 287; "brutal North that…": López, *José Martí*, 316.

[6] "the former slave…," "ill-gotten wealth," "New York is…": , Martí, *Selected Writings*, 323, 168, 131.

[7] "I saw it…": López, *José Martí*, 20–21.

[8] "blacks are considered…": Ibid., 239.

[9] "No man has…": Martí, *Selected Writings*, 318.

[10] "The Day of the Homeland": Vega, *Memoirs*, 75.

[11] "Everything binds me…": López, *José Martí*, 232.

[12] "We come from…": Gerald E. Poyo, "José Martí: Architect of social unity in the émigré communities of the United States," in *José Martí: Revolutionary Democrat*, eds. Christopher Abel and Nissa Torrents (London: Bloomsbury Academic, 2015), 29.

[13] "I never knew…," "they become laundrymen…": John Kuo Wei Tchen, *New York before Chinatown: Orientalism and the Shaping of American Culture, 1776–1882* (Baltimore: Johns Hopkins University Press, 1999), 251, 256.

[14] "practical self-help…": Cheryl D. Hicks, *Talk With You Like a Woman: African American Women, Justice, and Reform in New York, 1890–1935* (Chapel Hill, NC: University of North Carolina Press, 2010), 100.

Chapter Eight

"I Am a Working Girl": Upheaval in the Garment Trades

[1] "I am a…": Elizabeth Ewen, *Immigrant Women in the Land of Dollars: Life and Culture on the Lower East Side, 1890–1925* (New York: Monthly Review Press, 1985), 257.

[2] "Strike and let…," "this is more…": Richard A. Greenwald, *The Triangle Fire, the Protocols of Peace, and Industrial Democracy in Progressive Era New York* (Philadelphia: Temple University Press, 2005), 32, 53.

[3] "Righteousness" delivers from…," "In Russia for…": Hadassa Kosak, *Cultures of Opposition: Jewish Immigrant Workers, 1881–1905* (Albany, NY: State University of New York Press, 2000), 131, 156.

[4] "un-American": Ibid., 124.

[5] "The workhouse is…": Greenwald, *The Triangle Fire*, 40.

[6] "Great Revolt," "the preferential shop": Ibid., 26, 63.

[7] "the enlightened employer…": Ibid., 78.

[8] "Teaching the poor…": Goldman, *Living My Life*, vol. 1, 160.

[9] "I turned back…": Leon Stein, *The Triangle Fire, Centennial Edition* (Ithaca, NY: Cornell University Press, 2010), 39.

[10] "People had just…": David Von Drehle, *Triangle: The Fire That Changed America* (New York: Grove Press, 2003), 194; "I remembered their…": Stein, *The Triangle Fire*, 20.

[11] "We have tried…": Stein, *The Triangle Fire*, 144.

[12] "traveling road show of reform," "You can't tell…": Robert A. Slayton, *Empire Statesman: The Rise and Redemption of Al Smith* (New York: The Free Press, 2001), 94, 97.

[13] "The New Deal…": Greenwald, *The Triangle Fire*, 220.

[14] "all large-scale…": "Socialist Party Platform, 1912," in *No. 4 Socialist Documents*, ed. W. J. Ghent (Girard, KS: Appeal to Reason, 1916), 49.

Chapter Nine

"New York is the Battleground": The Campaign for Woman Suffrage

[1] "This is war…": Maureen Maryanski, *Leda Richberg Hornsby 1887–1939*, New-York Historical Society, August 25, 2016, http://www.womensactivism.nyc/catalog/566.

[2] "New York is…": Jacqueline Van Voris, *Carrie Chapman Catt: A Public Life* (New York: The Feminist Press, 1987), 78.

[3] "the value of…": Ellen Carol DuBois, *Woman Suffrage and Women's Rights* (New York: New York University Press, 1998), 198.

[4] "We must eliminate…": Ibid., 198.

[5] "It is the…": Ibid., 188.

[6] "Spoke outside of…": Nancy Schrom Dye, *As Equals and As Sisters: Feminism, the Labor Movement, and the Women's Trade Union League of New York* (Columbia: University of Missouri Press, 1980), 131.

[7] "WOMEN VOTE IN…": Margaret Finnegan, *Selling Suffrage: Consumer Culture & Votes for Women* (New York: Oxford University Press, 2014), 92.

[8] "For the long…": Frances Diodato Bzowski, "Spectacular Suffrage: Or, How Women Came Out of the Home and into the Streets and Theaters of New York City to Win the Vote," *New York History* 76, no. 1 (January 1995), 72.

[9] "chilled, scandalized feeling…": Jean H. Baker, *Sisters: The Lives of America's Suffragists* (New York: Hill and Wang, 2005), 199; "apple-cores, wet…": Finnegan, *Selling Suffrage*, 52.

[10] "Our sons are…": Bzowski, "Spectacular Suffrage," 90.

[11] "an immense debating…": Baker, *Sisters*, 212.

[12] "a stupendous stupidity": Ibid., 209.

[13] "silent sentinels": Ibid., 214.

[14] "arrest and martyrdom": Ibid., 219.

[15] "men and women…": Christine A. Lunardini, *From Equal Suffrage to Equal Rights: Alice Paul and the National Woman's Party, 1910–1928* (New York: New York University Press, 1986), 164.

[16] "Obscene Literature and…": John D'Emilio and Estelle B. Freedman, *Intimate Matters: A History of Sexuality in America*, third edition (Chicago: University of Chicago Press, 2012), 159.

[17] "I cannot promise…": Ellen Chesler, *Woman of Valor: Margaret Sanger and the Birth Control Movement in America* (New York: Simon & Schuster, 1992), 158; "absolute mistress of…": Virginia Coigney, *Margaret Sanger: Rebel with a Cause* (Garden City: Doubleday and Company, 1969), 68.

Chapter Ten

"The New Negro": Activist Harlem

[1] "The world must...": Anne-Marie Slaughter, "Wilsonianism in the Twenty-First Century," in *The Crisis of American Foreign Policy: Wilsonianism in the Twenty-First Century*, G. John Ikenberry, Thomas J. Knock, Anne-Marie Slaughter, and Tony Smith, eds. (Princeton, NJ: Princeton University Press, 2009), 94; "Mr. President, why...": Alessandra Lorini, *Rituals of Race: American Public Culture and the Search for Racial Democracy* (Charlottesville, VA: University Press of Virginia, 1999), 245; "We have fought...": Rebecca Meacham, "Lynching: Silent Protest Parade" in *Encyclopedia of the Harlem Renaissance*, vol. 2: K–Y, eds. Cary D. Wintz and Paul Finkelman, (New York: Routledge, 2004), 751.

[2] "Let the world...": Marcus Garvey, *Selected Writings and Speeches of Marcus Garvey*, ed. Bob Blaisdell (Mineola, NY: Dover Publications, 2004), 40.

[3] "all the Negro ...": Ibid., 3.

[4] "our most solemn...": Ibid., 19.

[5] "Africa for the..." Judith Stein, *The World of Marcus Garvey: Race and Class in Modern Society* (Baton Rouge, LA: Louisiana State University Press, 1986), 84; "Our children are...," "give up the...": Garvey, *Selected Writings*, 17, 179.

[6] "a spirit of...": Stein, *The World of Marcus Garvey*, 76.

[7] "If we had...": Garvey, *Selected Writings*, 28.

[8] "every single right...": Patricia Sullivan, *Lift Every Voice: The NAACP and the Making of the Civil Rights Movement* (New York: The New Press, 2009), 4.

[9] "was illegal there...": Groucho Marx, *Groucho and Me* (New York: Simon & Schuster, 1989), 210.

[10] "the metropolis of...," "enroll with us...": Ibid., 16, 31.

[11] "abolition of lynching...": *Report of the National Association for the Advancement of Colored People for the Years 1917 and 1918* (New York: National Association for the Advancement of Colored People, 1919), 68.

[12] "our first line...": Ibid., 77.

[13] "insult," "all public resorts..." : *Report of the National Association for the Advancement of Colored People for the Years 1917 and 1918*, 77, 19.

[14] "Rather die now...": Ibid., 40.

[15] "is a white...," "accept segregation with...": Stein, *The World of Marcus Garvey*, 154, 245.

[16] "pro-negro agitator": Ibid., 189.

[17] "By any means...": Malcolm X, *Malcolm X Speaks: Selected Speeches and Statements*, ed. George Breitman (New York: Grove Press, 1990), 96.

[18] "a sterner, longer...": Sullivan, *Lift Every Voice,* 84.

[19] "[E]very view, no...," "Communist Front": Samuel Walker, *In Defense of American Liberties: A History of the ACLU*, second ed. (Carbondale, IL: Southern Illinois University Press, 1999), 62, 232.

Chapter Eleven

Art is a Weapon: Activist Theater

[1] "There is nothing...": John Houseman, *Run-Through: A Memoir* (New York: Simon and Schuster, 1972), 261.

[2] "the audience found...," "there was a second's...", Ibid., 270, 274.

[3] "runaway opera": John Bush Jones, *Our Musicals, Ourselves: A Social History of the American Musical Theatre* (Waltham, MA: Brandeis University Press/Hanover, NH: University Press of New England, 2003), 111.

[4] "Art is a weapon": Albert Maltz, "What Shall We Ask of Writers?" in *Communism in America: A History in Documents*, ed. Albert Fried (New York: Columbia University Press, 1997), 351.

[5] "an escape from...": Houseman, *Run-Through*, 159.

[6] "The fantastic thing...": Jay Williams, *Stage Left* (New York: Charles Scribner's Sons, 1974), 87.

[7] "... [A]s a Jew...": Letter from Volunteer Hyman Katz to his mother, November 5, 1937, in *Facing Fascism: New York and the Spanish Civil War*, eds. Peter N. Carroll and James D. Fernandez (New York: Museum of the City of New York / New York University Press, 20070, 24.

[8] "KEEP THE NAZIS...": Richard Goldstein, *Helluva Town: The Story of New York City During World War II* (New York: Free Press, 2010), 208.

[9] "Get yourself a....": Williams, *Stage Left*, 96.

[10] "You hear? Seventeen...", "I'd have walked..." Ibid., 93, 117.

[11] "We'd drag ourselves...," "In the first," "Agit-prop plays...": Ibid., 132, 124, 43.

[12] "[A] shock of...," "Well, what's the...," "people went from...": Harold Clurman, *The Fervent Years: The Story of the Group Theatre and the Thirties* (New York: Harcourt Brace Jovanovich, Inc., 1975), 147–148.

[13] "What we want...": Joanne Bentley, *Hallie Flanagan: A Life in the American Theatre* (New York: Alfred A. Knopf, 1988), 193.

[14] "the new frontier...": George Kazacoff, *Dangerous Theatre: The Federal Theatre Project as a Forum for New Plays* (Pieterlen, Switzerland: Peter Lang, 2011), 320–321.

[15] "one more link...": John O'Connor and Lorraine Brown, *Free, Adult, Uncensored: The Living History of the Federal Theatre Project* (Washington, DC: New Republic Books, 1978), 31.

[16] "'Poor guys' like...": Clurman, *The Fervent Years*, 200.

Chapter Twelve

A Cold War: Activism and Anti-Communism in New York

[1] "a *real* American...": Philip Deery, *Red Apple: Communism and McCarthyism in Cold War New York* (New York: Fordham University Press, 2014), 80.

[2] "strongly surcharged with...": Ibid., 79.

[3] "to the social...": John Tirman, *The Deaths of Others: The Fate of Civilians in America's Wars* (Oxford: Oxford University Press, 2011), 64.

[4] "a network of...": Sidney Hook, *Out of Step: An Unquiet Life in the 20th Century* (New York: Harper & Row, 1987), 307.

[5] "begged me not...": Deery, *Red Apple*, 46.

[6] "Jim Crow practices," "aware of the...," "women and girls...": Clarence Taylor, *Reds at the Blackboard: Communism, Civil Rights, and the New York City Teachers Union* (New York: Columbia University Press, 2011), 267, 290–291, 247.

[7] "[N]o American could...": Stephen Petrus and Ronald D. Cohen, *Folk City: New York and the American Folk Music Revival* (New York: Oxford University Press and Museum of the City of New York, 2015), 77.

[8] "Then we went...": Ibid., 78.

[9] "an instrument of...," "even a teacher...": Taylor, *Reds at the Blackboard*, 164, 167.

[10] "would deny teachers...": Ibid., 173; "excesses and demagogic...": Hook, *Out of Step,* 498.

[11] "not given to...": Cedric Belfrage, *The American Inquisition: 1945–1960* (Indianapolis: Bobbs-Merrill, 1973), 226.

[12] "I will not...," "We will not...": Dee Garrison, "'Our Skirts Gave Them Courage': The Civil Defense Protest Movement in New York City, 1955–1961," in *Not June Cleaver: Women and Gender in Postwar America, 1945–1960*, ed. Joanne Meyerowitz (Philadelphia: Temple University Press, 1994), 210, 207.

Chapter Thirteen

"Gay is Good": The Rise of Gay Power

[1] "It had got...": Martin Duberman, *Stonewall* (New York: Dutton, 1993), 193; "'Gay Power!'": David Carter, *Stonewall: The Riots That Sparked the Gay*

Revolution (New York: St. Martin's Griffin, 2004), 147.

[2] "a public assertion...": Duberman, Stonewall, 205.

[3] "Something lifted off...": Ibid., 201.

[4] "in the closet": Carter, Stonewall, 236.

[5] "What we were...": John D'Emilio, Sexual Politics, Sexual Communities: The Making of a Homosexual Minority in the United States, 1940–1970, Second Edition (Chicago: University of Chicago Press, 1998), 102.

[6] "lewd and indecent...": Duberman, Stonewall, 111; "This is a ...": D'Emilio, Sexual Politics, 152.

[7] "their basic rights...": Duberman, Stonewall, 113.

[8] "indecent behavior": Ibid., 116.

[9] "We don't want...," "We have got...": Ibid., 211.

[10] "come out of...": Stephen Valocchi, "Gay Liberation Movement," in Men and Masculinities: A Social, Cultural, and Historical Encyclopedia, vol. I: A–J, eds. Michael Kimmel and Amy Aronson (Santa Barbara: ABC-Clio, 2004), 339; "mental disorder": Karla Jay, Tales of the Lavender Menace: A Memoir of Liberation (New York: Basic Books, 1999), 225.

[11] "U.S. Troops Out...": Nancy Zaroulis and Gerald Sullivan, Who Spoke Up? American Protest Against the War in Vietnam 1963–1975 (Garden City: Doubleday, 1984), 24–25.

[12] "THE WAR IS...": Ibid., 420.

[13] "We want free..." Donn Teal, The Gay Militants: How Gay Liberation Began in America, 1969–1971 (New York: Stein and Day, 1971), 140.

[14] "In New York...": Karla Jay, Tales of the Lavender Menace: A Memoir of Liberation (New York: Basic Books, 1999), 128.

[15] "the lavender menace," "man-haters": Ibid., 137; "A lesbian is...": D'Emilio, Sexual Politics, 236.

[16] "Both the women's...": Jay, Tales, 122.

[17] "I saw what...": Duberman, Stonewall, 280.

[18] "the problem that...," "I want something...": Betty Friedan, The Feminine Mystique (New York: W. W. Norton, 2001), 57, 78.

[19] "women's liberation," "instruments of torture," "Freedom Trash Can": Ruth Rosen, The World Split Open: How the Modern Women's Movement Changed America (New York: Viking, 2000), 84, 160.

Chapter Fourteen

"¡Basta Ya!": Young Lords and Puerto Rican Activism

[1] "The only choice...," "We all felt...": Miguel "Mickey" Melendez, We Took the Streets: Fighting for Latino Rights with the Young Lords (New York: St. Martin's Press, 2003), 105.

[2] "self control and...": Darrel Wanzer-Serrano, The New York Young Lords and the Struggle for Liberation (Philadelphia: Temple University Press, 2015), 48.

[3] "My neighbor, Pedro...": Melendez, We Took the Streets, 67.

[4] "It seemed that...": Iris Morales, "¡PALANTE, SIEMPRE PALANTE! The Young Lords," in The Puerto Rican Movement: Voices from the Diaspora, eds. Andrés Torres and José Velásquez (Philadelphia: Temple University Press, 1998), 210.

[5] "We want control...," "People's control of...," "urban removal": "13 Point Program and Platform of the Young Lords Organization (October 1969)," in The Young Lords: A Reader, ed. Darrel Enck-Wanzer (New York: New York University Press, 2010), 10.

[6] "WE WANT SELF-DETERMINATION...": Ibid., 9.

[7] "The men selected..." Iris Morales, "Women Organizing Women," in Through the Eyes of Rebel Women: The Young Lords, 1969–1976, ed. Iris Morales, 45; "WE WANT EQUALITY...": "13 Point Program and Platform of the Young Lords Organization (October 1969)" and "Young Lords Party 13-Point Program and Platform (revised November 1970)," in Enck-Wanzer, The Young Lords: A Reader, 10, 12; "[We] made it...": Denise Oliver-Vélez, "The Excitement Was in the Streets!" in Through the Eyes of Rebel Women, ed. Morales, 133.

[8] "We have to...": Brian Purnell, Fighting Jim Crow in the County of Kings: The Congress of Racial Equality in Brooklyn (Lexington, KY: University Press of Kentucky, 2013), 226.

[9] "100 skilled black...": Tamar W. Carroll, Mobilizing New York: AIDS, Antipoverty, and Feminist Activism (Chapel Hill, NC: University of North Carolina Press, 2015), 58.

[10] "From the time...": Young Lords Party and Michael Abramson, PALANTE: Young Lords Party, 1971 (New edition: Chicago: Haymarket Press, 2011), 40, 41.

[11] "[M]embers spent most...": Morales, "¡PALANTE, SIEMPRE PALANTE!," 222.

[12] "sea change in...": Pablo Guzmán, "La Vida Pura: A Lord of the Barrio," in The Puerto Rican Movement, eds. Torres and Velásquez, 158; "While some may...": Martha Arguello, "Woman, Dominican, Young Lord," in Through the Eyes of Rebel Women, ed. Morales, 142.

[13] "bold culture, unashamed...": Edward Iwata, quoted in William Wei, The Asian American Movement (Philadelphia: Temple University Press, 1993), 42.

Chapter Fifteen

"Don't Move! Improve!": The New Housing Activists

[1] "If you believe...": Samuel G. Freedman, Upon This Rock: The Miracles of a Black Church (New York: HarperCollins Publishers, 1993), 322.

[2] "let us build...": Holy Bible, King James Version, Nehemiah 2:17.

[3] "Remember... This land...": Freedman, Upon This Rock, 322.

[4] "Drugs really took...": Jill Jonnes, South Bronx Rising: The Rise, Fall, and Resurrection of an American City (New York: Fordham University Press, 2002), 190–191.

[5] "We needed everything...": Evelyn Gonzalez, The Bronx (New York: Columbia University Press, 2004), 133; "building by building...": Alexander von Hoffman, House by House, Block by Block: The Rebirth of America's Urban Neighborhoods (New York: Oxford University Press, 2003), 33.

[6] "We wanted to...": Jonnes, South Bronx Rising, 357.

[7] "Oh, mister," "It was fun...," "Don't move! Improve!": Ibid., 358, 363.

[8] "the media capital...": Jim Rooney, Organizing the South Bronx (Albany, NY: State University of New York Press, 1995), 83.

[9] "Don't worry... We...": Freedman, Upon This Rock, 325.

[10] "nurses' aides and...": Rooney, Organizing the South Bronx, 190.

[11] "is not just...": Ibid., 206; "My grandparents, parents...": Lee Stuart, "'Come, Let Us Rebuild the Walls of Jerusalem': Broad-Based Organizing in the South Bronx," in Signs of Hope in the City: Ministries of Community Renewal, revised edition, eds. Robert D. Carle and Louis A. DeCaro Jr. (Valley Forge, PA: Judson Press, 1999), 168–169.

[12] "If what you're...:" Tamar W. Carroll, Mobilizing New York: AIDS, Antipoverty, and Feminist Activism (Chapel Hill, NC: University of North Carolina Press, 2015), 141.

[13] "How do you...": Jay Blotcher, "AIDS on the Lower East Side," in Resistance: A Radical Social and Political History of the Lower East Side, ed. Clayton Patterson, 588.

Chapter Sixteen

"We are the 99 Percent!": Occupying Wall Street

[1] "Mic check!...": Todd Gitlin, Occupy Nation: The Roots, The Spirit, and The Promise of Occupy Wall Street (New York: Itbooks, 2012), 59–60.

2 "To take the...": Sarah van Gelder and the staff of *Yes! Magazine*, eds., *This Changes Everything: Occupy Wall Street and the 99% Movement* (San Francisco: Berrett-Koehler Publishers, Inc., 2011), 34.

3 "encourages deeper listening...": Ibid., 34.

4 "place where most...": Meghana Nayak, "The Politics of the 'Global,'" in *Occupying Political Science: The Occupy Wall Street Movement from New York to the World*, eds. Emily Welty, Matthew Bolton, Meghana Nayak, & Christopher Malone (New York: Palgrave Macmillan, 2013), 260.

5 "Look, I'm twenty-five...": Gitlin, *Occupy Nation*, 65–66.

6 "Are you ready...": Writers for the 99%, *Occupying Wall Street: The Inside Story of an Action that Changed America* (Chicago: Haymarket Books, 2012), 10; "There is no...": Gitlin, *Occupy Nation*, 14.

7 "micro-city": Matthew Bolton, Stephen Froese, and Alex Jeffrey, "This Space Is Occupied!: The Politics of Occupy Wall Street's Expeditionary Architecture and De-gentrifying Urbanism," in *Occupying Political Science*, eds. Welty et al., 136.

8 "who has lived near...": Gitlin, *Occupy Nation*, 154

9 "'spectacles' that can...": Ron Hayduk, "The Anti-Globalization Movement and OWS," in *Occupying Political Science*, eds. Welty et al., 236.

10 "assumption that the...": Emily Welty, Matthew Bolton, and Nick Zurowski, "Occupy Wall Street as a Palimpsest: Overview of a Dynamic Movement," in *Occupying Political Science*, 47; "You're sexy...": Matthew Bolton and Victoria Measles, "barricades dot net: Post-Fordist Policing in Occupied New York City," in *Occupying Political Science*, eds. Welty et al., 179.

11 "inundated with calls...": Writers for the 99%, *Occupying Wall Street*, 20.

12 "The people's mic...": Gitlin, *Occupy Nation*, 77; "Ivy Leaguers," "Brooklyn Hipsters": Bolton et al., "This Space is Occupied!," 149.

13 "we need to...," "I try to...": Susan Kang, "Demands Belong to the 99%? The Conflict over Demands, Issues, and Goals in OWS," in *Occupying Political Science*, eds. Welty et al., 69, 74; "The fact that...": Gitlin, *Occupy Nation*, 155.

14 "Occupy has had...": Hayduk, "Anti-Globalization," 238–239; "I felt something...": Bolton et al., "This Space is Occupied!," 154.

Colonial and Revolutionary New York: 1624–1783

Alexander, James. *A Brief Narrative of the Case and Trial of John Peter Zenger, Printer of "The New York Weekly Journal".* Edited by Stanley Nider Katz. Cambridge, MA: Harvard University Press, 1963.

Bailyn, Bernard. *The Origins of American Politics.* New York: Random House, 1968.

Bowne, John. *Journal of John Bowne, 1650–1694.* Edited by Herbert F. Ricard. New York: Friends of the Queensborough Community College Library/ New Orleans: Polyanthos, 1975.

Burrows, Edwin, and Mike Wallace. *Gotham: A History of New York City to 1898.* New York: Oxford University Press, 1999.

Butler, Jon. *The Huguenots in America: A Refugee People in New World Society.* Cambridge, MA: Harvard University Press, 1983.

Foote, Thelma Wills. "Crossroads or Settlement? The Black Freedmen's Community in Historic Greenwich Village, 1644–1855." In *Greenwich Village: Culture and Counterculture,* edited by Rick Beard and Leslie Cohen Berlowitz, 120–133. New Brunswick, NJ: Rutgers University Press and Museum of the City of New York, 1993.

Friedman, Ian C. *Freedom of Speech and the Press.* New York: Facts On File, Inc., 2005.

Gilje, Paul A. *The Road to Mobocracy: Popular Disorder in New York City, 1763–1834.* Chapel Hill, NC: University of North Carolina Press, 1987.

Haefeli, Evan. *New Netherland and the Dutch Origins of American Religious Liberty.* Philadelphia: University of Pennsylvania Press, 2012.

Jacobs, Jaap. *New Netherland: A Dutch Colony in Seventeenth-Century America.* Leiden: Brill, 2005.

Kammen, Michael. *Colonial New York: A History.* New York: Scribner, 1975.

Ketchum, Richard M. *Divided Loyalties: How the American Revolution Came to New York.* New York: Henry Holt, 2002.

Kluger, Richard. *Indelible Ink: The Trials of John Peter Zenger and the Birth of America's Free Press.* New York: W. W. Norton & Company, 2016.

Lepore, Jill. "The Tightening Vise: Slavery and Freedom in British New York." In *Slavery in New York,* edited by Ira Berlin and Leslie M. Harris, 57–89. New York: The New Press and New-York Historical Society, 2005.

Levy, Leonard W. *Emergence of a Free Press.* New York: Oxford University Press, 1985.

——, ed. *Freedom of the Press from Zenger to Jefferson.* Indianapolis: Bobbs-Merrill Company, Inc., 1966.

Linebaugh, Peter, and Marcus Rediker. *The Many-Headed Hydra: Sailors, Slaves, Commoners, and the Hidden History of the Revolutionary Atlantic.* Boston: Beacon Press, 2000.

Moore, Christopher. "A World of Possibilities: Slavery and Freedom in Dutch New Amsterdam." In *Slavery in New York,* edited by Ira Berlin and Leslie M. Harris, 29–56. New York: The New Press and New-York Historical Society, 2005.

Nash, Gary B. *The Unknown American Revolution: The Unruly Birth of Democracy and the Struggle to Create America.* New York: Viking Penguin, 2005.

——. *The Urban Crucible: Social Change, Political Consciousness, and the Origins of the American Revolution.* Cambridge, MA: Harvard University Press, 1979.

New York City during the American Revolution. Being a Collection of Original Papers (Now First Published) from the Manuscripts in the Possession of the Mercantile Library Association of New York City. New York, 1861.

Pybus, Cassandra. *Epic Journeys of Freedom: Runaway Slaves of the American Revolution and Their Global Quest for Liberty.* Boston: Beacon Press, 2006.

Rutherfurd, Livingston. *John Peter Zenger, His Press, His Trial, and a Bibliography of Zenger Imprints.* New York: Dodd, Mead & Co., 1904.

Schecter, Barnet. *The Battle for New York: The City at the Heart of the American Revolution.* New York: Penguin Books, 2002.

Smith, George Leslie. *Religion and Trade in New Netherland: Dutch Origins and American Development.* Ithaca, NY: Cornell University Press, 1973.

Stokes, Isaac Newton Phelps. *The Iconography of Manhattan Island.* 6 vols. New York: R.I I. Dodd, 1915–1928.

Tiedemann, Joseph S. *Reluctant Revolutionaries: New York City and the Road to Independence, 1763–1776.* Ithaca, NY: Cornell University Press, 1997.

Trebor, Haynes. *The Flushing Remonstrance (The Origin of Religious Freedom in America).* Flushing, NY: Bowne House, n.d., c. 1957.

Van Buskirk, Judith L. *Generous Enemies: Patriots and Loyalists in Revolutionary New York.* Philadelphia: University of Pennsylvania Press, 2002.

Van der Zee, Henri and Barbara Van der Zee. *A Sweet and Alien Land: The Story of Dutch New York.* New York: Viking Press, 1978.

Wertenbaker, Thomas Jefferson. *Father Knickerbocker Rebels: New York City during the Revolution.* New York: Scribner, 1948.

Young, Alfred F. *The Democratic Republicans of New York: The Origins, 1763–1797*. Williamsburg, VA: University of North Carolina Press for the Institute of Early American History and Culture, 1967.

Young, Alfred F., Gary B. Nash, and Ray Raphael, eds. *Revolutionary Founders: Rebels, Radicals, and Reformers in the Making of the Nation*. New York: Alfred A. Knopf, 2011.

Seaport City: 1783–1865

Alexander, Leslie M. *African or American? Black Identity and Political Activism in New York City, 1784–1861*. Urbana, IL: University of Illinois Press, 2008.

Anbinder, Tyler. *City of Dreams: The 400-Year Epic History of Immigrant New York*. Boston: Houghton Mifflin Harcourt, 2016.

———. *Nativism and Slavery: The Northern Know Nothings & The Politics of the 1850s*. New York: Oxford University Press, 1992.

Billington, Ray Allen. *The Protestant Crusade, 1800–1860: A Study of the Origins of American Nativism*. New York: The Macmillan Company, 1938.

Bridges, Amy. *A City in the Republic: Antebellum New York and the Origins of Machine Politics*. Ithaca, NY: Cornell University Press, 1987.

Burrows, Edwin G., and Mike Wallace. *Gotham: A History of New York City to 1898*. New York: Oxford University Press, 1999.

Douglass, Frederick. *My Bondage and My Freedom*. New York and Auburn: Miller, Orton & Company, 1857.

DuBois, Ellen Carol. *Feminism and Suffrage: The Emergence of an Independent Women's Movement in America, 1848–1869*. Ithaca, NY: Cornell University Press, 1978.

Foner, Eric. *Gateway to Freedom: The Hidden History of the Underground Railroad*. New York: W. W. Norton & Company, 2015.

The First Annual Report of the New York Committee of Vigilance, for the Year 1837, Together with Important Facts Relative to their Proceedings. New York: Piercy and Reed, 1837.

Gellman, David N. *Emancipating New York: The Politics of Slavery and Freedom, 1777–1827*. Baton Rouge: Louisiana State University Press, 2006.

Gellman, David N., and David Quigley, eds. *Jim Crow New York: A Documentary History of Race and Citizenship, 1777–1877*. New York: New York University Press, 2003.

Gilje, Paul A., and Howard B. Rock, eds. *Keepers of the Revolution: New Yorkers at Work in the Early Republic*. Ithaca, NY: Cornell University Press, 1992.

Greenberg, Joshua R. *Advocating the Man: Masculinity, Organized Labor, and the Household in New York, 1800–1840*. New York: Columbia University Press, 2009.

Hewitt, John H. "The Search for Elizabeth Jennings, Heroine of a Sunday Afternoon in New York City." *New York History* 71, no. 4 (October 1990): 386–415.

Hodges, Graham Russell Gao. *David Ruggles: A Radical Black Abolitionist and the Underground Railroad in New York City*. Chapel Hill, NC: University of North Carolina Press, 2010.

Hone, Philip. *The Diary of Philip Hone, 1828–1851*, 2 vols. Edited by Bayard Tuckerman. New York: Dodd, Mead and Company, 1889.

Hugins, Walter E. *Jacksonian Democracy and the Working Class: A Study of the New York Workingmen's Movement, 1829–1837*. Stanford, CA: Stanford University Press, 1960.

Laurie, Bruce. *Artisans into Workers: Labor in Nineteenth-Century America*. New York: Hill and Wang, 1989.

Litwack, Leon F. "The Abolitionist Dilemma: The Antislavery Movement and the Northern Negro." *The New England Quarterly* 34 (March 1961): 50–73.

McFeely, William S. *Frederick Douglass*. New York: W. W. Norton & Company, 1991.

Pessen, Edward. *Most Uncommon Jacksonians: Radical Leaders of the Early Labor Movement*. Albany, NY: State University of New York Press, 1967.

Peterson, Carla L. *Black Gotham: A Family History of African Americans in Nineteenth-Century New York City*. New Haven, CT: Yale University Press, 2011.

Porter, Dorothy B. "David Ruggles, an Apostle of Human Rights." *Journal of Negro History* 28, no. 1 (January 1943): 23–50.

Powell, W. P. "Escape from Slavery." *Seaport* 29, no. 3 (Fall–Winter 1995): 40.

Ratner, Lorman. *Powder Keg: Northern Opposition to the Antislavery Movement, 1831–1840*. New York: Basic Books, 1968.

Rock, Howard B. *Artisans of the New Republic: The Tradesmen of New York City in the Age of Jefferson*. New York: New York University Press, 1979.

———, ed. *The New York City Artisan: A Documentary History*. Albany, NY: State University of New York Press, 1989.

Sachs, Charles L. "A Good and Convenient House." *Seaport* 29, no. 3 (Fall–Winter 1995): 24–29.

Sorin, Gerald. *The New York Abolitionists: A Case Study of Political Radicalism*. Westport, CT: Greenwood Publishing Corporation, 1971.

Stansell, Christine. *City of Women: Sex and Class in New York, 1789–1860*. New York: Alfred A. Knopf, 1986.

Stott, Richard B. *Workers in the Metropolis: Class, Ethnicity and Youth in Antebellum New York City*. Ithaca, NY: Cornell University Press, 1990.

Walters, Ronald G. *American Reformers 1815–1860*, rev. ed. New York: Hill and Wang, 1997.

Wellman, Judith. *Brooklyn's Promised Land: The Free Black Community of Weeksville, New York*. New York: New York University Press, 2014.

Wilder, Craig Steven. *A Covenant with Color: Race and Social Power in Brooklyn*. New York: Columbia University Press, 2000.

Wilentz, Sean. *Chants Democratic: New York City & the Rise of the American Working Class, 1788–1850*. New York: Oxford University Press, 1984.

Wilson, Carol. *Freedom at Risk: The Kidnapping of Free Blacks in America, 1780–1865*. Lexington: University Press of Kentucky, 1994.

Wyatt-Brown, Bertram. *Lewis Tappan and the Evangelical War Against Slavery*. New York: Atheneum, 1971.

Gilded Age to Progressive Era: 1865-1918

Adickes, Sandra. *To Be Young was Very Heaven: Women in New York before the First World War*. New York: St. Martin's Press, 2000.

Argersinger, Jo Ann E. *The Triangle Fire: A Brief History with Documents*, second ed. Boston: Bedford/St. Martin's, 2016.

Avrich, Paul. *The Haymarket Tragedy*, Centennial ed. Princeton, NJ: Princeton University Press, 1986.

———. *The Modern School Movement: Anarchism and Education in the United States*. Princeton, NJ: Princeton University Press, 1980.

———. *Sacco and Vanzetti: The Anarchist Background*. Princeton, NJ: Princeton University Press, 1991.

Avrich, Paul, and Karen Avrich. *Sasha and Emma: The Anarchist Odyssey of Alexander Berkman and Emma Goldman*. Cambridge, MA: Harvard University Press, 2012.

Baker, Jean H. *Sisters: The Lives of America's Suffragists*. New York: Hill and Wang, 2005.

Beisel, Nicola. *Imperiled Innocents: Anthony Comstock and Family Reproduction in Victorian America*. Princeton, NJ: Princeton University Press, 1997.

Bencivenni, Marcela. "Fired by the Ideal: Italian Anarchists in New York City, 1880s—1920s." In *Radical Gotham: Anarchism in New York City from Schwab's Saloon to Occupy Wall Street*, edited by Tom Goyens, 54–76. Urbana, IL: University of Illinois Press, 2017.

Bloom, Nicholas Dagen and Matthew Gordon Ladner. *Affordable Housing in New York: The People, Places, and Policies that Transformed a City*. Princeton, NJ: Princeton University Press, 2016.

Boullosa, Carmen. "Notes on Writing in Spanish in New York." In *Nueva York: 1613–1945*, edited by Edward J. Sullivan, translated by Samantha Schnee, 122–135. New York: New-York Historical Society with Scala Publishers, 2010.

Burrows, Edwin G., and Mike Wallace. *Gotham: A History of New York City to 1898*. New York: Oxford University Press, 1999.

Bzowski, Frances Diodato. "Spectacular Suffrage: Or, How Women Came Out of the Home and into the Streets and Theaters of New York City to Win the Vote," *New York History*, LXXVI, no. 1 (January 1995): 56–94.

Carson, Mina. *Settlement Folk: Social Thought and the American Settlement Movement, 1885–1930*. Chicago: University of Chicago Press, 1990.

Castañeda, Christopher J. "Times of Propaganda and Struggle: *El Despertar* and Brooklyn's Spanish Anarchists, 1890–1905." In *Radical Gotham: Anarchism in New York City from Schwab's Saloon to Occupy Wall Street*, edited by Tom Goyens, 77–99. Urbana, IL: University of Illinois Press, 2017.

Chesler, Ellen. *Woman of Valor: Margaret Sanger and the Birth Control Movement in America*. New York: Simon & Schuster, 1992.

Clark, Sue Ainslie and Edith Wyatt. *Making Both Ends Meet: The Income and Outlay of New York Working Girls*. New York: The Macmillan Company, 1911.

Cott, Nancy F. *The Grounding of Modern Feminism*. New Haven, CT: Yale University Press, 1987.

Davis, Allen F. *Spearheads for Reform: The Social Settlements and the Progressive Movement, 1890–1914*. Oxford: Oxford University Press, 1967.

D'Emilio, John and Estelle B. Freedman, *Intimate Matters: A History of Sexuality in America*, third ed. Chicago: University of Chicago Press, 2012.

Dubofsky, Melvyn. *When Workers Organize: New York City in the Progressive Era*. Amherst: University of Massachusetts Press, 1968.

DuBois, Ellen Carol. *Harriot Stanton Blatch and the Winning of Woman Suffrage*. New Haven, CT: Yale University Press, 1997.

——. *Woman Suffrage and Women's Rights*. New York: New York University Press, 1998.

Dye, Nancy Schrom. *As Equals and As Sisters: Feminism, the Labor Movement, and the Women's Trade Union League*. Columbia, MO: University of Missouri Press, 1980.

Enstad, Nan. *Ladies of Labor, Girls of Adventure: Working Women, Popular Culture, and Labor Politics at the Turn of the Twentieth Century*. New York: Columbia University Press, 1999.

Ewen, Elizabeth. *Immigrant Women in the Land of Dollars: Life and Culture on the Lower East Side, 1890–1925*. New York: Monthly Review Press, 1985.

Feld, Marjorie N. *Lillian Wald: A Biography*. Chapel Hill, NC: University of North Carolina Press, 2008.

Ferguson, Kathy E. *Emma Goldman: Political Thinking in the Streets*. Lanham, MD: Rowman & Littlefield Publishers, Inc., 2011.

Fink, Leon. *Workingmen's Democracy: The Knights of Labor and American Politics*. Champaign, IL: University of Illinois Press, 1983.

Finnegan, Margaret. *Selling Suffrage: Consumer Culture & Votes for Women*. Oxford: Oxford University Press, 2014.

Fountain, Anne. *José Martí, the United States, and Race*. Gainesville, FL: University Press of Florida, 2014.

Gage, Beverly. *The Day Wall Street Exploded: A Story of America in the First Age of Terror*. New York: Oxford University Press, 2008.

Gallagher, Julie A. *Black Women and Politics in New York City*. Urbana, IL: University of Illinois Press, 2012.

Glenn, Susan. *Daughters of the Shtetl: Life and Labor in the Immigrant Generation*. Ithaca, NY: Cornell University Press, 1990.

Goldman, Emma. *Living My Life*. 2 vols. New York: Alfred Knopf, Inc., 1931.

Goyens, Tom. *Beer and Revolution: The German Anarchist Movement in New York City, 1880–1914*. Urbana, IL: University of Illinois Press, 2007.

——, ed. *Radical Gotham: Anarchism in New York City from Schwab's Saloon to Occupy Wall Street*. Urbana, IL: University of Illinois Press, 2017.

Gompers, Samuel. "Hostile Employers, See Yourselves as Others Know You," in *American Federationist*, XVIII, no. 5 (May 1911): 353–379.

Goodier, Susan. *No Votes for Women: The New York State Anti-Suffrage Movement*. Urbana, IL: University of Illinois Press, 2013.

Greenwald, Richard A. *The Triangle Fire, the Protocols of Peace, and Industrial Democracy in Progressive Era New York*. Philadelphia: Temple University Press, 2005.

Guglielmo, Jennifer. *Living the Revolution: Italian Women's Resistance and Radicalism in New York City, 1880–1945*. Chapel Hill, NC: University of North Carolina Press, 2010.

Haskell, Arlo. "Key West Should Be Known for This, too." *History News Network*, last modified November 26, 2017, http://historynewsnetwork.org/article/167386.

Helg, Aline. *Our Rightful Share: The Afro-Cuban Struggle for Equality, 1886–1912*. Chapel Hill, NC: University of North Carolina Press, 1995.

Hicks, Cheryl D. *Talk With You Like a Woman: African American Women, Justice, and Reform in New York, 1890–1935*. Chapel Hill, NC: University of North Carolina Press, 2010.

Jaffe, Steven H. *New York at War: Four Centuries of Combat, Fear, and Intrigue in Gotham*. New York: Basic Books, 2012.

Jones, Thai. *More Powerful Than Dynamite: Radicals, Plutocrats, Progressives, and New York's Year of Anarchy*. New York: Walker and Company, 2012.

Kessler-Harris, Alice. *Out to Work: A History of Wage-Earning Women in the United States*, 20th Anniversary ed. Oxford: Oxford University Press, 2003.

Kennedy, David M. *Birth Control in America: The Career of Margaret Sanger*. New Haven, CT: Yale University Press, 1970.

Kosak, Hadassa. *Cultures of Opposition: Jewish Immigrant Workers, 1881–1905*. Albany, NY: State University of New York Press, 2000.

Lasch-Quinn, Elisabeth. *Black Neighbors: Race and the Limits of Reform in the American Settlement House Movement, 1890–1945*. Chapel Hill, NC: University of North Carolina Press, 1993.

López, Alfred J. *José Marti: A Revolutionary Life*. Austin, TX: University of Texas Press, 2014.

Lunardini, Christine A. *From Equal Suffrage to Equal Rights: Alice Paul and the National Woman's Party, 1910–1928*. New York: New York University Press, 1986.

McCreesh, Carolyn Daniel. *Women in the Campaign to Organize Garment Workers: 1880–1917*. New York: Garland Publishing, Inc. 1985.

Malkiel, Theresa S. *The Diary of a Shirtwaist Striker*. Ithaca, NY: ILR Press, 1990.

Martí, José. *Selected Writings*, edited and translated by Esther Allen. New York: Penguin Books, 2002.

Maryanski, Maureen. "The 'Suff Bird Women' and Woodrow Wilson." *From the Stacks* (blog), *New-York Historical Society*, March 26, 2014, http://blog.nyhistory.org/the-suff-bird-women-and-woodrow-wilson/.

Matson, Cathy. "Permeable Empires: Commercial Exchanges between New York and Spanish Possessions before 1800." In *Nueva York: 1613–1945*, edited by Edward J. Sullivan, 82–95. New York: New-York Historical Society with Scala Publishers, 2010.

Nadel, Stanley. *Little Germany: Ethnicity, Religion, and Class in New York City, 1845–80*. Urbana, IL and Chicago: University of Illinois Press, 1990.

Orleck, Annelise. *Common Sense and A Little Fire: Women and Working-Class Politics in the United States, 1900–1965*, second ed. Chapel Hill, NC: University of North Carolina Press, 2017.

Pérez, Lisandro. "Cubans in Nineteenth Century New York: A Story of Sugar, War and Revolution." In *Nueva York: 1613–1945*, edited by Edward J. Sullivan, 96–107. New York: New-York Historical Society with Scala Publishers, 2010.

Pérez, Louis A., Jr. *Cuba Between Empires, 1878–1902*. Pittsburgh: University of Pittsburgh Press, 1983.

Poyo, Gerald E. "José Martí: Architect of social unity in the émigré communities of the United States," in Christopher Abel and Nissa Torrents, editors, *José Martí: Revolutionary Democrat*, edited by Christopher Abel and Nissa Torrents, 16–31. London: Bloomsbury Academic, 2015.

Remeseira, Claudio Iván, editor. *Hispanic New York: A Sourcebook*. New York: Columbia University Press, 2010.

Riis, Jacob A. *How the Other Half Lives: Studies Among the Tenements of New York*. New York: Charles Scribner's Sons, 1890.

Ross, Jack. *The Socialist Party of America: A Complete History*. Lincoln: Potomac Books and University of Nebraska Press, 2015.

Sánchez-Korrol, Virginia. *Feminist and Abolitionist: The Story of Emilia Casanova*. Houston: Arte Publico Press, 2013.

———. "Puerto Ricans in 'Olde' New York: Migrant Colonias of the Nineteenth and Twentieth Centuries." In *Nueva York: 1613–1945*, edited by Edward J. Sullivan, 108–121. New York: New-York Historical Society with Scala Publishers, 2010.

Schaffer, Ronald. "The New York City Woman Suffrage Party, 1909–1919," *New York History* Vol. 43, No. 3 (July 1962): 269–287.

Schneider, Dorothee. *Trade Unions and Community: The German Working Class in New York City, 1870–1900*. Champaign, IL: University of Illinois Press, 1994.

Seligman, Scott D. *The First Chinese American: The Remarkable Life of Wong Chin Foo*. Hong Kong: Hong Kong University Press, 2013.

Slayton, Robert A. *Empire Statesman: The Rise and Redemption of Al Smith*. New York: The Free Press, 2001.

Stein, Leon. *The Triangle Fire*, Centennial ed. Ithaca, NY: Cornell University Press, 2010.

Tchen, John Kuo Wei. *New York before Chinatown: Orientalism and the Shaping of American Culture, 1776–1882*. Baltimore: Johns Hopkins University Press, 1999.

Terborg-Penn, Rosalyn. *African American Women in the Struggle for the Vote, 1850–1920*. Bloomington, IN: Indiana University Press, 1998.

Van Voris, Jacqueline. *Carrie Chapman Catt: A Public Life*. New York: The Feminist Press, 1987.

Vega, Bernardo. *Memoirs of Bernardo Vega: A Contribution to the History of the Puerto Rican Community in New York*. Edited by César Andreu Iglesias. New York: Monthly Review Press, 1984.

Von Drehle, David. *Triangle: The Fire That Changed America*. New York: Grove Press, 2003.

Wald, Lillian D. *The House on Henry Street*. New York: Henry Holt and Company, 1915.

Wallace, Mike. *Greater Gotham: A History of New York City from 1898 to 1919*. New York: Oxford University Press, 2017.

———. "Nueva York: The Back Story." In *Nueva York: 1613–1945*, edited by Edward J. Sullivan, 18–81. New York: New-York Historical Society with Scala Publishers, 2010.

Yochelson, Bonnie. *Jacob A. Riis: Revealing New York's Other Half: A Complete Catalogue of His Photographs*. New Haven, CT: Yale University Press with Museum of the City of New York and Library of Congress, 2015.

Yochelson, Bonnie and Daniel Czitrom. *Rediscovering Jacob Riis: Exposure Journalism and Photography in Turn-of-the-Century New York*. New York: New Press, 2008.

Zimmer, Kenyon. "Saul Yanovsky and Yiddish Anarchism on the Lower East Side." In *Radical Gotham: Anarchism in New York City from Schwab's Saloon to Occupy Wall Street*, edited by Tom Goyens, 33–53. Urbana, IL: University of Illinois Press, 2017.

Zéndegui, Guillermo de. *Ámbito de Martí*. Madrid: Escuela Gráfica Salesiana, 1954.

Midcentury Metropolis: 1918–1960

Bayor, Ronald H. *Neighbors in Conflict: The Irish, Germans, Jews, and Italians of New York City, 1929–1941*. Baltimore: Johns Hopkins University Press, 1978.

Belfrage, Cedric. *The American Inquisition: 1945–1960*. Indianapolis, IN: Bobbs-Merrill, 1973.

Bentley, Joanne. *Hallie Flanagan: A Life in the American Theatre*. New York: Alfred A. Knopf, 1988.

Carle, Susan D. *Defining the Struggle: National Organizing for Racial Justice, 1880–1915*. Oxford: Oxford University Press, 2013.

Carroll, Peter N. *The Odyssey of the Abraham Lincoln Brigade: Americans in the Spanish Civil War*. Stanford, CA: Stanford University Press, 1994.

Carroll, Peter N. and James D. Fernandez, eds. *Facing Fascism: New York and the Spanish Civil War*. New York: New York University Press and Museum of the City of New York, 2007.

Caute, David. *The Great Fear: The Anti-Communist Purge Under Truman and Eisenhower*. New York: Simon & Schuster, 1978.

Clurman, Harold. *The Fervent Years: The Story of the Group Theatre and the Thirties*. New York: Harcourt Brace Jovanovich, Inc., 1975.

Cogley, John. *Report on Blacklisting II: Radio-Television*. The Fund for the Republic, Inc., 1956.

Deery, Philip. *Red Apple: Communism and McCarthyism in Cold War New York*. New York: Fordham University Press, 2014.

Denning, Michael. *The Cultural Front: The Laboring of American Culture in the Twentieth Century*. London: Verso, 1996.

Dossett, Kate. *Bridging Race Divides: Black Nationalism, Feminism, and Integration in the United States, 1896–1935*. Gainesville, FL: University Press of Florida, 2008.

Fast, Howard. *Being Red: A Memoir*. Boston: Houghton Mifflin, 1990.

Faulk, John Henry. *Fear On Trial*. New York: Simon & Schuster, 1964.

Flanagan, Hallie. *Arena: The History of the Federal Theatre*. New York: B. Blom, 1965.

Freeman, Joshua B. *Working-Class New York: Life and Labor Since World War II*. New York: The New Press, 2000.

Gallagher, Julie A. *Black Women and Politics in New York City*. Urbana, IL: University of Illinois Press, 2012.

Garrison, Dee. "'Our Skirts Gave Them Courage': The Civil Defense Protest Movement in New York City, 1955–1961." In *Not June Cleaver: Women and Gender in Postwar America, 1945–1960*, edited by Joanne Meyerowitz, 201–228. Philadelphia: Temple University Press, 1994.

Garvey, Marcus. *Selected Writings and Speeches of Marcus Garvey*. Edited by Bob Blaisdell. Mineola, NY: Dover Publications, 2004.

Grant, Colin. *Negro With a Hat: The Rise and Fall of*

Marcus Garvey. Oxford: Oxford University Press, 2008.

Hook, Sidney. *Out of Step: An Unquiet Life in the 20th Century*. New York: Harper & Row, 1987.

Houseman, John. *Run-Through: A Memoir.* New York: Simon & Schuster, 1972.

Jaffe, Steven H. "Legacies of the Spanish Civil War in New York." In *Facing Fascism: New York and the Spanish Civil War*, edited by Peter N. Carroll and James D. Fernandez, 170–183. New York: New York University Press and the Museum of the City of New York, 2007.

——. *New York at War: Four Centuries of Combat, Fear, and Intrigue in Gotham*. New York: Basic Books, 2012.

James, Winston. *Holding Aloft the Banner of Ethiopia: Caribbean Radicalism in Early Twentieth-Century America*. London: Verso, 1998.

Jones, John Bush. *Our Musicals, Ourselves: A Social History of the American Musical Theatre.* Waltham, MA: Brandeis University Press/Hanover, NH: University Press of New England, 2003.

Kanfer, Stefan. *A Journal of the Plague Years.* New York: Atheneum, 1973.

Kazacoff, George. *Dangerous Theatre: The Federal Theatre Project as a Forum for New Plays*. Pieterlen, Switzerland: Peter Lang, 2011.

Kwong, Peter. *Chinatown, N.Y.: Labor and Politics, 1930–1950*, revised ed. New York: New Press, 1979.

Lawson, Ellen NicKenzie. *Smugglers, Bootleggers, and Scofflaws: Prohibition and New York City*. Albany, NY: State University of New York Press, 2013.

Lerner, Michael A. *Dry Manhattan: Prohibition in New York City*. Cambridge, MA: Harvard University Press, 2007.

Lewis, David Levering. *W.E.B. Du Bois: The Fight for Equality and the American Century, 1919–1963*. New York: Henry Holt and Company, 2000.

Lorini, Alessandra. *Rituals of Race: American Public Culture and the Search for Racial Democracy*. Charlottesville, VA: University Press of Virginia, 1999.

McGirr, Lisa. *The War on Alcohol: Prohibition and the Rise of the American State*. New York: W. W. Norton & Company, 2016.

Maltz, Albert. "What Shall We Ask of Writers?" In *Communism in America: A History in Documents*, edited by Albert Fried, 350–353. New York: Columbia University Press, 1997.

Navasky, Victor. *Naming Names*. New York: Penguin, 1981.

O'Connor, John and Lorraine Brown. *Free, Adult, Uncensored: The Living History of the Federal Theatre Project*. Washington, DC: New Republic Books, 1978.

Okrent, Daniel. *Last Call: The Rise and Fall of Prohibition*. New York: Scribner, 2010.

Petrus, Stephen and Ronald D. Cohen. *Folk City: New York and the American Folk Music Revival*. Oxford: Oxford University Press and the Museum of the City of New York, 2015.

Schneider, Mark Robert. *"We Return Fighting": The Civil Rights Movement in the Jazz Age.* Boston: Northeastern University Press, 2002.

Schrecker, Ellen. *Many Are the Crimes: McCarthyism in America*. Boston: Little, Brown & Co., 1998.

——. *No Ivory Tower: McCarthyism and the Universities*. New York: Oxford University Press, 1986.

Stein, Judith. *The World of Marcus Garvey: Race and Class in Modern Society*. Baton Rouge: Louisiana State University Press, 1986.

Sullivan, Patricia. *Lift Every Voice: The NAACP and the Making of the Civil Rights Movement*. New York: The New Press, 2009.

Taylor, Clarence. *Reds at the Blackboard: Communism, Civil Rights, and the New York City Teachers Union.* New York: Columbia University Press, 2011.

Walker, Samuel. *In Defense of American Liberties: A History of the ACLU*, second ed. Carbondale: Southern Illinois University Press, 1999.

Wallace, Mike. "New York and the World: The Global Context." In *Facing Fascism: New York and the Spanish Civil War*, edited by Peter N. Carroll and James D. Fernandez, 18–29. New York: New York University Press and Museum of the City of New York, 2007.

Williams, Jay. *Stage Left*. New York: Charles Scribner's Sons, 1974.

The Sixties in New York: 1960–1973

Albrecht, Donald with Stephen Vider. *Gay Gotham: Art and Underground Culture in New York*. New York: Skira Rizzoli and the Museum of the City of New York, 2016.

Appy, Christian G. *American Reckoning: The Vietnam War and Our National Identity.* New York: Penguin Books, 2015.

Arguello, Martha. "Woman, Dominican, and Young Lord." In *Through the Eyes of Rebel Women: The Young Lords, 1969–1976*, edited by Iris Morales, 140–143. New York: Red Sugarcane Press, Inc., 2016.

Bausum, Ann. *Stonewall: Breaking Out in the Fight for Gay Rights*. New York: SPEAK, 2015.

Bell, Arthur. *Dancing the Gay Lib Blues: A Year in the Homosexual Liberation Movement*. New York: Simon & Schuster, 1971.

Biondi, Martha. *To Stand and Fight: The Struggle for Civil Rights in Postwar New York City.* Cambridge, MA: Harvard University Press, 2003.

Cannato, Vincent J. *The Ungovernable City: John Lindsay and His Struggle to Save New York*. New York: Basic Books, 2001.

Carroll, Tamar W. *Mobilizing New York: AIDS, Antipoverty, and Feminist Activism*. Chapel Hill, NC: University of North Carolina Press, 2015.

Carter, David. *Stonewall: The Riots That Sparked the Gay Revolution*. New York: St. Martin's Griffin, 2004.

Chauncey, George. *Gay New York: Gender, Urban Culture, and the Making of the Gay Male World, 1890–1940*. New York: Basic Books, 1994.

Cleaver, Kathleen and George Katsiaficas, eds. *Liberation, Imagination, and the Black Panther Party: A New Look at the Panthers and their Legacy*. New York: Routledge, 2001.

Cohen, Marcia. *The Sisterhood: The True Story of the Women Who Changed the World*. New York: Simon & Schuster, 1988.

Cohen, Stephan L. *The Gay Liberation Youth Movement in New York: "An Army of Lovers Cannot Fail."* New York: Routledge, 2008.

D'Emilio, John. *Sexual Politics, Sexual Communities: The Making of a Homosexual Minority in the United States, 1940–1970,* second ed. Chicago: University of Chicago Press, 1998.

Downs, Jim. *Stand By Me: The Forgotten History of Gay Liberation*. New York: Basic Books, 2016.

Duberman, Martin. *Stonewall*. New York: Dutton, 1993.

Echols, Alice. *Daring to Be Bad: Radical Feminism in America, 1968–1975*. Minneapolis: University of Minnesota Press, 1988.

Enck-Wanzer, Darrel. *The Young Lords: A Reader*. New York: New York University Press, 2010.

Faderman, Lillian. *The Gay Revolution: The Story of the Struggle*. New York: Simon & Schuster, 2015.

Fernandez, Johanna. "Between Social Service Reform and Revolutionary Politics: The Young Lords, Late Sixties Radicalism, and Community Organizing in New York City." In *Freedom North: Black Freedom Struggles Outside the South, 1940–1980*, edited by Jeanne F. Theoharis and Komozi Woodard, 255–285. New York: Palgrave Macmillan, 2003.

——, "The Young Lords and the Social and Structural Roots of Late Sixties Urban Radicalism." In *Civil Rights in New York City: From World War II to the Giuliani Era*, edited by Clarence Taylor, 141-160. New York: Fordham University Press, 2011.

Freeman, Joshua B. "Hardhats: Construction Workers, Manliness, and the 1970 Pro-War Demonstrations." *Journal of Social History*, vol. 26, No. 4 (Summer 1993), 725–744.

——. *Working-Class New York: Life and Labor Since World War II*. New York: New Press, 2000.

Friedan, Betty. *The Feminine Mystique*. New York: W. W. Norton & Company, 2001.

Gallo, Marcia M. *Different Daughters: A History of the Daughters of Bilitis and the Rise of the Lesbian Rights Movement*. Emeryville, CA: Seal Press, 2007.

Gitlin, Todd. *The Sixties: Years of Hope, Days of Rage*, revised trade ed. New York: Bantam, 1993.

Guzmán, Pablo. "*La Vida Pura:* A Lord of the Barrio." In *The Puerto Rican Movement: Voices from the Diaspora*, edited by Andrés Torres and José E. Velázquez, 155–172. Philadelphia: Temple University Press, 1998.

Haley, Alex. *The Autobiography of Malcolm X (As Told to Alex Haley)*. New York: Ballantine Books, 1965.

Halstead, Fred. *Out Now! A Participant's Account of the Movement in the United States Against the Vietnam War*. New York: Pathfinder Press, 1978.

Hoffman, Abbie. *The Autobiography of Abbie Hoffman*. New York: Four Walls Eight Windows, 2000.

Horowitz, Daniel. *Betty Friedan and the Making of the Feminine Mystique: The American Left, the Cold War, and Modern Feminism*. Amherst, MA: University of Massachusetts Press, 1999.

Jaffe, Steven H. *New York at War: Four Centuries of Combat, Fear, and Intrigue in Gotham*. New York: Basic Books, 2012.

Jay, Karla. *Tales of the Lavender Menace: A Memoir of Liberation*. New York: Basic Books, 1999.

Joseph, Peniel E. *Waiting 'Til the Midnight Hour: A Narrative History of Black Power in America*. New York: Henry Holt, 2006.

Kaiser, Charles. *The Gay Metropolis 1940–1996*. Boston: Houghton Mifflin Company, 1997.

Kornbluh, Felicia. *The Battle for Welfare Rights: Politics and Poverty in Modern America*. Philadelphia: University of Pennsylvania Press, 2007.

Kwong, Peter. *The New Chinatown*, revised ed. New York: Hill and Wang, 1996.

Lee, Sonia Song-Ha. *Building a Latino Civil Rights Movement: Puerto Ricans, African Americans, and the Pursuit of Racial Justice in New York City*. Chapel Hill, NC: University of North Carolina Press, 2014.

Marable, Manning. *Malcolm X: A Life of Reinvention*. New York: Viking Press, 2011.

Maristany, Hiram and Felipe Luciano. "The Young Lords Party 1969–1975." *Caribe*, VII, no. 4, ca. 1983.

Marotta, Toby. *The Politics of Homosexuality*. Boston: Houghton Mifflin Company, 1981.

McGarry, Molly and Fred Wasserman. *Becoming Visible: An Illustrated History of Lesbian and Gay Life in Twentieth-Century America*. New York: Penguin Studio, 1998.

Melendez, Miguel "Mickey." *We Took the Streets: Fighting for Latino Rights with the Young Lords*. New York: St. Martin's Press, 2003.

Morales, Iris. "¡PALANTE, SIEMPRE PALANTE! The Young Lords." In *The Puerto Rican Movement: Voices from the Diaspora*, edited by Andrés Torres and José E. Velázquez, 210–227. Philadelphia: Temple University Press, 1998.

——, ed. *Through the Eyes of Rebel Women: The Young Lords, 1969–1976*. New York: Red Sugarcane Press, Inc., 2016.

Morgan, Robin. *Sisterhood is Powerful*. New York: Vintage, 1970.

Nadasen, Premilla. *Welfare Warriors: The Welfare Rights Movement in the United States*. New York: Routledge, 2005.

Oliver-Vélez, Denise. "The Excitement Was in the Streets!" In *Through the Eyes of Rebel Women: The Young Lords, 1969–1976*, edited by Iris Morales, 127–139. New York: Red Sugarcane Press, Inc., 2016.

Pantoja, Antonia. *Memoir of a Visionary: Antonia Pantoja*. Houston, TX: Arte Público Press, 2002.

Perlstein, Daniel H. *Justice, Justice: School Politics and the Eclipse of Liberalism*. New York: Peter Lang Publishing, Inc., 2004.

Podair, Jerald E. *The Strike That Changed New York: Blacks, Whites, and the Ocean Hill-Brownsville Crisis*. New Haven, CT: Yale University Press, 2002.

Purnell, Brian. *Fighting Jim Crow in the County of Kings: The Congress of Racial Equality in Brooklyn*. Lexington, KY: University Press of Kentucky, 2013.

Randolph, Sherie M. *Florynce "Flo" Kennedy: The Life of a Black Feminist Radical*. Chapel Hill, NC: University of North Carolina Press, 2015.

Redstockings, *Feminist Revolution*. New York: Random House, 1975.

Rosen, Ruth. *The World Split Open: How the Modern Women's Movement Changed America*. New York: Viking, 2000.

Rudd, Mark. *Underground: My Life with SDS and the Weathermen*. New York: HarperCollins, 2009.

Shafer, Peter, ed. *The Legacy: Vietnam in the American Imagination*. Boston: Beacon, 1990.

Small, Melvin and William D. Hoover, eds. *Give Peace a Chance: Exploring the Vietnam Antiwar Movement*. Syracuse, NY: Syracuse University Press, 1992.

Steinem, Gloria. *Outrageous Acts and Everyday Rebellions*. New York: Holt, Rinehart, and Winston, 1983.

Sugrue, Thomas. *Sweet Land of Liberty: The Forgotten Struggle for Civil Rights in the North*. New York: Random House, 2008.

Swerdlow, Amy. *Women Strike for Peace: Traditional Motherhood and Radical Politics in the 1960s*. Chicago: University of Chicago Press, 1993.
Taylor, Clarence. *The Black Churches of Brooklyn*. New York: Columbia University Press, 1994.

Taylor, Clarence. *The Black Churches of Brooklyn*. New York: Columbia University Press, 1994.

——, ed. *Civil Rights in New York City: From World War II to the Giuliani Era*. New York: Fordham University Press, 2011.

——. *Knocking at Our Own Door: Milton A. Galamison and the Struggle to Integrate New York City Schools*. Lanham, MD: Lexington Books, 2001.

Teal, Donn. *The Gay Militants: How Gay Liberation Began in America, 1969–1971*. New York: Stein and Day, 1971.

Thom, Mary. *Inside Ms.: 25 Years of the Magazine and the Feminist Movement*. New York: Henry Holt, 1997.

Thomas, Lorrin. *Puerto Rican Citizen: History and Political Identity in Twentieth-Century New York City*. Chicago: University of Chicago Press, 2010.

Wanzer-Serrano, Darrel. *The New York Young Lords and the Struggle for Liberation*. Philadelphia: Temple University Press, 2015.

Wei, William. *The Asian American Movement*. Philadelphia: Temple University Press, 1993.

Wilder, Craig Steven. *A Covenant with Color: Race and Social Power in Brooklyn*. New York: Columbia University Press, 2000.

Wilkerson, Cathy. *Flying Close to the Sun: My Life and Times as a Weatherman*. New York: Seven Stories Press, 2007.

Young Lords Party and Michael Abramson. *PALANTE: Young Lords Party*, new ed. Chicago: Haymarket Books, 2011.

Zaroulis, Nancy and Gerald Sullivan. *Who Spoke Up? American Protest Against the War in Vietnam 1963–1975*. Garden City: Doubleday, 1984.

Urban Crisis and Revival: 1973–2011

Abu-Lughod, Janet L., ed. *From Urban Village to East Village: The Battle for New York's Lower East Side*. Cambridge, MA: Blackwell, 1994.

Alinsky, Saul D. *Reveille for Radicals*, Vintage Books ed. New York: Vintage Books, 1989.

———. *Rules for Radicals: A Pragmatic Primer for Realistic Radicals*. New York: Random House, 1971.

Bao, Xiaolan. *Holding up More Than Half the Sky: Chinese Women Garment Workers in New York City, 1948–92*. Urbana, IL: University of Illinois Press, 2001.

Blotcher, Jay. "Alphabet City Finishing School: The Education of an AIDS Activist." In *Resistance: A Radical Social and Political History of the Lower East Side*, edited by Clayton Patterson, 585–588. New York: Seven Stories Press, 2007.

Blumenkranz, Carla, Keith Gessen, Mark Greif, Sarah Leonard, Sarah Resnick, Nikil Saval, Eli Schmitt, and Astra Taylor, eds. *Occupy!: Scenes from Occupied America*. London: Verso Books, 2012.

Carroll, Tamar W. *Mobilizing New York: AIDS, Antipoverty, and Feminist Activism*. Chapel Hill, NC: University of North Carolina Press, 2015.

Castells, Manuel. *Networks of Outrage and Hope: Social Movements in the Internet Age*, second ed. Cambridge, UK: Polity Press, 2015.

Chomsky, Noam, ed. *Occupy: Reflections on Class War, Rebellion, and Solidarity,* second ed. Westfield, NJ: Zuccotti Park Press, 2013.

Freedman, Samuel G. *Upon This Rock: The Miracles of a Black Church*. New York: HarperCollins Publishers, 1993.

Gautney, Heather. "The Influence of Anarchism in Occupy Wall Street." In *Radical Gotham: Anarchism in New York City from Schwab's Saloon to Occupy Wall Street*, edited by Tom Goyens, 221–240. Urbana, IL: University of Illinois Press, 2017.

Gecan, Michael and Reverend Johnny Ray Youngblood. "A Housing Legacy." In *New York Comes Back: The Mayoralty of Edward I. Koch*, edited by Michael Goodwin, 98–103. New York: powerHouse Books in association with the Museum of the City of New York, 2005.

Gitlin, Todd. *Occupy Nation: The Roots, The Spirit, and The Promise of Occupy Wall Street*. New York: Itbooks, 2012.

Gonzalez, Evelyn. *The Bronx*. New York: Columbia University Press, 2004.

Gregory, Steven. *Black Corona: Race and the Politics of Place in an Urban Community*. Princeton, NJ: Princeton University Press, 1998.

Greif, Mark, Dayna Tortorici, Kathleen French, Emma Janaskie, and Nick Werle. *The Trouble is the Banks: Letters to Wall Street*. New York: n+1 Foundation, 2012.

Horwitt, Sanford D. *Let Them Call Me Rebel: Saul Alinsky—His Life and Legacy*. New York: Alfred A. Knopf, 1989.

Jaffe, Steven H. and Jessica Lautin. *Capital of Capital: Money, Banking and Power in New York City*. New York: Columbia University Press and Museum of the City of New York, 2014.

Jonnes, Jill. *South Bronx Rising: The Rise, Fall, and Resurrection of an American City*. New York: Fordham University Press, 2002.

McGarry, Molly and Fred Wasserman. *Becoming Visible: An Illustrated History of Lesbian and Gay Life in Twentieth-Century America*. New York: Penguin Studio, 1998.

Martinez, Miranda J. *Power at the Roots: Gentrification, Community Gardens, and the Puerto Ricans of the Lower East Side*. Lanham, MD: Lexington Books, 2010.

Mele, Christopher. *Selling the Lower East Side: Culture, Real Estate, and Resistance in New York City*. Minneapolis, MN: University of Minnesota Press, 2000.

Patterson, Clayton, ed. *Resistance: A Radical Social and Political History of the Lower East Side*. New York: Seven Stories Press, 2007.

Rooney, Jim. *Organizing the South Bronx*. Albany, NY: State University of New York Press, 1995.

Schulman, Sarah. *The Gentrification of the Mind: Witness to a Lost Imagination*. Berkeley, CA: University of California Press, 2012.

Snyder, Robert W. *Crossing Broadway: Washington Heights and the Promise of New York City*. Ithaca, NY: Cornell University Press, 2015.

Stuart, Lee. "'Come, Let Us Rebuild the Walls of Jerusalem': Broad-Based Organizing in the South Bronx." In *Signs of Hope in the City: Ministries of Community Renewal*, revised ed., edited by Robert D. Carle and Louis A. DeCaro Jr., 158–169. Valley Forge, PA: Judson Press, 1999.

———. "Redefining the Public Sphere: South Bronx Churches and Education Reform." In *Signs of Hope in the City: Ministries of Community Renewal*, revised ed., edited by Robert D. Carle and Louis A. DeCaro Jr., 170–182. Valley Forge, PA: Judson Press, 1999.

Stuart, Lee with John Heinemeier, "The Nehemiah Strategy." In *Making Housing Happen: Faith-based Affordable Housing Models*, edited by Jill Suzanne Shook, 196–213. St. Louis, MO: Chalice Press, 2006.

Susser, Ida. *Norman Street: Poverty and Politics in an Urban Neighborhood*, updated ed. Oxford: Oxford University Press, 2012.

Thabit, Walter. *How East New York Became a Ghetto*. New York: New York University Press, 2003.

Van Gelder, Sarah and the staff of *Yes! Magazine*, eds. *This Changes Everything: Occupy Wall Street and the 99% Movement*. San Francisco: Berrett-Koehler Publishers, Inc., 2011.

Von Hoffman, Alexander. *House by House, Block by Block: The Rebirth of America's Urban Neighborhoods*. New York: Oxford University Press, 2003.

Walker, Samuel. *In Defense of American Liberties: A History of the ACLU*, second ed. Carbondale: Southern Illinois University Press, 1999.

Welty, Emily, Matthew Bolton, Meghana Nayak, and Christopher Malone, eds. *Occupying Political Science: The Occupy Wall Street Movement from New York to the World*. New York: Palgrave Macmillan, 2013.

Writers for the 99%. *Occupying Wall Street: The Inside Story of an Action that Changed America*. Chicago: Haymarket Books, 2011.

Pages 4, 15, 23, 53 (top left), 67, 70 (top left), 84 (middle right), 91, 93, 94, 98, 100, 108, 111 (bottom right), 116 (middle left), 117, 127 (top), 134 (top left), 134 (top right), 134 (middle left), 142, 144 (middle left), 144 (bottom left), 145, 146, 148 (bottom), 150, 151, 152, 158, 160, 172, 175, 188, 202 (no. 5), 202 (no. 7), 228, 229: Library of Congress, Prints & Photographs Division; 6, 168–169, 174, 183: Everett Collection Historical/Alamy Stock Photo; 8–9, 35 (bottom right), 52 (top center), 70 (top right), 70 (middle left), 84 (middle left), 111 (top left): The Miriam and Ira D. Wallach Division of Art, Prints and Photographs, The New York Public Library, Astor, Lenox, and Tilden Foundations; 13, 119, 148 (top), 173, 197, 245: Author's collection; 14: Cal Vornberger/Alamy Stock Photo; 17 (29.100.709), 24–25 (29.100.1572), 40 (X2012.61.24.61), 48 (bottom, 29.100.2077), 55 (29.100.1777), 71 (29.100.2425): Museum of the City of New York, gift of J. Clarence Davies; 18 (52.100.30), 63 (top, 52.100.16): Museum of the City of New York, bequest of Mrs. J. Insley Blair in memory of Mr. and Mrs. J. Insley Blair; 20, 135: New York State Archives; 22 (#1909.2, framed: 29 1/4 x 25 in.), 32 (# 81452d), 76–77 (#78927d), 84 (top left, #74637, 7 1/2 x 5 3/4 in.), 140 (#71412), 170 (bottom right): Collection of the New-York Historical Society/Photography © New-York Historical Society; 25, 99 (bottom right), 101: GRANGER— All rights reserved; 26: The Metropolitan Museum of Art, New York, gift of Henry Walters, 1917, 17.37.184; 27: Rijksmuseum, Amsterdam; 28, 38, 42, 64: Sarin Images/ GRANGER — All rights reserved; 29 (X2011.5.184), 66 (56.124.1), 92 (top, X2011.34.3319), 114 (bottom left, X2010.11.6781), 114 (bottom right, X2010.11.6775), 144 (top left, 99.7.2), 149 (X2011.11.1), 156 (X2010.11.11361), 218 (2017.20.60), 259 (X2010.11.6488): Museum of the City of New York; 30: Collection Amsterdam City Archives; 31 (F2011.33.1467), 54 (F2011.33.694): Museum of the City of New York, Postcard Collection; 35 (top left): Collection of the National Gallery of Ireland, Purchased, 1993/Photo © National Gallery of Ireland; 35 (top right): Brooklyn Museum, purchased with funds given by John Hill Morgan, Dick S. Ramsay Fund, and Museum Collection Fund, 43.196; 35 (bottom left): Museum of the City of New York, gift of William Hamilton Russell, 50.215.3; 36: British Museum, Purchased from Edward Hawkins, 1868/© Trustees of the British Museum; 37, 47, 48 (top), 80–81: Art and Picture Collection, The New York Public Library, Astor, Lenox, and Tilden Foundations; 39: Collection of the New-York Historical Society Library, #95527d; 41, 70 (bottom left): Rare Book & Manuscript Library, Columbia University in the City of New York; 43: Museum of the City of New York, gift of Isoline D. Ray, 32.382B; 44: Museum of the City of New York, gift of Mrs. Gordon Cadwalader, Mrs. John Wightman, and Mr. William L. Nicoll, 48.250.2; 46 (76.79), 133 (2016.1.1): Museum of the City of New York, museum purchase; 49 (left, 55.6.32), 49 (right, 55.6.33), 78 (55.6.10): Museum of the City of New York, gift of Francis P. Garvan; 50: Museum of the City of New York, Portrait Archive, F2012.58.1251; 51: Museum of the City of New York, gift of Mrs. Edwin Tatham, 33.295; 52 (top left): Museum of the City of New York, bequest of Elizabeth Mary Frelinghuysen, 67.113.2; 52 (top right): Museum of the City of New

York, gift of Mrs. Wendell T. Bush, 28.153.137; 53 (center): Museum of the City of New York, Portrait Archive Print Collection, F2012.56.146; 53 (top right): Museum of the City of New York, gift of Mrs. Alexander Hamilton and General Pierpont Morgan Hamilton, 71.31.3; 57: Museum of the City of New York, gift of Lou Sepersky and Leida Snow, 97.227.3; 58 (top and bottom): Museum of the City of New York, gift of W. Prescott Barker, 27.114AB; 60: Museum of the City of New York, gift of Miss Sarah F. de Luze, 39.253.11; 63 (bottom): Smithsonian Institution Archives; 65: Kilroe Ephemera Collection, Rare Book & Manuscript Library, Columbia University in the City of New York; 68 (56.300.816), 75 (right, 56.300.1011), 87 (56.300.681): Museum of the City of New York, gift of Mrs. Harry T. (Natalie) Peters; 69: Museum of the City of New York, gift of Harry Shaw Newman, 46.415; 70 (middle right): University of California Libraries; 70 (bottom right): INTERFOTO/Alamy Stock Photo; 72, 170 (middle left): Boston Public Library, via the Internet Archive; 75 (left): Negro Almanac Collection, Amistad Research Center at Tulane University; 79: Kansas State Historical Society; 80 (left): National Portrait Gallery, Smithsonian Institution; 82–83: The Metropolitan Museum of Art, The Edward W. C. Arnold Collection of New York Prints, Maps, and Pictures, Bequest of Edward W. C. Arnold, 1954, 54.90.13; 84 (top center): Randolph Linsly Simpson African-American Collection, James Weldon Johnson Collection in the Yale Collection of American Literature, Beinecke Rare Book & Manuscript Library; 84 (top right), 84 (bottom right), 115, 116 (top right), 116 (bottom left), 164, 170 (top left): Manuscripts, Archives and Rare Books Division, Schomburg Center for Research in Black Culture, The New York Public Library, Astor, Lenox, and Tilden Foundations; 84 (bottom left); 84 (bottom center): Jean Blackwell Hutson Research and Reference Division, Schomburg Center for Research in Black Culture, The New York Public Library, Astor, Lenox, and Tilden Foundations; 84 (center), 116 (bottom right), 118, 121 (bottom), 157, 161, 162, 170 (top right), 170 (middle right), 170 (bottom left), 202 (no. 8): Photographs and Prints Division, Schomburg Center for Research in Black Culture, The New York Public Library, Astor, Lenox, and Tilden Foundations; 86: Collection of the Massachusetts Historical Society; 88 (90.13.2.10), 97 (90.13.1.149), 105 (90.13.2.303), 106 (90.13.1.290), 107 (90.13.2.297), 126 (left, 90.13.1.156), 130 (top, 90.13.1.387): Museum of the City of New York, gift of Roger William Riis; 89 (93.1.1.244); 92 (bottom, 93.1.1.15418); 127 (bottom, 93.1.1.18396): Museum of the City of New York, gift of Percy Byron; 96: World History Archive/Alamy Stock Photo; 99 (top left): University of Michigan Library, Joseph A. Labadie Collection; 99 (top right), 111 (bottom left): Pictorial Press Ltd/Alamy Stock Photo; 99 (middle left), 102: American Labor Museum, Haledon, NJ; 99 (middle right): The Newberry Library/© Man Ray Trust/Artists Rights Society (ARS), NY/ADAGP, Paris 2017; 99 (bottom left), 134 (bottom right), 144 (top right), 190, 200, 241: Tamiment Library, Robert F. Wagner Labor Archives, New York University; 104: *The Modern School* magazine; 111 (top right): Museum of the City of New York, gift of Mrs. Henry H. Whitlock, 32.179.16; 112: University of Michigan Library, via

Acknowledgements

No single book can hope to cover all aspects and episodes of New York City's activist history, a truly encyclopedic topic. This book is intended as an introduction and prompt for further thinking, recording, and preserving of a history that refuses to sit still. As the "Director's Foreword" makes clear, many people helped make this book. I would also like to thank some of them here.

Perry, Gladys, and Neal Rosenstein of the Puffin Foundation have waited a long time for this book's completion, and I hope they feel that their patience has been rewarded. Led by Peter N. Carroll, the Puffin Foundation's advisory committee offered trenchant comments and questions that strengthened the book's arguments.

Sarah M. Henry and Susan Henshaw Jones invited me to write this companion volume to the *Activist New York* exhibition. Whitney W. Donhauser has been equally supportive as the book has neared completion. As usual, Sarah M. Henry's keen historical and editorial insights—along with her rare ability to keep multiple balls in the air, and her unfailing good cheer—greatly enhanced the final product. Likewise, this book would not have reached fruition without the intelligence, hard work, professionalism, and coolness under fire of Susan Gail Johnson.

My other colleagues at the Museum of the City of New York helped in innumerable ways, whether they realized it or not. In particular, Sean Corcoran, Curator of Prints and Photographs, facilitated the use of some of this book's most striking images, and photographer Victoria Martens did a beautiful job of reproducing them. I relied on Sarah Seidman, Puffin Foundation Curator of Social Activism, to answer numerous questions as the book came together. Thanks are due to her and to Marcella Micucci, Andrew W. Mellon Curatorial Post-Doctoral Fellow, who has assisted Dr. Seidman in curating the *Activist New York* gallery and *Beyond Suffrage: A Century of New York Women in Politics*, another MCNY exhibition that enriched this book.

Lastly and as always, I thank Jill, Toby, and Matt for their love and their ability to keep me laughing.